ABOVE THE CLOUDS

Also by Anatoli Boukreev

The Climb (with G. Weston DeWalt)

Translated from the original Russian
by Natalia Lagovskaya and Barbara Poston

Collected and edited by Linda Wylie

Foreword by Galen Rowell

ANATOLI BOUKREEV

ABOVE THE CLOUDS

THE DIARIES OF
A HIGH-ALTITUDE MOUNTAINEER

ST. MARTIN'S PRESS ∾ NEW YORK

www.stmartins.com

Dedication page art and maps on pages xxv–xxvii are by Julie Kandyba.

Library of Congress Cataloging-in-Publication Data

Boukreev, Anatoli.
    Above the clouds : the diaries of a high-altitude mountaineer / Anatoli Boukreev;
  translated from the original Russian by Natalia Lagovskaya and Barbara Poston;
  collected and edited by Linda Wylie; foreword by Galen Rowell.—1st ed.
       p. cm.
    ISBN 0-312-26970-6
    1. Boukreev, Anatoli. 2. Mountaineers—Kazakhstan—Diaries. 3. Mountaineering
expeditions—Himalaya Mountains.   I. Wylie, Linda (Linda Elaine).   II. Title.

GV199.92.B69 A3 2001
796.52'2'092—dc21
[B]

                                                                          2001041614

First Edition: October 2001

10   9   8   7   6   5   4   3   2   1

All religions, all teachings, are synthesized in the Himalayas.

—NICHOLAS ROERICH, *SHAMBHALA*

For Anatoli

CONTENTS

FOREWORD

Many doubts rushed through my mind when Anatoli Boukreev asked me to join him on a winter ascent of the South Face of Annapurna in December 1997. That it would be his last climb was not among my fears. He seemed to possess that rare balance of boldness tempered by self-restraint that keeps so many great climbers alive. If he failed on Annapurna, I expected it to be the result of his own wise decision not to continue.

My doubts were mostly about my own abilities. Nearing sixty, I would be no match for his Olympian level of fitness. I didn't want to prevent his making the summit. Attempting the huge wall in winter without fixed ropes or camps was radically more difficult than the siege-style first ascent done by Britain's best climbers in the prime season.

Anatoli would need unusually good winter conditions plus an unusually strong partner, or he would have to leave a weaker partner behind, hopefully by mutual agreement. Was I prepared to wait it out up high or possibly descend alone in winter?

After he listened to my concerns about the extreme nature of his goal, my ability compared to his, and my previous commitment to guide a photography trek in Patagonia, he told me not to come with him if it didn't feel right to me. Then he suddenly switched topics. What was I doing next July? Would I join him in Pakistan to climb two 8,000-meter peaks by standard routes in summer conditions? I instantly accepted and set aside two months on my 1998 calendar.

Had we done those climbs together, I would have come to know Anatoli well enough to write about him in the third person with a literary facade of objectivity, as if I really could assess the meaning of his life apart from my own experience. I was taught that to promote oneself or one's own philosophy is the cardinal sin of writing reviews or biographical essays. Yet I feel the need to present much of my own philosophy and related experience to evoke what Anatoli's spirit meant to me and should mean to mountaineers of the future. I believe that I come up short in the obvious parallels between Anatoli's bold decisions and those by which I remain alive today. Anatoli lived his short life to the fullest and packed more into thirty-nine years than almost anyone who lives to be one hundred.

If this book were to be distributed only among fellow mountaineers, a review of Anatoli's achievements combined with a few anecdotes would suffice as a foreword. But why should armchair mountaineers, who might only know Anatoli as the inarticulate Russian villain depicted in a bestseller about the 1996 Everest tragedy, care to know more about his life and letters? It is that perspective that I want to convey here.

Though the latent greatness that Anatoli possessed cannot be compared to the unquestionable genius of a Mozart, Anatoli's fine mind was far more in tune with its body, which it rightly recognized as part of, rather than separate from, the natural world. For Anatoli, mountains were altars where "I strive to perfect myself physically and spiritually. In their presence I attempt to understand my life, to exorcise vanity, greed, and fear. . . . I view my past, dream of the future, and with unusual acuteness I experience the present moment. . . . On each journey I am reborn."

Based on his Himalayan record alone, Anatoli was indisputably a great man, but few Americans outside his circle of friends know about the breadth of his humanity or how deeply he suffered during the last year and a half of his life because of negative publicity about his role as a guide on the infamous 1996 tragedy on Mount Everest. Unlike genius, which is a personal quality that often comes to naught, greatness implies a recognition of unusual human endeavor by the minds of others. It always comes after the fact, and all too often posthumously. Besides involving a continuum of accomplishments, greatness seems to require humility and a willingness to wait for the world to make its judgments.

I dwell at length on greatness because I believe Anatoli was robbed of it during his lifetime. As I wrote in a *Wall Street Journal* review of climber/journalist Jon Krakauer's book *Into Thin Air,* readers of the number-one bestseller are drawn "toward conclusions that erase heroism from the Himalaya as surely as modern journalism erases greatness from the American presidency." Though I praised the book as having "rare eloquence and power that could remain relevant for centuries," I strongly objected to the author's unfair treatment of Anatoli. Though Krakauer grants Anatoli certain strengths, "he never paints the big picture of one of the most amazing rescues in mountaineering history performed single-handedly a few hours after climbing Everest without oxygen by a man some describe as the Tiger Woods of Himalayan climbing."

After going from tent to tent, pleading for help, Anatoli headed out alone at night in a blizzard from the South Col to rescue three lost climbers. After descending from Everest, no other guide, Sherpa, or client (including Krakauer) could muster the necessary strength or courage to accompany Anatoli. That this amazing man who saved lives high on the mountain came to be characterized as an arrogant Russian villain in the subsequent made-for-TV movie based on the book is as woeful a modern outcome as any fictional tragedy of the past conjured up by Shakespeare or Dostoyevsky. Sadly, the *New York Times* report on Anatoli's death a year and a half later included the dark cloud of unresolved Everest controversy: "Krakauer accuses Boukreev . . . of compromising his clients' safety to achieve his own ambitions . . . and endangered them by making the exhausting climb without the aid of bottled oxygen. . . . However, Krakauer credits Boukreev with bravely saving the lives of two [*sic*] climbers."

Only by understanding how Anatoli suffered as he came to be demonized, in the same media feeding frenzy that brought Himalayan mountaineering into the forefront of American consciousness, can a reader begin to comprehend the forces that put Anatoli into the path of death two years in a row. I've previously published my strong opinion that the presence of a journalist on assignment from *Outside* magazine on the most fatal commercial Everest venture was no coincidence. The two competing guides who died high on the peak felt extreme pressure to get positive free ink in a big national magazine story that they believed would attract lots of clients to pay $65,000 fees to the most successful guide.

I'm also haunted by a strong suspicion that the second tragedy, so soon after the first, was also not coincidental. Were it not for the untoward media criticism directed at Anatoli after Everest, I doubt he would have felt the need to prove himself yet again in a world in which he had already outperformed every other climber of his generation.

In early December 1997, just after Anatoli left for Annapurna, he received a special award for heroism in absentia at the annual meeting of the American Alpine Club.

At the time of the award, Jim Wickwire, a highly respected Himalayan climber, clearly stated that the committee weighted "all of the information that was readily available to us" and that "Jon Krakauer's book was just one source." Wickwire explained that the committee carefully considered Anatoli's "nonuse of oxygen as well as his quick descent ahead of the Mountain Madness clients." In the end, "despite what some, but by no means all, would consider to be actions inconsistent with so-called 'standard' guiding practice, Boukreev's actions met the committee's award criteria, including the higher standard imposed when professional climbers are involved."

More than enough said, but the controversy continued to escalate. I was among the dozens of people who began receiving e-mail copies of accusations and rebuttals between Jon Krakauer and Anatoli's coauthor, Weston DeWalt, who had helped Anatoli publish a strikingly different account of events on Everest than what had been written in *Into Thin Air.*

Because the Alpine Club had previously asked me to review *The Climb,* I decided to enter the fray and pose a question directly to Krakauer about the astounding claim in one of his e-mails "that virtually every Sherpa on Everest in 1996 blames that entire tragedy on Boukreev." I asked Krakauer how he reconciled that statement "with the fact that every one of Boukreev's clients survived without major injuries, while all the clients who died or received major injuries were members of your party."

On December 20, Krakauer answered that the survival of Anatoli's clients was primarily due to their greater strength, but he curiously added: "I think the Sherpas are absolutely wrong to blame Anatoli, which is why I didn't mention their point of view in my book. . . . They blame him, I think, because they hate him so intensely."

Neither DeWalt nor I had ever heard this claim before. Since I was planning a trip to Nepal in March, I decided to do a fact-finding journey of my own to interview Sherpas in the Everest area. Though that journey didn't happen until after Anatoli's death, it seems best to report the results out of chronological sequence here. At Everest Base Camp, I talked to more than thirty Sherpas who had been on Everest in 1996 as well as three commercial expedition leaders who were also there at the time. No one expressed the belief that Anatoli was responsible for the tragedy, nor knew of any Sherpa who had ever expressed such a belief. Speculations that the late Lobsang Jangbu might have blamed Anatoli for not staying high enough long enough to help his close friend Scott Fischer were put to rest by a climber who had tented with Lobsang on a small expedition shortly before his death.

When I boarded a flight for South America just before Christmas, I expected not to hear anything more about Anatoli until I returned a month later. On the morning after Christmas at a remote lodge in Patagonia, a barely legible fax was brought to my door.

When I saw the names Anatoli and Annapurna, my first thought was that he had kindly asked someone to notify me about his successful climb. As I looked more closely at the rain-soaked paper, I saw that it said "missing and presumed dead in an avalanche on 25 December." A wave of grief rushed through my entire body as I walked out to the shore of a glacial lake filled with icebergs. There beneath the wild peaks of Torres del Paine, I stood alone, trying to make sense of wildly conflicted emotions. I didn't know Anatoli that well, and never would, yet I felt as deep a sense of loss as if a member of my own family had died. We would never climb an 8,000-meter peak together, or any other mountain.

Looking out over the blue icebergs, motionless beneath an angry Patagonian sky, I thought about how their floating tips represented the intense physicality that was all that many people knew of Anatoli. Invisible beneath the surface was the unseen spirituality that I had come to know in my conversations with him. We shared a diffident sacredness about life, friends, and simple things that comes across in the pages of his journals. It's something that permeates the being of many a mountaineer after decades of personal challenge in the natural world.

A more selfish reason for my extreme sense of loss struck me as I walked back to my cabin. There but for the grace of God went I. Despite our cultural gulf, Anatoli and I had an uncanny amount in common. I, too, had been a geology whiz kid who had moved from collecting rocks to climbing them. I, too, had moved on to become a physics major, hoping to better understand how the world worked, but instead finding ever more questions to ask. I, too, suffered from asthma, found relief in the clean air of higher altitudes, and went on to make fast ascents in the mountains. Lungs stressed by childhood asthma sometimes become conditioned to process oxygen better than normal lungs in later life. A classic example is Jim Ryun, who held the world record for the mile run, yet also suffered from childhood asthma.

I also felt quite conflicted by my good fortune not to have been with Anatoli on Annapurna. Was I just luckier than he, or would the two of us together have somehow sensed the avalanche danger and avoided it? I had quite a history of narrowly avoiding avalanches, as well as of extracting myself out of some minor ones before they swept me down. Did that make me more likely or less likely to die in one in the future? I had no clear answer, but I did ponder whether the circumstances that had led Anatoli to try such an extreme climb in winter might further have influenced his decisions on that fateful Christmas Day.

I recalled my own attempt to solo a lower peak in the Annapurna region in winter conditions, and how I'd instinctually retreated from an open slope, gone to its very edge, climbed up a few feet, jumped hard into the snow, and set off a slab avalanche that had cracked a curving arc up and over my original route, releasing tons of ice and snow. I later contemplated whether I would have sensed the danger and tested the slope if I'd had an eager partner with me, or if something about being there alone had allowed me to be more in tune with the mountain. I had few outside influences spurring me on—no sponsors to satisfy nor an agenda of summits to climb that year.

If I had been there with Anatoli on Christmas Day, would either of us have sensed the impending doom? Such a question is unanswerable, yet appropriate to contemplate privately as a phantom survivor who had dropped out before the adventure began.

Years earlier, I had dropped out of guiding Himalayan peaks, partly because of an increased ability to make a living through photography, but more because of witnessing too many times the fine line between triumph and tragedy while climbing with people I would otherwise not have chosen as partners. In 1977, I led the first American-guided ascent of a 7,000-meter Himalayan peak. A fellow guide roped to two clients was descending from the summit far too slowly into the night when the weakest member stumbled and fell on an ice slope. The guide held both men in a two-hundred-foot fall. Luckily, no one was injured, but few people outside our party realized how close our triumph had come to tragedy.

The reverse—triumph instead of tragedy—could have happened on Everest in 1996 with just minor differences, such as a slightly earlier start or turning around weaker clients sooner. A smaller, more experienced, or more tightly organized group of Everest climbers would have been back at the South Col well before the brunt of the afternoon storm. Indeed, a French woman ascended neighboring 27,923-foot Lhotse that same day in the same weather conditions without incident. Though some say that Anatoli could have saved more lives by remaining near the summit for several more hours, waiting around so high while climbing without oxygen did not seem like the best choice at the time for Anatoli.

Hindsight is always twenty-twenty, but impending avalanches often defy prediction. In 1989, I was leading two clients across a glacial bowl at twenty thousand feet on Gasherbrum II when a distant avalanche began to fall off a lower peak. Judging its path, I yelled, "Run for it now!" Thirty seconds later, the tracks where we had been walking, as well as the empty nearby high camp of a women's expedition, were buried under tons of ice. We were coated in blowing snow, but unscathed.

How close we came was driven home to me when another guide from our expedition arrived roped to a weaker, more argumentative client who, I realized then and there, might not have instantly obeyed my command. That tiny sort of life-or-death difference influenced my decision not to participate in any more guided 8,000-meter expeditions. On the other hand, I immediately agreed to climb two 8,000ers with Anatoli in the summer of 1998. Had I been roped only to Anatoli that day on Gasherbrum, I like to think that we both would have run for it, roped together, without a spoken word.

Since that 1989 trip, I haven't been back to an 8,000-meter peak. For me, serious mountaineering is all about trust; trust in oneself and trust in one's companions. Mountaineering has no formal code of conduct, as there is with law or medicine. Philosophies constantly evolve, especially for those who excel. The old proverb "Good judgment comes from experience; experience comes from bad judgment" is nowhere more true than in high-altitude mountaineering. With your life on the line, you must constantly reassess your values, your decisions, your future goals, as Anatoli does so eloquently within these pages.

Another truism is that human beings tend to explain away their failures as due to circumstances beyond their control, usually by blaming someone else. Unusual success, however, whether their own or someone else's touted in the media, must be the result of exceptional personal ability. Thus Einstein was a born genius to come up with the theory of relativity (though he did poorly in school), and Reinhold Messner was a born superman to be the first to climb Everest without oxygen and to summit all the world's 8,000-meter peaks (though physiologists who tested him afterward concluded that he was well trained, but physically quite normal). Had I not known Anatoli personally, I might have bought into the media myth that he was just a genetically gifted and narrowly trained Russian speed climber.

When I met Reinhold Messner in the Himalaya and again in Alaska well before his Everest climbs, I realized that, above all else, he possessed an unusually inquiring and decisive mind. He wanted to know whether there was a yeti and all about Tibetan Buddhism as much as he wanted to summit high peaks. Messner is a survivor who has moved on to become deeply involved in European politics and to write more than thirty books.

Anatoli had a similar breadth and power of mind, but in a far more genetically gifted body. He rarely experienced the pain and suffering often described as an inherent part of climbing into the "death zone" above eight thousand meters. Thus the high Himalaya became Anatoli's playground, a place where he experienced supreme joy from simply being there as well as occasional greatness when he seized the proper moment to launch his long-prepared body and mind into action. Though best known to the public for climbing Everest, his performance above eight thousand meters on many other Himalayan peaks, often alone and in extreme conditions, remains unparalleled. He climbed Gasherbrum II in ten hours, Dhaulagiri in seventeen hours, Makalu in forty-six hours, Manaslu in winter, and traversed all four summits of Kanchenjunga in a single push. After just two days' rest from his 1996 Everest rescue, he soloed 27,923-foot Lhotse in the record time of twenty-one hours.

Climbing Mount Everest was second nature for Anatoli, even the first time he reached its summit. In these pages from his private journals, he describes undertaking "an easy acclimatization climb" above the South Col in preparation for his first climb of the peak as a speed ascent from Base Camp in 1991. He and a friend set off casually without oxygen and with just their ski poles at 8:30 A.M., long after the typical midnight starts for summit bids. For him, the climbing was "easy going, not particularly a struggle." By two o'clock, "rather unexpectedly, we found ourselves on the South Summit." While his partner descended back to camp in high winds, Anatoli crawled up the infamous Hillary Step without an ice ax and "almost by accident. I arrived on the summit at 3 P.M."

Had Anatoli revealed these inner thoughts to a journalist in 1991, out of context they could have been made to sound highly arrogant. What kind of person would express such casual regard for an adversary so formidable that its very name—Everest—has become a global metaphor for supreme challenge? Between the lines of his journal is the answer to that question never asked. Everest was simply a different mountain for Anatoli.

Everest is separated from other great peaks of the world not so much by its ascent height as by its thin air, in which Anatoli performed extremely well. Alaska's Mount McKinley rises thousands of feet higher above its base to just 20,320 feet. Even 14,495-foot Mount Whitney rises almost as high above a valley in California as Mount Everest does above the Khumbu Valley in Nepal.

What matters far more than a mountain's height or vertical rise is an emergent quality related to each human being's ability to ascend under his or her own power. It is this that gives Everest such charisma and mystique. To see it rising 10,800 feet above the trekkers' viewpoint at Kala Pattar is ever so psychically different from seeing Mount Whitney rising 10,600 feet above the Owens Valley. Every human being assesses natural terrain, from the most humble hilltop to the highest mountain, by a subconscious measure of the time it would take to get to the top under one's own power.

I was in my thirties when I first looked up at Everest's summit from below and naturally visualized it in the expanded geography of time. With the techniques of the day and my abilities, it would have taken me at least three weeks to get to the top.

Back home in California, I looked up about the same distance to the top of Mount Whitney. I had recently run the tourist trail to the summit in three hours. What a comparison to my three-week estimate for Everest! I let my youthful urge to mathematically quantify the world run rampant and calculated my personal psychic height for Mount Everest by multiplying the 168 hours in a week by the 14,495-foot height of Mount Whitney. The result was a staggering 2,435,160-foot mountain. A more conservative estimate might compare the difference between a guided client's 250-foot-per-hour pace above the South Col on Everest to a 1,000-foot-per-hour pace on Whitney. That would make Everest's psychic altitude only four times its measured height, or 116,140 feet. For Anatoli, however, Everest's psychic height was far lower, within the limits of a hard day's outing in good conditions. But was the mountain truly diminished for him? In psychic height yes, but in psychic reward, absolutely not.

When Hillary and Tenzing first climbed Everest in 1953, media pundits predicted that no one would ever climb it again, now that it had been conquered. While the mountain will never again be viewed as the world's most pristine and immutable point, there are good reasons why many top climbers return to it again and again after first reaching the summit. Human experience over time with proper motivation can infuse a landscape with a spiritual quality that every enduring culture describes in a hauntingly similar way. It is the essence of the long history of Himalayan pilgrimage, where physical hardships are undertaken for spiritual reward, rather than material gain. It also helps clarify the Everest dichotomy that engulfed Anatoli. The public knew him as a guide climbing Everest for material gain, yet he did so to fund his private passion to do other climbs for spiritual reward.

When I first met Anatoli more than a decade ago, I felt an instant kinship with him on my favorite morning trail run in the Berkeley Hills. Rather than push the pace, which he could so easily have done, he paused to contemplate the sun breaking through fog-draped Monterey pines, patterns in the windblown grass, and the tall buildings of San Francisco rising in the distance over the blanket of fog. We hardly spoke about these things as our heads turned together and our bodies slowed down while the particular visions remained in view.

At the time, Anatoli's English was so broken that I knew him better by gesture and body language than by the few words we had in common. Not until after he died did I fully realize how much this lack of fluency in English contributed to his being misunderstood in America. Our increasingly troubled journalism is ever less satisfied with basic reporting. Events must be validated by eyewitness regurgitations of emotions that supposedly occurred at the moment, but more likely came to mind when the press asked for an interview. The British Everest climber Doug Scott may have been the first to openly state that great thoughts rarely if ever occur to mountaineers on summits, but frequently surface afterward while celebrating over beers with one's mates. The same principle applies to tragedies.

The language problem is at least part of the reason why Anatoli's "great thoughts" are wholly absent in *Into Thin Air*, and only weakly present in his own book, *The Climb*, which is based on interviews conducted in English. Anatoli's personal philosophies—from simple truisms to profound insights about the human condition—come across clearly in the book you are now reading because he wrote them in his native language. As I read them, they evoke strong memories of the young Anatoli, fresh to America, who asked me all about my first one-day climb of Alaska's Mount McKinley.

Pushing my personal limits, I had done the climb in 1978 with the late Olympic cross-country skier Ned Gillette, from a pass at about ten thousand feet where the peak connects to Mount Foraker. Anatoli wanted to do it from where bush planes normally land climbers at seven thousand feet, not because it would better our record, but because to him this seemed to be a more natural starting point. Only after we had spent an hour talking all about the climb did he ask if I thought we could have done it faster.

"Not much faster that day," I answered, "but we weren't trying to set a speed record. We'd come from sea level two days before and weren't acclimatized. Our goal was to pace ourselves and experience the mountain as a day climb—unencumbered with all the extra stuff between us and the mountain that we otherwise would have brought to spend nights in the cold or wait out storms."

"It is same for me," Anatoli said. "At home I do competitions, but when I climb for me, my experience is not about the record, even when I break it. It is how I am with the mountain in that special way. You understand?"

I did then, and more than ever, I do now. What set Anatoli apart from most other Himalayan climbers was far more than the combination of fortuitous genes, intensive training, and raw experience that rendered him able to climb 8,000-meter peaks in less than a day or to rapidly retreat in the face of advancing weather. The breadth of his humanity surpasses his physical exploits. It is that quality that makes this book of his personal journals so compelling.

Linda Wylie's splendid introduction sets the stage for understanding Anatoli's emergence from what she summed up to me as "the Soviet experiment that was not all Stalin and bad things," as so many Americans believe. She also summed up how that same society "nurtured his purest desire to achieve spiritual and physical perfection" to a degree that American society did not during the same era.

It would be a mistake to leave readers with the impression that all this controversy over style and motives on Mount Everest is uniquely contemporary. While books and articles may emphasize satellite telephone calls and Internet postings from the mountain as well as the personal eccentricities of wealthy clients, in a larger sense these are simply modern manifestations of states of affairs as old as humanity and nothing new on Mount Everest. The great British mountaineer, explorer, and writer Eric Shipton directly anticipated the style of expedition that met with tragedy in 1996 in the following words he wrote after his own 1938 attempt:

> The ascent of Everest, like any other human endeavor, is only to be judged by the spirit in which it is attempted. . . . Let us climb peaks . . . not because others have failed, nor because the summits stand twenty-eight thousand feet above the sea, nor in patriotic fervor for the honour of the nation, nor for cheap publicity. . . . Let us not attack them with an army, announcing on the wireless to a sensation-loving world the news of our departure and the progress of our subsequent advance.

Shipton made several attempts on Everest before World War II with lightweight expeditions that reached over twenty-eight thousand feet without oxygen, much in the style that Anatoli preferred to climb. After the war, Shipton was summarily removed as leader of the 1953 successful climb because the Royal Geographical Society thought his style didn't bode high enough odds for a British success. The society found a military leader, Colonel Hunt, to assemble the far larger, oxygen-supported effort that was victorious.

Had Shipton succeeded on Everest without oxygen and an army of Sherpas, the history of high-altitude climbing would have unfolded entirely differently. Huge, overequipped Himalayan expeditions to big peaks—private and commercial alike—would have been hard to justify and harder to finance. And Anatoli might still be alive, pursuing Shipton's dream of climbing the wild peaks of Asia with a few friends and a few classic tools.

—GALEN ROWELL

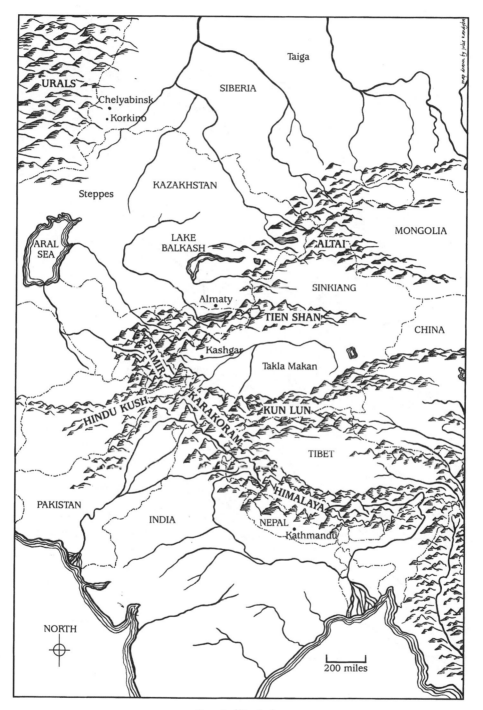

Anatoli's Asia

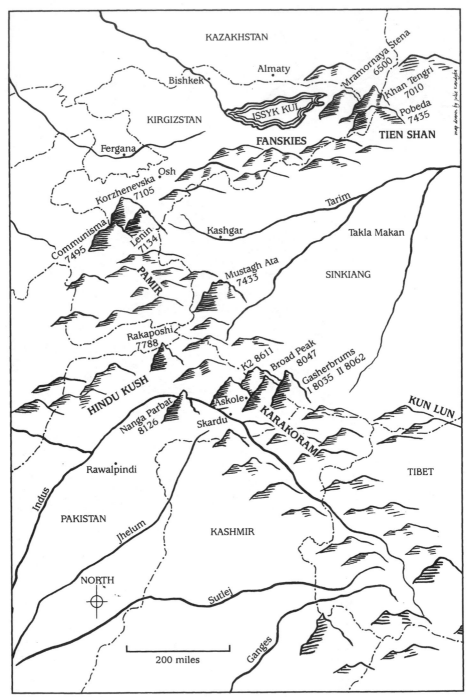

Central Asian Ranges

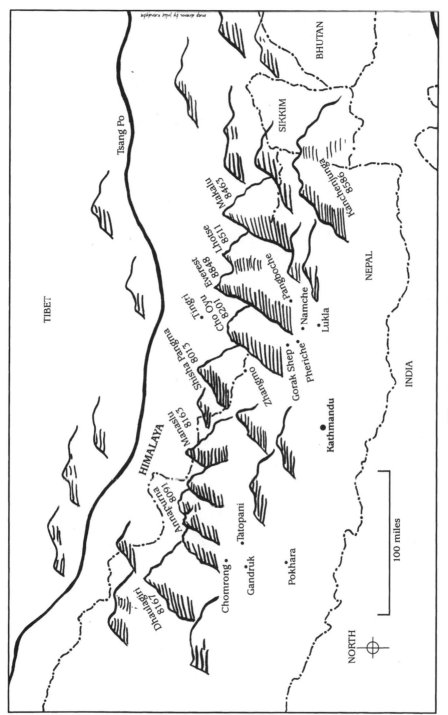

map drawn by Julie Kendrick

TIBET

Tsang Po

BHUTAN

SIKKIM

Kanchenjunga 8586

Makalu 8463

Lhotse 8511

Everest 8848

Cho Oyu 8201

Tingri

Shisha Pangma 8013

Manaslu 8163

Annapurna 8091

Dhaulagiri 8167

HIMALAYA

Pangboche

Namche

Lukla

Gorak Shep

Pheriche

Zhangmo

Chomrong

Gandruk

Tatopani

Pokhara

Kathmandu

NEPAL

INDIA

100 miles

NORTH

Himalayas of Nepal

ABOVE THE CLOUDS

INTRODUCTION:

TO RUSSIA WITH LOVE

On Christmas Day in 1997, the rumble of falling rock and ice disturbed the cathedral silence in Annapurna Sanctuary. On the ramparts of the Western Wall a cornice collapsed and scoured an eight-hundred-meter-long couloir. Car-sized blocks of ice gathered speed and swept three men to the glacier below. The life of internationally renowned Russian mountaineer Anatoli Boukreev ended in the embrace of natural forces.

Far away, in the world of record books, Anatoli left a list of accomplishments unparalleled in the sport of high-altitude mountaineering. To his credit were twenty-one successful attempts on eleven of the world's fourteen highest peaks, including speed records on Lhotse, Dhaulagiri, and Gasherbrum II, as well as new routes up Central Kanchenjunga and the West Wall of Dhaulagiri. He is one of thirteen men who can claim the tops of the highest and hardest mountains on earth: Everest, K2, Lhotse, Kanchenjunga, Makalu, Dhaulagiri, and Manaslu. In 1989, as a member of a history-making team from the Soviet Union, he traversed the ridge of the four 8,400-meter-plus summits that form the Kanchenjunga Massif. All these challenges—except for the traverse of Kanchenjunga and the

1997 Indonesian climb of Everest—he surmounted without the relief of supplemental oxygen.

During a 1997 summer interview in Kazakhstan, Reinhold Messner appraised him as "one of the strongest mountaineers in the world."
Respected American filmmaker and mountaineer David Breashears
echoed that assessment in a CNN television interview with Larry
King. "Anatoli is gifted," Breashears said, "one of a handful of men
who could have succeeded in rescuing clients from the death grip of
a storm on the South Col of Mount Everest in 1996." In an obituary
in *Outside* magazine, premier alpinist Ed Viesturs remembered his
peer as the "consummate mountaineer."

Mountain climbers like Anatoli are a breed apart. Like a latter-
day Ulysses, he journeyed in a world of cataclysm and giants, armed
only with wit and strength, to meet destiny unafraid. The recognition of his peers would have meant more to Anatoli than any laurel
for literary achievement. And though Anatoli was the first to admit
he was no Dostoyevsky, his unique personal history and the magnitude of his accomplishments give his journals a compelling authority. In the following chapters you will find an uncompromising
picture of the forces at work above the clouds. Even for the uninitiated these writings clarify the complex challenge of high mountains
for the men and women who climb them. As history these journals
chronicle the ten years when one of the earth's pure inviolate fron-
tiers became an unlikely commercial business: the pricey peak experience. For the Western reader, they personalize a nationality and are
a window into a Russian man's quest for meaning in life.

The financial security and patronage that would have allowed
him to express his full capacity eluded Anatoli. His greatest achievements went unrewarded in Kazakhstan and Russia. While Western
alpinists of high caliber, such as Messner, Loretan, and Carsolio, returned to countrymen who took their successes to heart, Anatoli's
bent for individual accomplishments made him an anomaly in the
USSR. When he was thirty-three, the collapse of the Soviet Union
shattered the fabric of his life. At the peak of his physical potential,

political instability and economic chaos opened like a great yawning crevasse, swallowing opportunity and destroying the ethic that supported his athleticism. His role as an Honored Master Athlete in Soviet society evaporated.

Ill prepared for the pitfalls of capitalism but unwilling to give up a quest that had charted his course in life since the age of sixteen, he turned to the mountains. That trail would lead him to America, to the Karakoram, to the Himalayas, and then always home in search of a place in his motherland. Fifteen years of hard-won experience earned him work as a guide in an emerging international marketplace: the world's 8,000-meter peaks. During the spring of 1996 on Mount Everest the game turned deadly. Anatoli Boukreev found himself center stage, thrust into a spotlight of attention created by an American journalist's interpretation of the tragedy. A popular outdoor magazine rushed to publish an article that held Anatoli accountable for the Damoclean forces of nature and a complex web of ambitions that had spun beyond his control. There followed a storm of controversy that threatened to eclipse his brilliant career and unquestionable bravery. He was fortunate to meet and collaborate with writer Weston DeWalt on *The Climb*. Anatoli's version of the 1996 Everest tragedy was published by St. Martin's Press only two months before his death. The scope of that work was necessarily narrow and investigative. It could not communicate the depth of Anatoli's contribution to mountaineering or his measure as a man.

Soviet citizens lived out values and ethics molded in a society that is little understood in the West. A generation ago, the Russian faces we knew were those of Khrushchev and Stalin: stolid, humorless, unknowable for most people. Anatoli was born in January of 1958, three months after the successful launch of *Sputnik* marked a milestone in human scientific achievement. For Russians, it validated their arrival in the twentieth century. Their scientific success provoked a respectful wave of paranoia in America: we headed for the moon. In the sixties and seventies our two nations' rivalries were played out on different stages. Soviet education and their science of human performance produced dazzling results. Adept prodigies captured the imagination of audiences on international platforms, with their music and ballet and with their athletic prowess and grace on Olympic playing fields. There were cracks in the wall, but fear and suspicion contorted the humanity glimpsed from both sides. For Americans, the varied population that inhabited one-sixth of the world's landmass was reduced to a few stereotypes.

In 1991, when the walls came down, generations of Russians were left standing in the shambles of their country to sort out who they were if they were not Soviet. God and the czar were far away. Who would they be without the ideology of Communism, and how should they act in the world? The idealism and inner strength that Anatoli possessed are common among his people. These values endure in the population of average citizens independent of the strange political machinations that have played out throughout their history. Anatoli was not ashamed of his Soviet upbringing. He salvaged what was positive from his culture, marrying the bewildering political and social contradictions into something exemplary, something uniquely Russian.

Deprived of the political context that had created his role in Soviet society, he went out in the world to make his own place. Ingrained in him was a conservative, utilitarian view of materialism. He never mistook the accumulation of objects for wealth or freedom. Direct physical experience was refined into meaning. Most of what he needed he learned to carry on his back. Monastic simplicity lent Anatoli a paradoxical kind of elegance. His motives for climbing reflected a rich interior world with a bedrock of idealism that seemed more grounded in the mystical tenets of his mother's Orthodox faith than in his indoctrination as a Communist.

Big mountains are a completely different world: snow, ice, rocks, sky, and thin air. You cannot conquer them, only rise to their height for a short time; and for that they demand a great deal. The struggle is not with the enemy, or a competitor like in sports, but with yourself, with the feelings of weakness and inadequacy. That struggle appeals to me. It is why I became a mountaineer.

Every summit is different, each a different life that you have lived.

You arrive at the top having renounced everything that you think you must have to support life and are alone with your soul. That empty vantage point lets you reappraise yourself and every relationship and object that is part of the civilized world with a different perspective.

On the anvil of his self-realization, life hammered out a man who in most ways had more in common with Tibet's ascetic poet Milarepa than with superathletes like Michael Jordan.

In the autumn of 1994, Anatoli Boukreev walked into a lodge in the village of Pheriche in the kingdom of Nepal. Though he entered without pretension, he was impossible to ignore. A big man, he moved with the grace of something wild, and his presence filled the room. His composure was complete: at once cautious and curious. An unwavering gaze and the amused interest playing in his blue eyes offered me windows to his soul. Coincidentally we were thrown together at Lhotse Base Camp. Our days passed in idle conversation. Attentively generous, Anatoli shared sections of a mysterious, never-ending supply of mandarin oranges and he talked—modestly fitting the pieces of his life into a picture. Those conversations were the beginning of this book.

Our friendship became a collaborative partnership in 1996. Together, we began sorting and translating the stack of notebooks, diaries, and journals that had collected in his closet in Almaty. Composing and editing material for magazine articles, speaking engagements, and his contributions to *The Climb* refined a mutual vocabulary. A year of difficult personal circumstances and climbing forged a deeper understanding. When the avalanche fell in December of 1997, I could thank Anatoli for a broader view of the earth's horizon. In his way he had given me the golden light of the Russian steppes and the celestial mountains of Central Asia. This introduction reveals what

Anatoli shared with me of the people and events that influenced his life. The journals are as much as he had time to say about his motives and his experience of climbing mountains.

To be Russian in the sense that Anatoli spoke of himself is to be tied to a vast landscape with a complex history. He grew up a thousand miles from Moscow, past the Rubicon that divides Europe from Asia, and all his adult life, his home was in Almaty, a city that had once welcomed travelers who strayed from the Silk Road. The town of his birth is located at the southeast end of the Ural Mountains on the edge of the steppes. That vast grass highway extends away from Korkino for a thousand miles in three directions. As a child Anatoli explored Scythian barrows and learned the details of a long history that wove his people into the fabric of the land. Anatoli insisted the Mongol word *Kazakh* was derived from the Russian word for cossack, and that Kazakhstan gained its name from the czar's soldiers, who were stationed in the Russian colony in the early 1700s. Over the next three hundred years a stream of Russian explorers and immigrants brought the trappings of Western civilization and diluted the area's nomad populations. In the Siberian northland surrounding his birthplace, expansive wilderness and extreme forces of nature affected the psyche of new settlers. In cities to the south, Russian immigrants melted into a polyglot society of Turks and Mongols, where mature urban customs and attitudes reflected the ameliorating influences of twelfth-century Persian humanism.

Anatoli resisted canonizing the political vicissitudes of perestroika that made him Russian one day and Kazakh the next. That change occurred too quickly for him to make any peace with it. At the beginning of the twentieth century the standard of excellence set by Russians in architecture, art, music, literature, theater, and ballet put his country in the vanguard of international creativity. Pride in that rich legacy was transferred to him during his adolescent education as he was raised on Russian classics. The likes of Dostoyevsky, Gorky, Tolstoy, and Pushkin colored his life view and sense of place in the world. Just as certainly as he inculcated values from Russian culture, he acknowledged that growing up past the Urals made him an "Eastern" man. He was cautious and did not like to hurry. In business, he expected to bargain and negotiate, his word being his bond. In relationships, he appreciated modesty and honesty. To him the peoples who had washed across Central Asia and Siberia in history's waves were Soviet. Time, circumstance, and geography had forged their union. Anything less deprived him of his country. More than once, Reuters reporter Elizabeth Hawley, the doyenne of Himalayan mountaineering history, became exasperated with his dual passports and ambivalent national identity.

His hometown, Korkino, had dubious beginnings. The founding father was a prisoner who had escaped a czarist chain gang in the late 1800s. In a lush part of the steppes he carved out a home beyond convenient reach of the authorities, dryly naming his outpost after the Russian word for "last crust of bread." The area's subsequent settlers were fugitives as well. Until the turn of the century the superstitious inhabitants filled in their wells when the water mysteriously turned black, thinking the phenomenon was a sign that they had been cursed by the devil. In fact, the town would develop haphazardly on top of some of the largest coal deposits on the Eurasian continent.

By the mid-1930s Korkino's coal was firing Stalin's lurching industrialization. Ranking high on Soviet pay scales, workers operated Pit Korkinski around the clock. Until the coal became of a poorer quality and more difficult to extract, citizens enjoyed the benefits of a stable economic base. In the twenties and thirties, upper-class peasants whom the Communists had designated for reeducation were relocated and assigned new occupations. Korkino was the site of one of Stalin's gulags.

Unlike many of their neighbors, Anatoli's family did not suffer the brunt of Stalin's paranoia. His mother and father were poor and were never Party members. Likely it was emancipation of the serfs or the czar's work details that had moved his great-grandparents to the Chelyabinsk Oblast before the turn of the century. The details of their personal circumstances were lost to family historians. Anatoli was of the *narod,* the common people, and such ancestral amnesia is not unusual in Russia.

In 1948, Nikolai Boukreev and Valentina Shipitsina married and moved from rustic homes in the Chelyabinsk countryside to Korkino. Valentina's war-widowed mother came with them. Around a three-room wooden house, they fenced off enough land for a kitchen garden and a small orchard. By the time Anatoli was born, the city had grown to a population of sixty-five thousand. The old center of town had a certain charm, thanks to the large log houses that were the architectural pretension of the upper-class peasants. New classic Stalin-style buildings were constructed with a low profile to prevent the blasts at the mine from knocking them down. Residential streets were mud more often than they were dirt. Individual homes lacked indoor plumbing. Water was available from hand pumps at communal wells. The open-pit mine, which by then was five hundred meters deep and larger than any other in Europe, had drained the local lakes and significantly despoiled the environment. With characteristically sardonic humor, Anatoli replied to a reporter from the *Chelyabinsk Worker's News,* who asked how he had come to love mountains, that it was Korkino's towering slag heaps that had first inspired him to climb.

By the late 1950s the environment developed other malignant problems. Radiation leaks from the Mayak Nuclear Waste Storage Unit located one hundred kilometers away were a regular occurrence. One of the first things Anatoli told me about himself was "it was only luck that I was born." In 1957 a massive release from Mayak dosed his mother and the rest of the population with levels of radiation higher than those from the reactor explosion at Chernobyl. He grew up with two maladies common in local children. Until he was twenty-one, chronic nephritis plagued him with a form of hypertension, and his allergies caused asthma. His older sister, Luba, died of breast cancer at age thirty-five. Anatoli was convinced that her disease was linked to a lifetime of exposure to the radiation leaks from Mayak.

The potential effects of his childhood environment haunted

Anatoli, and over the years he developed a preoccupation with his health, which extended far beyond his strict fitness regimen for mountaineering. He incorporated into his daily routine health practices recommended by American nutritionist Paul Bragg and Russian pulmonologist Constantine Buyteko. His friend Elliott Robinson remembered, "We talked a lot about keeping healthy the natural way through fasting, good diet, and training. He always believed that while Americans had a great medical system, they did not fully understand the body's ability to heal naturally." Anatoli believed in the beneficial effects of sauna, massage, and icy plunges. Laughing at me when my expression implied that some of his prescriptions were too extreme, he would insist that we must "work for our health, and the discomfort is very good training for climbing mountains."

One way or another his health always threatened to jeopardize his athletic ambitions. Aside from the asthma, which was exacerbated by a night bivouac on the South Col of Everest in 1991, he was hospitalized for three months in 1981 with meningitis. He survived an auto accident in 1989, and underwent treatment for liver abscesses in 1990. Returning from Cho Oyu in 1997, a bizarre bus crash decapitated the man sitting in front of him and would have decapitated Anatoli if he had not been slumped forward behind the seat to sleep. In September of 1997 he remarked to a Moscow interviewer that from his experience, life below four thousand meters was more risky for him than the sobering odds he faced above that elevation.

I saw Anatoli angry only once, and that was for but a short time. Usually he ventilated frustration with a dry, earthy sense of humor and exercise. He looked at life differently, took personal responsibility for situations, and was alive to the opportunity of the present moment. His sense of humor and peculiar self-awareness, coupled with a master's sense of timing, authored some hilarious stories.

Scottish expedition leader Henry Todd tells a great story that is classic Anatoli:

I had a Tibet-side Everest permit for the spring of 1995. Some of my younger team members were very impressed by

Anatoli and had endless questions for him. Patiently responding to their after-dinner inquiries, he would sit with a tea-
spoon in his forefingers spooning down small portions of an
entire jar of jam, while he slowly related some tale in his
heavily accented Russian-English. These stories were always
peppered with colorful, unusual metaphors. Finally every
evening he would take a sip from a tiny brown bottle. This
routine and Anatoli's little bottle had a special fascination for
one member. "What is it? What does it do?" were part of a
nightly interrogation.

"The ingredients are a secret," Anatoli maintained, adding
something irresistible to the mystery: "But this is the source
of my power."

The game of cat and mouse went on for several weeks.
Finally the young man asked for a sample of the precious
elixir, on the pretext of needing extra power during his summit bid to begin the following day.

Relenting with a spark in his eye, Anatoli filled his hastily
wiped jam spoon with the thick, red liquid.

It was dispatched with a shudder of distaste, followed by
the obvious question.

"What is it?"

The mess tent was silent. Anatoli had drawn us all into
the drama.

Pausing, he intoned with exaggerated resonance, "Blood
of woman."

Everyone collapsed laughing.

The cruel contradictions of Soviet life provided the material for
many jokes that were so darkly ironic only a Russian could laugh. On
the whole he was not harshly critical of his country's political philosophy. He tended to view the shortcomings in all political systems
as the outcome of individual character flaws and human weakness.
"The main thing wrong with Communism turned out to be the
Communist," he maintained dryly. After perestroika things weren't

much different in his mind: "Before tyrants controlled what we thought with their fists; now, with their fists full of money, the same tyrants control people economically—the freedom which has come to the average person is the freedom to struggle desperately for survival." Friends described him as "apolitical," obstinately individualistic but steel-bound by an sensitivity and family-mindedness not uncommon among Russian people. The attention to detail and iron discipline that authored his phenomenal endurance underwrote his ethical behavior. Don't waste, live up to your commitments, respect life— those things were concrete in his character. Anatoli gave a lot of credit to the educational system that had nurtured his potential and guided his development.

By the time he reached school age, his nation's priorities had shifted to higher education and patronage of human excellence in sports, the arts, and sciences. Farmers, steelworkers, and miners extended the luxury of self-perfection to the ballerina, the scientist, and the athlete. Anatoli grew up believing his personal effort contributed to the cultural elevation of the whole society. He never thought what he did was more important than what his brother did as a coal miner. It was just different. That concept of social reciprocity, with its implied humility, was fundamental to the way he rationalized his striving for athletic self perfection. It was the basis for his value as a unit in his society.

Secondary functions of the Soviet educational system were to nurture idealism, natural ability, and initiative. There were many avenues for self-expression. Even in a town like Korkino, where most children were destined to end up in the mines, there was an art and music academy. Individual sports such as gymnastics, rock climbing, skating, and cross-country skiing had coaches and community support. Anatoli gratefully acknowledged that his success as a mountaineer was due to the Soviet mentoring system, which refined his natural ability with discipline and technique.

He grew to manhood in the most enlightened years of the Communist experiment. After Stalin's death, as the country emerged from twenty-five years of silent self-annihilation, a generation of

poets and philosophers survived to affect Party politics. In the brief
window when an officially sanctioned version of Solzhenitsyn's *One
Day in the Life of Ivan Denisovich* was published, citizens acknowledged
publicly that Stalin had charted a dehumanizing course to achieve
their humanitarian goals. Actor and songwriter Vladimir Vysotskii
became the voice for average people. A starring role as a mountaineer
in a movie called *The Height* catapulted him to popular fame. Despite
a season in Siberia for reeducation, he gave free rein to his opinions
in poems and songs. Audiocassettes of his lyrics were reproduced in
secret and made available underground to millions of fans throughout
the Soviet Union. In the nineties, Anatoli's American friends received
these tapes as gifts and puzzled over the significance and appeal of
Vysotskii's gravely guttural voice. During Anatoli's politically forma-
tive years, Vysotskii in Russia, like Bob Dylan in America, encouraged
humanistic individualism, which the state sought to disallow. Vysotskii
was one of Anatoli's heroes.

Young people in Russia had a huge appetite for things Western;
Levi's jeans and disco seemed to define the freedom they were after. For
twenty years a complex turbulence—at once base and noble—propelled the Soviet Union toward more permeable borders. Anatoli was
not completely comfortable with the face of change he saw in Moscow
and St. Petersburg in the late eighties. Musing about this in 1990, he
recorded in his diary: "Something terrible is happening to young
people in my country: drugs, alcohol, and spiritual degeneration."

East of the Urals, priorities were different from those in the urban centers that incubated classical Russian culture and political ambition. In the late sixties, authors raised on the Eastern frontier found
their voice in a characteristic genre of literature. The "village prose
writers" asked the Soviet public to look at the environmental price
Russia was paying for progress both in her devastated landscapes and
on their interior geography. Nature's profound beauty and the moral-
ity of common people who eked out a living in the Siberian outback
inspired writers such as Valentin Rasputin. Attempting to recall the
positive mooring for Russian identity, these writers celebrated traditional wisdom, human compassion, and the land. Anatoli's mother

and father might have provided the role models for the values these writers championed.

Anatoli proudly described his parents as "simple people," saying that "my father had golden hands and my mother devoted her life to the needs of her children." Despite the hardships of difficult circumstances, Nikolai Boukreev and his wife, Valentina, raised their five children gently and with respect. Handicapped by a childhood bout of polio, Nikolai's withered legs barely functioned; he walked only with the aid of crutches. The family's income was dependent on his industry, discipline, and the fastidious quality of his work. In a small Korkino street kiosk, he repaired clocks, mechanical objects, and musical instruments; later on he became a shoemaker. His skill as a musician and his beautiful singing voice softened the austerity of life at home. He infected his son with a love of music. Singing was a way Anatoli remembered his father. Nikolai died in December of 1995 while his middle son was in Nepal climbing Manaslu. When Anatoli called to tell me that sad news in January of 1996, I imagined the man he mourned, so steady and generous of spirit he could sing a love song to his wife of forty-five years before he slipped away into death's quietness.

A single word in Anatoli's language, *umilenie,* is used to describe a complex emotion: the combination of tenderness, sadness, and exaltation. It is wonder that falls just short of tears. The man or woman who is unable to respond to beauty that deeply, Russians believe, has missed the point of being human. For them the scope of beauty is wide and deep: like the presence of courage in the old, the innocence of children, nature, and great music or art. Often Anatoli presented a composed reserve, for he was an intensely private man, but he appreciated life with that depth of feeling. When the barrier of language frustrated communication, he sang, celebrating these things that are universal in human experience: love, beauty, and loss. He was a romantic who took pleasure in small things and graceful behavior. I can only surmise that the refined sensitivity I saw consistently operate in his character was grounded in the tender regard of his parents and the quality of his Russian upbringing.

Although the Boukreev children never heard their father complain about his disability, it caused hardship for the big family. The kitchen garden and orchard provided a crucial supplement to the family's diet. Household chores fell on Anatoli and his two older siblings. The older boys hauled water and coal, Luba and Irina helped with washing and housework. There was never a surplus of food or money for luxuries. Their childhood privations marked the children in different ways; they were not all happy.

Anatoli, for his part, was never ashamed or angry about the hard work that denied him an easy childhood. His chosen lifestyle would effect a kind of loneliness. He required nothing from his family but the grounding of their honest affection, and as an adult he was that kind of friend. He took the time to write and made an effort to maintain important relationships. Like his father, he was a perfectionist. A pedantic attention to detail could be maddening when translated into the fast-paced lives of American friends, but in the mountains it kept him alive. He expressed an earnest concern and appreciation for others and a generosity that was startling in one whose life came to depend so much on his own initiative. I asked Irina, his younger sister, to describe him as a child. She remembered that as a boy he refused the money his father offered the children for ice cream, reasoning that "it was better for our family to buy bread." That child became the adult who was satisfied to hand-wash the two shirts that served every occasion, who repaid every loan or gave you the biggest portion of food he had cooked after an exhausting day of climbing.

If Nikolai was the model for his manhood, Anatoli's mother provided the stable, abiding love that anchored him in the world. Valentina gave her affection and acceptance equally to her children. She nurtured their differences, and no one was deprived of tenderness, kindness, or care. Until the end of her life she would be there to absorb their troubles. Her second son she christened Anatoli, "from the east," and for a time after his birth, in recognition of his size and health, she called him "the giant slayer." In those ways Anatoli said she put names on his destiny. Valentina protected his independence, nurturing the notion that his inner thoughts could shape the world around him. She defended his decision to become a teacher when his pursuit of a career in engineering or geophysics would have been more advantageous for the family. In 1979, when it became apparent that mountains and not physics were his first love, Valentina encouraged Anatoli to follow his dreams to Almaty, Kazakhstan.

Dreams and premonitions psychically connected them. The delicate golden crucifix Anatoli took care to wear around his neck was his mother's talisman. He expressed guilt about the risks he faced as a source of stress for her. When his great efforts left him transparent with exhaustion and longing for human contact, he would go home to Korkino. For a few days he would absorb Valentina's affection, feeding that place in himself that required the essential refuge of belonging. In May of 1996, while Anatoli struggled up Mount Everest to attempt to rescue Scott Fischer, his mother suffered a heart attack. In the weeks that followed she seemed to recover. Anatoli spoke with her often by telephone. During an especially poignant conversation on July 3, she seemed to try to prepare Anatoli for her death. We made reservations for him to fly home. A sudden complication sent Valentina to the hospital that night. Hours later, news of her passing shattered Tolya like a piece of glass.

Anatoli's reserve was mostly shyness. As a child, to those outside the family he was "Buka," a nickname that implied he was a bit aloof and too introverted. Even though he was a precocious reader, his first years of school were traumatic. Teachers ridiculed his inability to roll r's, refusing to acknowledge Buka until he could speak properly. His pride made him internalize a complex of emotions; he became withdrawn and careful socially. In adult life, when pressed into some social situation in which he intuitively felt maligned or ridiculed, he would withdraw into a stony, intimidating silence. At home he lived in an imaginative world of his own creation. His closest friends were his two sisters, Luba and Irina; for them he was the pet and hero. For a short time when he was young, Valentina was the custodian in the local library. Anatoli enjoyed keeping her company at work: in the shelves of books he found his escape from drab reality. Irina told me they spent many hours on the warm shelf of the Russian stove in the living room, Anatoli lost in the pages of some adventure story. American authors O. Henry and Jack London were his favorites. Though his sensitivity and introversion were protected at home, the only freedom for such eccentricity, in the system that controlled Anatoli's life beyond those walls, was coupled with academic excellence. He demonstrated aptitude for math and science, and by the seventh grade his diligence won him recognition as an academic prodigy.

When a thin, tall, red-haired boy flawlessly presented his ideas concerning the significance of one of the local archaeological ruins for a geology science fair, the adult judges were so impressed that twelve-year-old Anatoli was invited to become the youngest member of the geology section of the Young Pioneers. Field trips to the crags in the Urals were his homecoming. The feelings fostered by his interactions with nature resonated with his deep-seated individuality. He confessed, "Membership in the club gave me an appreciation for life in the collective and rescued me from the potential to become an egoist." The partnerships of climbing ended his social isolation, and the camaraderie around evening campfires cemented lifelong friendships.

One of his comrades from those days, Serge Segov, remembered Anatoli as "headstrong, argumentative, and fiercely competitive." Everything he did, he did to win. Watching Olympic competitions with his buddies, he had no trouble projecting that he would wear the uniform of the USSR and compete on the world stage. He treated girls like his sisters; shyness and Old World manners prevented anything else. Stellar academic performance in geochemistry and physics courses earned him special opportunities outside the classroom. His field trips became longer, more involved. The biggest bonus hidden in the invitation to join the geology club was that the group's twenty-five-year-old coach, Tatiana Dmitrievna Retunskaya, was a respected Soviet mountaineer.

Like all sports activity in the Soviet Union, mountaineering and rock climbing were regulated. A prescribed body of knowledge had to be mastered, and along with that good judgment, teamwork, and leadership skills were developed in practical application. Individual initiative and ability determined how far you went on the road from novice to Master of Sport. Aside from the skills needed for climbing, first aid, weather patterns and snow conditions, map reading, and geology were all components of a mountaineer's education. Information became more complex with each grade. To advance a rating, one had to demonstrate dynamic mastery by applying practically new information and skill in climbing situations. The candidate was assigned an objective and given the leadership role in a team composed of more advanced climbers. An individual extended his personal limits protected by a safety net of experience. In a system of limited resources, the opportunity for advanced instruction was won by competition.

In Tatiana Retunskaya, Anatoli found the combination of mentor and friend who could channel his adolescent energy. She taught basic rope and climbing techniques during her field trips. Those opportunities and her personal interest in her new twelve-year-old protégé introduced Anatoli to the world that became his life. She encouraged him to take up cross-country skiing. His body was perfectly suited to the sport, and early success fed a competitive passion. Their relationship thrived on his achievements. He mirrored her passion for nature and revived her outgrown mountaineering ambitions.

She indulged the streak of independence in him, once covering up that he and his friend Serge Segov had ditched the bus that returned campers from a weekend field trip. The two adolescents ran wild in the wilderness for six days, surviving on bread and berries. "With Anatoli," she said, "I came to expect such things." She had an unfailing belief in his ability and his drive and went so far as to fudge the details on medical records that would have excluded him from climbing competitions. When a three-month bout of meningitis threatened to end his career in 1981, Tatiana included him on a summer trip to the Caucasus Mountains and helped him regain his edge of fitness. Given free rein, he performed illegal solo speed ascents on the 5,000-meter peaks while she kept the rest of her team in line. For ten years she was his advocate. She focused his drive and ambition, pulling strings that provided him with the opportunities to climb higher.

In 1974 his skiing skills added the edge that earned him a trip to Talgar Mountaineering Camp in the Zaalyskiy Ala Tau near Almaty, Kazakhstan. The camp was located deep in the wilderness and surrounded by towering 5,000-meter peaks. Under the eye of Retunskaya's old coach Irvand Illinski, Anatoli climbed real mountains for the first time. He came home to Korkino's slag heaps dreaming of a life close to the craggy summits. Only the rare child in Korkino escaped some kind of work in the coal mines. As Illinski would remember, "Anatoli's dreams were not castles in the air; his feet were always on the ground." Friend Segov said, "His goals were concrete, and he was patient: for him it was just a matter of time."

High school academic performance earned him a physics scholarship at Chelyabinsk Pedagogical University. He was the first member of his family to attend college. The trip to Talgar had made it clear to him that a life indoors would be intolerable, but he knew that teaching would give him a winter holiday and summers free for the mountains. Wages as a night watchman in a trucker's warehouse paid his bills. "Fortunately," he said, "the only requirement for that job was that I had to be a light sleeper." He began college studying physics six hours a day and training as a competitive ski racer for two, and he admitted that by the time he graduated in 1979 his passion and priorities had reversed. The dynamics of human endurance and speed fascinated him. He added courses in sports physiology to his schedule. "By the end," he said, "I was grateful physics was only a four-year program." When I inquired about girls, he laughed, saying, "I wasn't much of a catch. All my energy was spent training. Studying filled up my nights, and when I did go to parties, I was usually so exhausted I fell asleep in the corner." He graduated with honors, earning a bachelor of science degree in physics, and was certified to coach cross-country skiing. After four summers of college climbing, he became a candidate for Master of Sport in mountaineering.

Two years of mandatory military service awaited him after graduation. Tatiana lobbied Irvand Illinski, requesting that Anatoli be assigned to the Central Asia Mountaineering Unit he supervised. The sports club provided mountaineering training for the regular army soldiers who were headed for the Afghanistan war. Illinski pulled the necessary strings, and Buka joined the Sports Club of the Army as a military recruit. When his service commitment was over, Illinski invited him to join the club as a civilian.

The first time I saw him in action I marked to myself the huge potential he revealed with his initiative. No one could stand up to his standards of endurance and speed in the mountains. He was a fanatical sportsman, strictly training according to his own schedule. Several times due to accident or severe illness I thought his career was over, but always he came back. On our teams when complicated situations arose—those situations which are not always predictable or preventable in the high mountains—Anatoli always had the strength and willingness to help. His character was not simple; he was very thorough in everything he decided to undertake. With some he built very close relationships, but he could be obstinate and that antagonized others. Though Anatoli worked as an individual at mountaineering, he was a graduate of the old school. He was proud of that.

Soviet mountaineering had a respectable fifty-year history. In the 1950s the 8,000-meter peaks in the world were about as accessible as outer space. Everest and other high peaks challenged the imagination of individuals and nations. At the same time, training at high altitude was hard to come by. Americans, Europeans, and the British had to go a long way to find a mountain higher than five thousand meters. The Soviets had a great geographic advantage. Locked up behind the Iron Curtain, in the endless ranges of the Pamirs and Tien Shan Mountains, were unnumbered peaks higher than six thousand meters and five giants higher than seven thousand meters. By 1960 Soviet climbers had worked out the hardest routes on most of the highest ones. That bank of experience was passed on to Anatoli's generation from veterans who became coaches in the main state-sponsored sports clubs. The Soviet Ministry of Sports sponsored competitions in all the mountain regions. Each year there was national recognition for the best team ascents in three categories—technical high-altitude climbing, classical high-altitude mountaineering, and technical mountaineering.

Physiologists and doctors kept track of the effects altitude and exertion had on sportsmen so that by 1980 a significant body of scientific data had been collected. When Nickoli Tchorny, the assistant head coach of the USSR's second International Expedition, gave me his files detailing the Soviet training routines, he shook his head. "This information was once classified as top secret," he said, and wondered aloud if anyone in the West knew it existed or the price Soviet athletes had paid for it. Soviet coaches incorporated the results of their basic research on acclimatization, diet, and rest into their training programs. Veterans like Tchorny, Irvand Illinski, Serge Efemov from Ekaterinburg, and Vladimir Shataev from Moscow were as respected and well known in the Soviet Union as the likes of Chris Bonington, Reinhold Messner, and Jim Whittaker were in the West.

Mountaineering was popular in the Soviet Union. In the eighties, summers found as many as thirteen thousand climbers with sports vouchers on holiday in the many International Mountaineering Camps. The support services provided in base camp included physicians who specialized in high-altitude medicine and special rescue units were available to assist with air evacuation in emergencies.

Established in the late sixties with Illinski as head coach, from the beginning Almaty Army Sports Club teams earned the highest of all Soviet mountaineering awards for their efforts above sixty-five hundred meters. Though Illinski had to be a bureaucrat to survive, Anatoli remembered "he was a sportsman at heart." He was fair, had an absolute respect for excellence, and was not afraid to skate out onto the thin ice of what was not officially sanctioned. By the undeniable superiority of their performance, his climbers overcame the prejudice and favoritism that cornered opportunity for Moscow and St. Petersburg athletes.

Membership in the club committed Anatoli to a demanding

training schedule: three sessions a week of two hours with weights, followed by long cross-country runs, and a weekend speed ascent of one of the local 4,000-meter peaks. It provided him with a $30-a-month reserve officer's salary and covered his transportation and expenses on group expeditions. Within the club Illinski let men form climbing partnerships according to personal preference. There was no shortage of talent in the old guard; Zinur Halitov, Grigori Luniakov, Kazbec Valiev, and Andrei Seleschev represented Almaty on the Soviet's first International Expedition to Everest in 1982. When Anatoli was invited to join the club in 1981, the roster included many rising Soviet stars: Valeri Khrichtchatyi, Vladimir Suviga, Rinat Khaibullin, and Yuri Moiseev. Illinski nostalgically recalled: "In those days I had fifty strong candidates, all men who could lead. My biggest problem was eliminating that group down to sixteen for an expedition."

Anatoli arrived from the provinces with a reputation as a ski racer. Initially he was looked upon as an outsider. Rinat Khaibullin, his sports-club climbing partner until 1992, recalled the circumstances of their first meeting:

We were invited to join the Sports Club of the Army as civilians at the same time. This was a big honor for both of us as it had the reputation as one of the best in all of the Soviet Union; practically it meant our training expenses would be covered by the state. In the summer of 1982 we were required to take part in a technical climbing competition in the Fanskie Mountains in Kirgizstan. The rest of the team went to Artuch Base Camp before us. I was held up by my college exams, and Anatoli was delayed due to the demands of his coaching work. We made arrangements to meet in Osh, ride to the trailhead, and hike to Base Camp together.

I knew Anatoli only as a skier. I was a rock climber; for my ego that was an important difference. Neither of us was familiar with the way to Base Camp, but we decided, being such strong men, that we could make a three-day hike in one day. We left the trailhead with towering backpacks full of mountaineering gear. Anatoli's pace was punishing, but for the sake of my pride, I forced myself to keep up. At the last pass before camp, we stopped to rest. In silent disbelief, I watched Anatoli liberate a whole watermelon from his pack. There were two reasons for my amazement: as a rock climber we never carried more weight than absolutely necessary; and I had been struggling to keep up with him for more than eight hours.

By and large Anatoli's personal ideology left him oblivious to the petty infighting for position in the club. He never spoke of it. Even among stars, he was different: "a white crow" they called him, making sure to add, "He is our white crow." During a time when most of his peers treated vodka and cigarettes like vitamins, his knowledge of sports physiology influenced him to give up smoking. He was never a big drinker. His personal life set him apart. He remained single, preferred to live twenty kilometers from the city, did not drive a car, and did not socialize much. At times his fanatic commitment to training was perceived as strange and alarming, even to Illinski. Hearing his young protégé was running the mountain trails in winter in shorts and a tank top, Illinski suggested that even training was good only in moderation. That admonition did not faze Anatoli, who had his own ideas about conditioning. No one argued with his results.

To remain in the club after his service commitment was completed, Anatoli found paying work as a ski coach at a collective farm on the outskirts of Almaty. He bought an orchard and a small, dilapidated wooden house in nearby Mountain Gardener. Right outside his door was a vast pristine wilderness; trails laced the towering conifer taiga, crossed alpine meadows and ridges to the summits of four-thousand-meter peaks. For the next ten years he coached and climbed mountains.

He began a ski program at Mountain Gardener with a group of novices aged eight to thirteen and implemented his personal system of aerobic-fitness and endurance-training routines. Starting the program from scratch burdened Anatoli with the responsibility of providing equipment for his growing athletes—a big problem on a $100-a-month salary. In the former Soviet Union, the supply of consumer goods dropped off right outside Moscow. For ten years Anatoli's kids ran and exercised in work boots. The supply officer at the Talgar Sports Camp was impressed with the local coach's determination. Alex Severnuk passed on to Anatoli used skis from the store of supplies earmarked for the relatively well-heeled Moscow and St. Petersburg clubs. His patronage paid off. During the time that Anatoli was their coach, five of his protégés became champions of Kazakhstan in their respective distance races. Three girls represented Kazakhstan as members of the combined team from all republics of the Soviet Union and competed for places on the Soviet team in Olympic trials. Over the same period, an astounding number of mountaintops were put behind Anatoli. He summited more than two hundred 5,000- and 6,000-meter peaks and made thirty ascents of the 7,000-meter giants in the Pamirs and the Tien Shan.

In 1986 the Soviets began a series of competitions aimed at selecting athletes for their second International Expedition. Vladimir Frolov, a current member of the Sports Club whom I met in Kathmandu after he had summited Everest in 1997, gave me a sense of what those competitions were like:

> In the old system, the main focus was on team climbing, a spirit of comradeship, a reliance on the strength in a teammate's shoulders and a sense of responsibility for one another. In general, it was good. I personally experienced the value of our system when climbing with friends. You knew you were not alone on a peak, there were others who were ready to help if something happened. We are proud of being brought up in this tradition, proud of what our Soviet climbers have achieved.
>
> But there was also quite another side to all this. The words "be responsible for one another" were taken literally. Climbers watched each other vigilantly when climbing, or

even drinking beer. Some men looked for one false step to remember something negative that could be used at an opportune moment. These things happened.

When the big Himalayan expeditions became a reality, after the Iron Curtain had lifted a little to let our people climb the highest mountains, the big question was "Who will have the opportunity to go?" The state provided money for those expeditions, but not enough for every qualified climber to go. Individuals had to compete with one another and with the system. Some chose the wrong methods to eliminate rivals: blackmailing, slander, and libelous anonymous letters to the authorities. This is not an exaggeration.

Illinski sent nine men to the competitions in the Caucasus where one hundred twenty candidates from all the major clubs were reduced to sixty climbers in twenty days of grueling events. All nine of the Almaty team survived the cut. Medical tests followed at the cosmonauts' training center outside Moscow. Rock-climbing champion Evgeny Vinogradski and Anatoli told hair-raising stories about those exams. No one had any secrets after the investigation. The worst test required each man to jog on a treadmill in a compression chamber. Gradually the chamber changed the atmosphere to simulate conditions at 8,500 meters. Altitude tolerance was evaluated with cardiac monitors, kidney-function tests, and respiratory flow rates. If you passed out, you failed, and many did. Each man was required to collect his urine output for twelve hours after the session in the chamber: for that, one-liter bottles were issued. Rinat Khaibullin remembers:

The next morning we showed up holding modest specimens; none of us had more than a liter. Then Anatoli walked in with three full bottles. At first we thought he was playing a joke and we were incredulous at the boldness of his levity. No one could keep a straight face. Tolya just shrugged his shoulders and grinned sheepishly. We sobered up when the doctor walked in the room to find out what was going on.

Moscow officials took themselves so seriously, fooling around like that would have been a ticket home.

Sixty athletes were reduced to thirty-five by the physical exam, then to twenty-six in a series of high-altitude training races. All kinds of political intrigue followed. Raisa Gorbacheva lobbied to include a woman on the team. Katerina Ivanova performed well in competitions with the men. She moved to Almaty to train under Illinski. In the end, chauvinism and concerns about female endurance overrode Gorbacheva's patronage. The Moscow and St. Petersburg coaches resented that the competition results left such a heavy representation from Almaty. When it was suggested that the thirty-one-year-old ski coach from the Kazakh backwoods might be eliminated, Coach Tchorny balked. He pointed out that not only had Anatoli won both high-altitude endurance races up two 7,000-meter peaks and completed a twenty-five-kilometer traverse above seven thousand meters, he had finished among the top five men in every other selection category.

In the spring of 1989, twenty-six men headed for the Himalaya; Anatoli was one of them. They spent three weeks trekking through the jungles of Nepal with two hundred porters and just about as many "assistant coaches" on sabbatical from Moscow and laid siege to the third-highest mountain in the world. Their successes were staggering. Kanchenjunga had bowed her head sixty-three times before. But that spring there were more than one hundred successful summit attempts on all four peaks of the massif, all of which are higher than 8,400 meters. Anatoli, Serge Arsentiev, and Vladimir Balyberdin surprised the coaches. After hauling heavy loads of oxygen canisters to a supply camp, they pioneered a route to the summit of Central Kanchenjunga. In the end, Anatoli and eight other men traversed the massif from end to end. Tchorny refused to let Anatoli attempt the climb without supplemental oxygen. Though he respected Tchorny, Anatoli later expressed his resentment of the inflexibility that had denied him the opportunity to succeed without it.

For Anatoli the first taste of the world beyond Soviet borders was intoxicating. Kathmandu was full of international climbers. Starved of a world perspective, he soaked up information like a sponge. In 1989 some of it was late news, but the details of ascents by mountaineering avatars like Messner, Kukuczka, and Loretan captured his imagination. At age thirty-one he entered that short window of time when peak power and experience let climbers dream of their most daring accomplishments. The top of Kanchenjunga let him see where he stood in the world.

Weeks later, in a capital enjoying the dizzy pinnacle of perestroika, Mikhail Gorbachev presented Anatoli with the Order of Personal Courage, then awarded him the gold pin of an Honored Master of International Sports. Those were the highest honors his country bestowed on private citizens and athletes. From that vantage point Anatoli's future as an alpinist was assured. He was determined to follow Messner's magic road, to carry his nation's flag to the summits of the world's fourteen highest peaks. Past that, he aspired to perfect a level of endurance and strength in himself that would raise the standard of human achievements a rung higher for all men in the mountains. Fate had other challenges in mind.

After Kanchenjunga, resuming a normal routine was difficult for Anatoli; life as a coach paled in the shadow of his experiences. He spent the summer of 1989 climbing in the Pamirs. Returning home, he was in a serious auto accident and was airlifted to Almaty. X rays diagnosed a cracked vertebra and two fractured ribs. After five days in the hospital, he strapped on a neck brace and walked the twenty kilometers home to Mountain Gardener.

During that time his four-year relationship with skier Olga Sevtevka ended. She had been one of his athletes and had become his first love. Olga waited through the four years of training that interrupted their lives before Kanchenjunga, but when Anatoli returned and could only talk of future climbs instead of a car, a home, and a better salary, she ended the relationship. He resumed training, setting his sights on an October race up Mount Elbrus sponsored by *Alpinist*. In the more relaxed political atmosphere, Kanchenjunga teammate Vladimir Balyberdin chartered a new cooperative aimed at developing private-sector support for Soviet mountaineers. An invitation from Balyberdin brought respected American rock climber and adventure photographer Beth Wald to the Caucasus to watch the competition.

Anatoli won the Elbrus race and caught Beth's eye. He met her during the later part of her Russian tour, and their friendship blossomed. Beth Wald became Anatoli's champion in the United States. Until the end of his life she was his advocate and a valued personal friend. She introduced him to the American public in an article called "Back in the USSR" published in the October 1989 issue of *Climbing* magazine.

Thanks to Beth Wald's vision, work, and initiative, Anatoli and two other Russians, Alex Rogozhyn and Anatoli Shkodin, were provided with an opportunity to come to United States in the spring of 1990. Leaning on personal connections in the elite community of American mountaineers and rock climbers, Beth found venues for a series of slide shows and sponsors in six Western cities. A Soviet-American cultural exchange was on. She went out on a limb, lobbying respected alpinist Michael Covington to provide Anatoli with work on a McKinley expedition. "In 1990," Anatoli said, "that opportunity was about as likely for a Russian climber as flying to the moon."

His impressions of America were varied. After a long trip to New York from Moscow, bad weather forced the cancellation of the flight to Denver. The airline company provided the three Russians with a hotel room near the airport in New York. Tired from travel, Anatoli fell asleep early. He woke up at 4 A.M. because of the TV noise. Alex Rogozhyn stayed up all night watching "sex," he reported in his diary. The bill for Alex's entertainment was $21 and Anatoli was nonplussed:

Twenty-one dollars is a huge sum of money for us, one-third of a month's salary. So thanks to Alex, we learned our first lesson here. You can have anything, but you must pay for it.

Things are concrete, not abstract. There is some sort of cruelty in a system that does not make allowances for human weakness. At the same time choice allows a person to be stronger; maybe that is good.

Later Anatoli noted he was impressed with the "high level of culture" he observed while wandering the streets in Berkeley and Boulder—every house was different, nature was protected, and the environmental accommodations invited people to exercise. He liked the music of Dire Straits and the Grateful Dead. Mountaineers Galen Rowell and Gary Neptune earned his respect with their endurance and skill. "The trip to Yosemite was like a fairy tale," he wrote. The Black Hills of South Dakota reminded him of the southern Urals. He was embarrassed more than once by his rock-climbing performance with Beth's high-powered friends, and he vowed he would return to America able to do better. The variety and quality of the sports equipment he saw left him openmouthed with desire. Anne Kirck at North Face and Gary Neptune outfitted him with skis, Gore-Tex clothes, and One Sport boots. Their generosity humbled him. He was embarrassed by his own overreaching need and by the "desire" that came from nowhere looking at the never-ending supply of good gear. Elliott Robinson recalled Anatoli's introduction to the Bay Area:

I met Tolya in Berkeley at a dinner party during his first trip to America. He told me that night that he had no plans to go to Yosemite. We had such a blast struggling to talk with one another, describing our regions. Somehow my effort to speak English with a broken Russian accent worked, and I became Tolya's translator.

Among other things I learned was how personally he loved the mountains above Almaty. He described a beautiful wilderness that went on forever, forest and mountains where you could still encounter snow leopards. It amazes me I got so much out of that conversation because we really did not speak the same language. Anyway I insisted that he see Yosemite, a region I felt as strongly attached to.

We decided to climb El Capitan. What made it all the more enchanting, besides the weather and language, was Tolya's absolute vigor in a new environment. His experience had been in the mountains, not on the cliffs. Between our instincts we pulled off a spring climb of the East Buttress of El Capitan in a rainstorm, with the temperature dropping. Despite a struggle with "friends," a piece of equipment that was new to him, he went up in beautiful form. I can still hear him roaring like a bear as we scurried down the slabs to the east ledges during our descent. That trip we experienced the rain and cold as they are best enjoyed, without the protection, convenience, and predictability that people now impose on nature.

In the years that followed, his acquaintances with the likes of Kevin Cooney, Elliott Robinson, Bob Palais, Jack Robbins, and Neal Beidleman evolved into trusted friendships. Anatoli climbed with all of them. But some made a special effort to meet him on Russian turf, and that cemented a deeper understanding. Reflecting on what he found unique about Anatoli, Elliott recalled:

He could jog all day. But when I went with him, his pace was my pace. He never made me feel like I had less power than he did. Tolya always brought me closer to the world, and with him I experienced it in a more wild and genuine way, whether it was looking back over the distance we could cover when I accompanied him on a small fraction of his long runs through the East Bay hills or on our tours of Moscow. For Tolya a trip to the Kremlin or churches wasn't so important. What was important was riding in his friend Victor Danilin's boat down the Moscow River to an island in the industrial part of town where we met a few friends and drank tea. Or a hot sauna at Serge Zaiken's workplace (for the life of me, I still believe that Serge worked in the firm that maintained

Moscow's sewers) and a few glasses of Armenian brandy. And of course, his ever-present guitar and Vysotskii or Rosenbaum ballads brought the Russian spirit to life.

Anatoli left America in 1990 with a network of people who became the keel of social support that sustained him through the storm of financial chaos that was brewing in his country. The fallout from the collapse of the Soviet Union pushed him toward a world driven by commerce. Anatoli spent the next years trying to reconcile the necessities of earning a living with his idealism.

The following chapters are Anatoli's accounts of his life and climbs from Kanchenjunga until Annapurna. Resting after each expedition, he wrote as a way to decant his experiences. While he recovered his strength and the memories were fresh, he drafted long narratives from terse day journals, charts, and philosophical ruminations. He talked a lot to friends about writing a practical guide for those who aspired to be climbers, a book that would discuss training methods and acclimatization. Due to changing political fashion, Russian mountaineering history seemed destined to disappear before it had been written. That was an insult to Anatoli and it ignored the sacrifices of many great men. Every piece he wrote included a tribute to the climbers who had pioneered the science of Russian mountaineering.

By 1997, no borders restricted his passage. In the arc of his accomplishments Anatoli had transmuted the painful contradictions of his county's recent history. In nine years of international climbing, he earned a voice among the world's alpinists and set a standard of endurance that will be hard to raise. Idealistically, he believed in the fundamental value of mountaineering and thought it cultured something valuable in the human psyche, something that was too fast becoming an anachronism. In an environment that most people find restrictive and intimidating in its harshness, Anatoli was free. And I believe that of all things he loved freedom best. Two months before he died he prepared these remarks for an audience at the Festival of Mountain Culture at Banff, Canada:

Mountaineering is a model of the ordinary life of all human beings placed in an extreme environment. We strip away all the polite layers that make it easy to ignore the truth. We work hard, deny ourselves comfort, and face the uncertain future with our skills. What comes of this effort is that we can know ourselves better. That is what we offer the public. Everyone in his or her life must ask the questions "Who am I?" "What am I doing here?" If we are honest and fair, this is what we can report from our adventure that is important.

It is the rare man or woman who faces the existential paradox of meaning and mortality as squarely as the alpinist. Athleticism allowed Anatoli to experience a greater measure of what is possible for a human being on earth. Ultimately, we die because we live. He dreamt the avalanche nine months before it came, dreamt it in disturbing detail. Only the name of the mountain was missing. We could not stand on the edge of that abyss with much composure. Reeling, resisting, I groped for some alternative. Sadly teasing, he asked me to come to him.

"How long would I lie here on your couch doing nothing before you could not love me? Mountains are my life . . . my work. It is too late for me to take up another road."

Somehow from his mouth the word *work* lost all mundane character and was elevated to an existential act of creation. Human life was separate neither from the mystical nor from reality.

"Will you suffer?"

"I am not afraid."

That reply exhausted every option.

In the wake of the avalanche, "Why?" echoed loudly in my ears. Many answers came back to me. Close to the second anniversary of Anatoli's death, I received a letter from Vladimir Frolov.

In the old school he was one of the strongest climbers, one of the most deserving. Everyone knew it. Once I asked him about his methods of training. They were a way of life: a whole complex of ways to be stronger. He was a great example for the younger generation. His mentality and discipline made him stand apart from his contemporaries. He was better than most of them. To tell the truth, they did not like him very much; he was a rival and his Western point of view exasperated them. Not so for my generation; for us he was an example of how it is possible to find your own way, free of the bias that exists in our society.

Petty intrigues were beyond Anatoli's ideology; his philosophy was above slander and libel. What was important to him was the love of mountains and climbing. He was the first "white crow" to show himself as different from all those who had gotten used to obeying the system. He just wanted to climb and he did. He loved the Himalayas. For him that was enough.

It is possible to achieve what Anatoli did if you know what you want and work hard. He showed us that the Iron Curtain was in our minds. Money is a problem, but Anatoli managed, and we believe because of his example that we can manage.

A human life is like a poem with a rhyme and meaning that is revealed most clearly in retrospect. It is not so strange that the man I knew, as those who can recall his name fall silent, still compels me to share his story.

—LINDA WYLIE, August 2000

THE JOURNALS

PROLOGUE:

DECEMBER 1989

*I*n *the fall of 1997, Anatoli unloaded a small stack of loose pages and several weathered notebooks from his pack. "You will like this," he said, and handed me a poem. "Working on them, you will be busy while I climb Annapurna." Laughing a modest apology, he added, "Someone must work." Those were the last bits and pieces of writing that had collected in his apartment in Almaty over the years. This short introduction was among them. Titled "Prologue," it was dated December 1989.*

Six months have passed since the members of the national Soviet team returned from our traverse of Kanchenjunga. The Himalayas are far away. The celebrations with friends and family and the honors bestowed on us in Moscow are only memories of the past. So much has changed for me in such a short time. When I returned home, I plunged into the responsibilities and problems of my coaching work, but the mountains did not release my soul. Still I feel strangely separated from events and the people around me. My thoughts and dreams wander to transcendental summits. In comparison to those heights, the ruts of my everyday life are uninspiring.

In October I won first place in a high-altitude race up Mount

Elbrus. I entered that race not necessarily to win. My participation was my way of showing support for the entrepreneurial efforts of my Kanchenjunga teammate Vladimir Balyberdin. For me a team reunion in the Caucasus Mountains seemed like a fitting memorial to our participation in the USSR's obsession with achievement in the Himalaya. For six years each of us renounced the desire for an easy life and familiar pleasure to earn the chance to journey through Kanchenjunga's icy cloisters. Athletic tests, like the Elbrus race, prepared us to face her challenges.

Now, recalling Kanchenjunga's storehouses of snow makes my heart ache like memories of a love that has been lost. Six years, not six months, will pass and I know that I will feel the same way. She possessed a purity and grandeur that are incomparable. Her summits provide reasons that make the human struggle for physical and spiritual perfection meaningful, motivators that are more profound than vain aspirations for fame or wealth. Perhaps this sounds idealistic, but my experiences on Kanchenjunga make those reasons seem shallow and vulgar.

Confronted with the petty concerns of my ordinary life, I feel empty, as if I am wasting a priceless gift . . . the brief time that is allotted to each human for creativity. Days pass and my work does not generate the strength and eagerness to live, which memories of the mountain inspire in me. Perhaps this melancholy will pass when there is another magnificent peak. In truth I do not know. Can this longing and restlessness be the price that mortals pay for daring to trespass in the houses of the Gods . . . the price you pay for disturbing the peace of God?

I never aspired to have the laurels given to a talented writer. Rather I want to achieve something essential in life, something that cannot be measured by wealth or position in society. I want to respect myself as a man and to earn the respect of my friends and family. Clearly, it was my fate to be an athlete. With the gift of that ability, I must strive to realize my potential as a human being.

Mountains are not stadiums where I satisfy my ambitions to achieve. They are cathedrals, grand and pure, the houses of my religion. I approach them as any human goes to worship. On their altars I strive to perfect myself physically and spiritually. In their presence I attempt to understand my life, to exorcise vanity, greed, and fear. From the vantage of their lofty summits, I view my past, dream of the future, and with unusual acuteness I experience the present moment. That struggle renews my strength and clears my vision. In the mountains I celebrate creation, for on each journey I am reborn.

My first ratings as an alpinist were earned climbing on technical routes in the Caucasus. In 1980 I found myself in the Pamir Range ascending 6,000- and 7,000-meter peaks for the first time. There I experienced a different kind of mountaineering. The challenge of climbing above six thousand meters is more than surmounting the complexity of the route. It is about man's struggle to overcome his innate weakness. From the first day, I knew that I belonged in those heights, that it was my destiny to climb high. I knew that, for me, mountaineering would be about the human struggle with altitude.

1

AMERICA, McKINLEY, SPRING 1990

*I*n America, Anatoli's eyes opened to a world full of possibility. Access *to current climbing publications allowed him to appreciate what inter-national climbers considered the cutting edge in mountaineering. Dur-ing his three-month stay this view of the world helped him to refine a plan for personal accomplishment.*

Responding to a request from Beth Wald, well-known American mountaineer Michael Covington provided the thirty-two-year-old Soviet star with a working berth on a Mount McKinley expedition. In the last hours of his stay in Alaska, without permission from authorities in his country, Ana-toli set in motion events that would stretch both him and Michael to the limit.

TALKEETNA, ALASKA, MAY 19, 1990

Tomorrow I fly to the Base Camp on the glacier below Mount McKinley. Many hours of training have gone into realizing this dream. The training is over and the last stage of the journey is before me. It has not been easy to create this opportunity, and the last few days of organization have been especially difficult. My backpack is full of trouble; twenty kilos is too heavy. Experienced backwoodsmen would be surprised to hear my thoughts. In their trips to the mountains, that amount of weight is nothing to carry. For a speed ascent, it will be a big problem.

This giant of rock and ice has seen nothing like what I want to do. I treat this mountain with a lot of respect, though I have success on many higher peaks behind my shoulders. Last year my teammates and I raised the ceiling of our abilities on Kanchenjunga, the third-highest mountain in the world. Maybe we set a new standard of endurance for all human beings. That exploit is the theme for a different conversation; tomorrow I face a challenge that is no less serious. I want to climb from the base of McKinley to the summit in one day.

Because it is located near the arctic circle, and relatively close to the ocean, rapidly changing weather patterns often create conditions on this mountain that are more severe that those we endured in the Himalaya. My rate of ascent will be faster, and going alone, if there are unforeseen difficulties or my body becomes disabled, there will be no teammates to rely on. Alone in this hotel room in Talkeetna, suddenly I am aware of my total solitude. What happens from now on will be up to me.

My patron left me this evening. Michael Covington, the owner of Fantasy Ridge Mountain Guides, has looked after me during this, my first visit to Alaska. Working the last twenty-five days, I believed that I helped him as well. With my assistance, Michael led four paying clients to the top of Mount McKinley via the Cassin route. Mountain historians can record our climb as the second successful ascent by a group of nonprofessionals on the difficult route. That was not my success, it was Michael's, and I have to thank him for teaching me the ropes of guiding paying clients.

Michael Covington is a real professional; throughout the expedition I was impressed with his endurance and his judgment. In the beginning he was a puzzle for me. Though I sensed his professionalism, I felt uneasy with him. That feeling stayed with me for a long time.

We met at the airport in Anchorage on the nineteenth of April two days before his clients arrived. He took me along on a shopping trip for expedition supplies. That market amazed me. Though it was early spring in Alaska, the counters in the Anchorage store were crammed and bending under the weight of fresh fruits and vegetables. Such a variety of produce could not be found in Almaty's Green Bazaar even during the peak summer growing season. As well as providing ordinary food for the local people, the store had a whole section with special products for use by outdoorsmen. Michael purchased a mountain of supplies; everything we needed was to be found in that one store.

Four clients arrived in Anchorage on the twenty-first of April. They were from a variety of professions and included an oil businessman, an engineer, a moviemaker, and a university professor. Their ages, twenty-six to thirty-three, put them at the peak of human physical ability. I was curious about how Michael screened candidates for such a hard route. He told me that he had assessed their technical ability while ice climbing with them in Colorado. Each of the men had experience climbing high mountains in other parts of the world, and two of them had previously summited McKinley via the normal route. I was informed that another, no less important criterion was an individual's ability to write a check for a large sum. A client had to be pretty well-off financially to afford to pay one or two month's wages for a vacation. Michael charges more to guide on the Cassin route than he charges for climbing via the normal one. Because of that, I understood the men on our team had sportsmen's appetites for adventure.

We flew to Talkeetna, the Alaskan village where all McKinley expeditions begin and end. After picking up the necessary gear from Michael's equipment storage, we boarded small planes that flew us to a camp on the glacier below McKinley. The cold temperature left us with no doubts that we were in Alaska.

During the first days of the climb, Michael made an effort to explain his schedule to me using a photograph. I saw four camps on the glacier and seven camps marked on the mountain slopes, but my poor command of English prevented me from understanding the details of his plan. Seven days into the expedition, when I found myself sleeping at Camp I for the second night, I began to grasp Michael's tactics. Some confusion at dinner helped to clarify the situation.

The sleds we dragged behind us across the glacier were piled high with enormous loads of supplies. Based on my past experience, taking into account the size of the mountain, I was sure we had about three times as much food as we could eat. Therefore, I saw no reason to limit consumption at mealtime. I can never complain about my appetite in the mountains. Among the stores were many foods that had never been available to me on a mountaineering expedition: freeze-dried strawberries, ice cream, many different kinds of tasty drink mixes, soups, and entrées. Each item was in a beautiful, colored package. My curiosity about those packages had a life of its own.

At mealtime Michael gave me a frequent notice: "Tolya, it is a ration."

I thought he was saying "Russian." So I would answer, "Okay, Michael, it is Russian." For several nights, with a mysterious grin, he had allowed the conversation to end there. After his usual declaration on night seven, I watched his patience come to an end. Asking for my dictionary, he looked up the word *ration*. Thanks to that English lesson, during the next twenty days the team did not run short of food. By the end of the climb I was eight kilograms lighter.

Twenty-five days is a long time to work on climbing a 6,000-meter-high peak. The American school of thought regarding acclimatization is dramatically different from ours. On Michael's schedule, there were no preliminary trips to higher elevation to adjust to the altitude. Two or three nights were spent in each of seven successively higher camps; that is how our bodies adjusted to increases in elevation.

Michael and I worked on the route or hauled up supplies between each advance. The clients did not express much eagerness to carry loads, and because they were not properly trained, the necessary technical work was beyond their ability. Guaranteed safety and reliable support, each of them had paid big money to Fantasy Ridge Mountain Guides so they could feel like real mountaineers on a complicated route. In general, there is nothing wrong with that. Enjoying a vacation in exotic circumstances, each man moved up the mountain securely connected to fixed rope, with ample free time to take a lot of pictures. Michael and I worked hard. Despite the hardship imposed by our route and episodes of bad weather, on May 14 we made it to the summit. The thermometer registered minus thirty degrees centigrade.

We flew back to Talkeetna on the seventeenth. Before they left for home, I exchanged addresses with my teammates and invited them to my region for climbing. We stayed up late drinking beer and talking in the hotel bar. Saying good-bye, I could see they were immersed in the problems of their normal lives. Though they were good men, the mountains are the only things we had in common. Surviving here is very different from in Russia. Here people face different problems; you sense the struggle in every encounter. Even the most basic requirements of life have a price. Work earns you the money to pay for things; and that is the only way to live a full life. This constant struggle makes things more interesting for the individual.

When it was over, Michael asked me what I thought about the climb. Mostly I enjoyed learning about the technological advances in our sport; some of the equipment I used was completely new to me. Michael had French rope that absorbs the shock of falling. Boots are available that are designed specially for rocks or providing protection in extremely low temperatures. Crampons and ice axes are available that accommodate any degree of steepness on a slope. Comparable Soviet items do not meet the same high standards for safety and quality. The best in every category can be purchased in any mountaineering store in America. My experiences have made it clear that the technical support provided for Soviet mountaineers is far from good. The compensation for us is that we have peaks that rise above seven thousand meters in our beautiful mountain regions. Our expertise is built on experience. I did not find this climb with clients to be challenging, but only hard work.

Last night at dinner, I flabbergasted Michael and another team member, Bill Pierson. When I delivered the not so pleasant news that

I wanted to attempt to reclimb McKinley alone, Michael thought I was showing off. Slowly, I watched as his face registered the seriousness of my intention. Gruffly, he said that he had no time or money to be occupied with my problems. Probably he is tired of my straightforward requests for help and my unpredictability. He must think that I want too much. My request creates problems for him, and his work is hard enough already. From his tense response I understood that the picture did not look so good. With only obstinacy to rely on, I decided to bring the subject up again after dinner. Michael has an interesting character, a little strange in the way of all mountaineers. He lit a cigarette, so I lit a cigarette. We talked; he relented. He decided that I could stay at the guesthouse without paying, that I had to leave for the glacier as soon as possible. Flight arrangements were up to me. Kindly, Bill Pierson offered to help me with the organizational problems that stood in my way.

Unable to sleep after that conversation, I walked the streets of Talkeetna alone. I find it humiliating to rely on others for what happens in my life. The burden of my ambition has fallen on Michael, and I know that he has no money to help me. The mountaineering equipment I brought from home to sell during my trip has not generated much interest. I have a bag full of axes and ice-screws and very little American money to make my plan a reality.

Determined to fight on till the end, I went to the airport this morning armed with the issue of *Climbing* magazine that contained Beth Wald's article about my Elbrus victory. Loren, a nice woman who controls the office, had some sympathy for the ambitions of a penniless Russian; she agreed to give me a free seat on one of the air flights to the glacier tomorrow morning.

During a breakfast discussion regarding my tactics, Michael tried to talk me out of making the speed ascent up the West Rib. Timewise, he thinks it would be better for me to start on the West Buttress; the routes join on the upper part of the mountain. That approach does not suit me. I want to try to ascend the line on the Rib from beginning to end. I appreciated that Michael was uneasy about letting me go through the glacier alone, and I know that it is risky. If the weather conditions are bad, I promised him that I would consider changing my mind. He left it at that. I ate the food on my plate quickly, and still hungry, I asked for more. That request made Michael boil; he said that I could pay my own food bill. I was a little surprised by his reaction, but did not show it.

My supplies cost $70; there is very little money left. The stove I borrowed from Michael's storage works differently from the system I am accustomed to. At park headquarters, Bill Pierson registered me for the "Ration" West Rib, No Problem expedition. The rangers asked me what I would do alone with no radio if I fell into a crevasse.

"No problem," I said, "I can sing."

Though it was funny at the time, only the future will tell if this solo climb will be "no problem." Saying my good-byes to Michael and Bill this afternoon, I sensed that they were both pretty tired of me.

⋅   ⋅   ⋅

Though I stayed up until 5 A.M. writing and thinking, I woke at eight and jogged to the airport the morning of May 20. By noon, I was in a seat on a flight to the glacier. I thanked Loren and the pilot with some small souvenirs from Russia. Loren gave me two canisters of gas for Michael's stove. Two hours after touchdown, I walked past the place where the West Rib route diverges from the easier route up the Buttress. Stopping about 5 P.M. near a group of Colorado skiers with two guides named Bob, I set up my camp. The Bobs patiently showed me how to operate Michael's stove. Snow started falling; heavy accumulations made unloading the tent necessary twice during the night. Fog and snow all day long on the twenty-first reduced the visibility to zero. Since it was impossible to go on, I took the precaution of relocating my tent in a more protected spot.

After breakfast on the twenty-second I said good-bye to the two Bobs. All their efforts to discourage my departure were useless. Soon the camp was far behind and I was left one-on-one with the knee-deep snow and the crevasses. Being attentive and careful, I struggled breaking a new trail for five hours. A couple descending from the West Rib passed me and reported that the couloir, the most dangerous part of my route, was in good condition. That was all I needed to know. Following in their tracks, I relaxed a little. Suddenly the snow dropped out from under me. Wedged in a crack, I sensed only emptiness beneath my feet. Unclipping my pack to decrease my weight, inch by inch I crawled to safety, then hauled the pack out. I was lucky that I had not disappeared down that hole. I proceeded more carefully, intending to finish what was normally a two-day crossing before dinner. Wading through the deep snow exhausted me. My level of fatigue was a clear indication to me that I had not fully rehabilitated from working on the previous expedition. Though I would not say that I starved on that trip, my weight was down to 74 kilograms from my normal eighty-two kilograms. Ahead of me was an unusual effort. A team would take about twenty days and acclimated mountaineers might take three or four days to do what I hoped to accomplish in one. My plan was simple: to climb continuously until I reached the summit.

By evening I threw down my tarp at the base of McKinley's West Rib. The sky looked as if the weather would cooperate. In a good mood, I fixed a huge dinner and visited with two Anchorage mountain guides who shared my campsite. The nights here are only a little darker than the day, so time loses meaning. I woke at 5 A.M. on the twenty-third and might have started out earlier, but I was fatigued from the work the day before. Still feeling the full effects of dinner, I ate a light breakfast. As I packed up, firsthand knowledge of McKinley's penetrating cold and mercurial weather patterns prevented me from lightening my load. With the sleeping bag, stove, gas, and tent, my pack weighed twenty kilograms or more. I began the assault at exactly 7:30 A.M.

The bottom of the couloir was not steep; I had the trail left by previous climbers to follow. My speed was good, but I was not going at full strength. Soon the snow ended and I began to climb sound, crisply ringing ice. Denali, as Alaska natives call their mountain, made me cautious. Past the steep ice, I came onto a snowy crest. One more hour of effort and I passed Camp I. Rushing on for two more hours, I arrived at Camp II. During a five-minute rest, I explained my mission to the climbers I met there. Surprise registered on their faces. An hour later at Camp III, I stopped for a ten-minute rest with another Fantasy Ridge expedition. They had started out on May 16. (The only way I can explain such slow progress is that the Americans sit too long and don't climb in bad weather.) Again I told my story and asked the group members to take a few pictures of me. The next section was not so steep. My sharp crampons dug into the frozen, bare rocky terrain. By the time I reached the elevation of 4,800 meters, my shoulders and arms were numb from the weight of my pack. Somewhere about 5,000 meters I passed the last group of climbers that I would meet before the summit ridge. Three hundred meters farther on, I understood that I had to stop. I sat for fifteen minutes, ate a small snack, and fixed myself a hot drink.

Only snow-covered slope lay between the summit crest and me, but it was steep and the crust was hard. I was a little apprehensive because slabs of snow break off easily in those conditions. After seven hours of continuous work my pack felt unbearably heavy, and the slope seemed to stretch on to infinity. The only comforting thought was that somewhere above me it would all end. After the West Rib joined the West Buttress the final journey to the summit was not so steep. After that I could go down.

The last meters on that slope were difficult, hard going for me. Wearily, I traversed left and came around a corner. Then I saw people slowly climbing to the summit. Dragging myself to the flag-marked path, I abandoned the unbearable weight of my pack. I started to the summit. The wind blew strongly and the cold was incredible. I was not sorry that I had taken the time to put on my down jacket. Silently, I was grateful for the mittens one of Michael's clients had given me. With dogged determination I passed eight climbers. I arrived on the top in the company of an Englishman, ten and one-half hours from the time I'd started out. We photographed one another for posterity, and my fingers became instantly numb without the protection of the mittens.

Right away, I started down. After recovering my pack, I followed a flagged trail on the West Buttress. A team of climbing instructors camped at 5,000 meters gave me a mug of hot tea. Steering the unfamiliar course by following the fixed rope, finally I arrived on a big plateau where many groups were camped. It looked strange, a lone Russian coming down the mountain. People asked me a lot of questions. Cached food that I had hidden at the trail junction on the glacier was my destination. I only wanted to eat and drink. When I arrived, I was so exhausted that I had no power to look for the food or to put up my tent. Trying to melt the water for tea, I fumbled and the temperamental stove caught fire. I managed to put out the flames, gulped a meager amount of water. Using the last of my strength, I crawled into my sleeping bag.

I had done it. In less than one day I had completed a route that would normally have taken five camps. I fell asleep thankful that the night was not too cold.

Climbing *magazine noted the ten-and-one-half-hour solo ascent of McKinley by Anatoli Boukreev in the October 1990 issue. It was the fastest ascent of McKinley in the history of the mountain. The Denali Park rangers would add* unreal *to the list of adjectives describing the "Ration" West Rib, No Problem expedition.*

2

FROM ELBRUS TO ELDORADO, FALL 1990

The familiar sounds of Russian conversation woke me from my sleep. All around me in the New York airport were people with huge bags of goods, things purchased during their visit to America. They talked of homecoming; like me, everyone was absorbed with his or her return to the motherland. At the check-in counter, the clerk informed me that I owed $32 more for the extra weight in my baggage. Digging in my pockets for money, I found less than $10. I attempted to explain my predicament. The airline official decided not to be too strict and allowed my luggage to be loaded on the plane without the extra charge.

That was just one of the many times during my first visit when I had cause to appreciate the remarkable kindness and generosity of Americans. Perhaps the country's general affluence allows its citizens to be this way. On the flight back to Moscow, I sat next to the assistant director of a Moscow champagne factory. He could not stop talking about how wonderful life was in the USA. After three months of traveling I did not need him to tell me what was good and what was not.

I don't believe that the United States is free of problems. Everything has a price. Survival depends on the individual's initiative; there no one is promising you anything. There is some cruelty in a system that makes no allowances for human weakness, but at the same time, the people are forced to be stronger. Factors that affect life are concrete, not abstract. Maybe that is for the best. At home all our attempts at humanism have gotten us to the place where no one remembers how to work hard and there is no motivation to strive for a better life. Something terrible is happening to the young people in my country: drug and alcohol addiction and other signs of moral degradation are common. I think these problems are growing faster in the USSR than they are in America. Now there are problems with every aspect of Soviet existence. Average people should be inspired by the opportunities in their lives, but they are not. The field of sports is no exception. Athletes like me need ways to become self-supporting.

In America I observed a phenomenon that was new to me. Masses of people use running to keep fit. In Colorado on the weekends the countryside was crowded with groups enjoying hiking or rock climbing. Few of those people were training to be professional athletes. Daily sports activity is used to relieve the stress of work or as a way to socialize or commune with nature. A passion for the outdoors enriches the quality of their lives. In that way sports produces stronger citizens, people who appreciate the harmony of nature and are motivated to get more out of their free moments than rest from work. Those are the essential benefits of sports activity on the psychology of the masses. Europe and America have far more people than we do who understand my point, but in those countries it is possible to earn enough money to finance the luxury of active leisure.

My passion for sports has led to its becoming my profession. I live about forty kilometers from Almaty, Kazakhstan, in the midrange of the Zaalyskiy Ala Tau Mountains. When I am not climbing, I work as the coach of the skiing program at a collective farm in the village of Mountain Gardener. The pay is miserable, $100 a month, but my work allows me to maintain a schedule of training. Climbing and coaching has been my life for eight years. In that time I progressed from a mountaineer of the first category to Master of Sports, International Class. Over the same period, three of my protégés rose from rank novices to become members of the Combined National Ski-Racing Team and finalists for the Olympic team from the USSR.

For fifteen years I have been a proponent of cross-country running for fitness. For anyone who conditions this way, shoes are the most important item of equipment. During my first trip to America, I found out that there are specially designed sports shoes, which make even steep downhill tracks a pleasure. When I jog, I am usually not alone; members of my ski team run with me, but they have no special shoes. When I visited American stores, my eyes devoured the racks of special equipment that is available to anyone. In the USSR even top-caliber athletes can only find work boots for training.

Beyond the borders of our country, a variety of extreme sports have gained popularity. Success in those events is won by exploring the limits of human ability. On adventures such as climbing the highest peaks, sailing alone around the world, in triathlons and supermarathons, individuals are setting new standards for human endurance. Businessmen from many companies in Europe and America understand the advertising benefits of sponsoring competitions and professional athletes. Foreign climbing publications are full of record-setting reports. Italian Ermanno Salvaterra climbed five difficult routes in the Alps alone and in a day. Americans storm Yosemite's sheer rock faces, speeding up routes that once took days in a matter of hours. There is a record time for climbing Everest. French climber Marc Batard made it up in twenty-two hours and thirty minutes. A rumor has it that he will try to better his record next year. It will not be too difficult for him to find a sponsor for that ambition.

Since McKinley, the idea of challenging Batard's record has inspired me. Of necessity that goal is set somewhere in the future. Before one can break records, first there must be the opportunity to climb the highest mountain in the world. The permit alone is $3,200. Add to that the expenses of living in Nepal for several months, the cost of equipment for preparing the route, and wages for the porters, and climbing in the Himalayas becomes an expensive proposition for a ski coach with my salary.

Respected Boulder, Colorado, mountaineer Kevin Cooney is interested in joining me on an Everest speed ascent. He is a professional triathlon competitor and a strong rock climber. Now Kevin is looking for sponsors. For training and to generate some interest in our plans, we decided to compete in several high-altitude races. Vladimir Balyberdin is trying to get financing from the Soviet Ministry of Sports to undertake an Everest-Lhotse expedition in the fall of 1991; the speed ascent appealed to him as well. To show his support for us, he arranged for the official invitations that allowed Kevin and another Colorado friend, Patrick Healey, to come to the Soviet Union to compete in the Second International Elbrus Race. In October, I returned to America to run the Basic Boulder Marathon, the high-altitude competition that Kevin sponsors.

Last summer the Everest idea inspired me to undertake two speed ascents in the Tien Shan. A month after the McKinley climb I was still weak. Back at home I was diagnosed with an infectious illness: a case of giardiasis had progressed to a critical stage and I had abscesses in my liver. Initially, I had intended to challenge the speed records set by our teams climbing Khan-Tengri and Pobeda, but in no way was I committed to paying the ultimate price for such a victory. To climb solo safely, I needed to be strong enough to carry everything required for a bivouac on either route. The weather in the Tien Shan is unpredictable. Two months passed before I felt that I had regained enough strength to make the climbs feasible. Though in the West solo climbing is considered a high level of accomplishment, in the USSR such climbs are prohibited by Soviet mountaineering rules. To use the facilities at Base Camp, official permission was required. Fortunately, the coach of my sports club, Irvand Illinski, is an innovator by nature and a true sportsman in his soul. He resolved the problem with a compromise: he would not officially sanction my speed ascents, but neither did he forbid me from making them.

In the summer of 1990, for the first time our mountaineering camps were open for the use of international teams. When I stepped off the helicopter at Khan-Tengri Base Camp, I could see that so many climbers were attempting my route, there was not much possibility of ascending the technical portions quickly. I had to be satisfied with gaining a good acclimatization and a speed ascent from 5,800 meters. Leaving the last camp early, I had the steep route to the top to myself. After four hours of effort I was standing on the 7,010-meter-high summit. Encouraged by my body's performance, I moved up the South Ilynichk Glacier to the base of Pobeda, expecting a harder challenge.

Pobeda Peak is a more complicated mountain, and climbing it alone proved to be a difficult test for me psychologically. The day that I began my ascent, the sky changed in the late morning and showed signs that the weather might deteriorate. Worried about that eventuality, a group of Italians turned back at 6,700 meters. I was left alone with the mountain. About 2 P.M. while eating lunch, I studied the sky. Conditions were not changing rapidly. I decided to go on. By 3 P.M. I topped Vasha Pshavel, a subsidiary peak on the huge Pobeda Massif. From that point, a three-kilometer traverse along an undulating 7,000-meter-high ridge separated me from the base of the summit pyramid. To spare my back some weight and increase my speed, I stashed my sleeping bag and extra supplies in a depression about midway across the traverse. With me I carried a gas stove, a pot for melting snow, a headlamp, and my ice tool. The altitude wasn't causing any problem and I did not feel tired. About 6 P.M. I began ascending the last five hundred vertical meters. Looking at the sky, I thought my only nemesis was the coming nightfall. The summer sun set beneath the clouds as I reached the 7,439-meter summit. Grateful that my old Pentax camera was working in the low evening temperatures, I took a few photos and quickly descended. In the fading twilight I began the traverse—somewhere in the middle of the ridge, my sleeping bag, shovel, and extra food were in a snow depression. The wind picked up, erasing my trail. In the dark of night heavy clouds descended, obscuring the relief. Recovering the food and sleeping bag became critical. Somehow I located the pack. Past the summit of Vasha Pshavel, I gave up and took shelter in a snow cave.

The storm raged all night. At noon the next day I resumed my descent down slopes burdened with a deep, dangerous layer of unconsolidated snow. In places I waded in powder up to my waist; moving forward was difficult. Eleven hours later, exhausted, I reached the safety of the International Mountaineering Camp. I was lucky and grateful to be alive. As a welcome home my thoughtful comrades had heated up the *banya* (Russian sauna) for me.

One month before the Elbrus race, I returned to my dacha in Gorni Sadovod (Mountain Gardener). Soon I was able to enjoy easy runs with my team of skiers on the cross-country trails through the taiga. During those late-summer days, I relaxed and made my final preparations for the trip to the Caucasus.

In 1989, I had protected my feet with several pairs of socks and wore lightweight track shoes with cleats to win the Elbrus race. Last year the finish line had not been at the top of the mountain; the 1990 race was set to end on the east summit. In late September I expected that the daytime temperatures on the route would be below freezing. Beth Wald had reported on my unusual footgear in her *Climbing* magazine article. I learned that my American friends were coming to compete in the race armed by Nike with "secret weapons," specially fitted track shoes. My search for the right-size shoes in Almaty was fruitless; I was forced to run the race in trekking boots and crampons.

On race day the officials lined us up in front of the Hotel Priyut, at 4,200 meters. We took off, and Vladimir Balyberdin started his stopwatch, standing on the summit finish 1,440 meters higher. With the excellent acclimatization from my summer efforts, I ran without feeling the altitude. The official record time went down in the books: one hour and forty minutes. I finished first and Kevin was second, losing to me by only twelve minutes.

When I said good-bye to Kevin, I had my official invitation to America in my hand and twenty days to obtain authorization to leave the USSR, a visa, and a ticket to the USA. Only a Soviet citizen can appreciate such a mission. Illinski decided that my trip to America was a personal initiative. Without an official sponsor, permission to leave the country was a problem, and all the trip expenses had to come out of my pocket.

Unfortunately, in our country a regular citizen going abroad, es–

pecially to the United States, is about as likely as flying to the moon. That is a joke, but a bitter one. Finally Balyberdin agreed to sponsor me through [his business] Alpinist, but my exit visa came through only one day before I was supposed to be in New York to pick up a ticket to Boulder. By that time only a first-class seat was available from Moscow, which cost me twice as much as a regular fare. That had a dramatic impact on my finances.

Because of the bureaucratic tangle, in those twenty days I managed to make only one long-distance training exercise for the marathon. Though that beautiful eighty-kilometer run over two mountain passes from Almaty to Lake Issyk-Kul was an intense, difficult effort, it was nothing like a competition. At any whim, I stopped to drink from the mountain streams and rested in the warm sun. My lack of experience running the marathon distance made it impossible for me to judge my strength during the actual race.

On October 20, about one hundred people came out to compete in the Basic Boulder Marathon. The trail conditions were bad, icy slush and mud. Just before the start of the race the route was changed. I ran in fifth place for most of the distance. After the steep uphill section, Kevin, Patrick Healey, and Neal Beidleman passed me. I was disgusted with myself for being in such pitiful shape. At a rest stop, I paused and ate a little. When the food kicked in, my strength came back. Toward the end of the race I sped up, but lost time negotiating the unfamiliar trail. I finished in eighth place; if I had not gotten lost, my place would have been sixth. Some would say that was not so bad for my first marathon, but those results weren't anything that impressed a sponsor or me. Kevin felt sick before the race and finished ten minutes behind me in thirteenth place. After it was over, I could see from looking at him that he was satisfied with his performance.

The thing that struck me most after the race was the attitude of the participants. No matter what place they took, everyone seemed satisfied with his time. Each person finished the race beating his main rival, himself. You could see that the motivation for these people was a love of running, the mountains, and nature; the race was a way to celebrate life. The run through the beautiful spurs of the Rocky

Mountains was a kind of holiday. Now I believe that everywhere there are humans who cannot live without regular athletic pursuit.

I am starting to understand a lot more about the way things work here. Visiting in America, you must be ready to live according to local standards. One must respect the customs and lifestyle. I have a good impression of the people that I met during my first trip, especially Bob Palais and Elliott Robinson. My relationships with Beth Wald, Kevin, and Patrick Healey have become more complex. They are interesting people. During this time, the biggest problem for me has been my poor command of the English language. Even Kevin, whom I lived with, sometimes seems like a complete stranger. From our training sessions, I know that like me he has a deep love for running and will make a good climbing partner on Everest. We have that in common, but really very little else. Often during this visit a Russian saying has come to mind: "An uninvited guest is worse than a Tartar." A month has passed since the race and my soul is feeling empty. I guess that I am homesick.

Though it was expensive for me, and I wish that some things had gone differently, coming here was not a waste of time. Now I understand that I need to work harder on bringing climbers and travelers to the Union. Though strong people are respected in America, to obtain sponsorship as a sportsman, one must have a famous name. By Russian standards I earned good money working at a laborer's job, but if I hope to coach or interest sponsors in my climbing ambitions, I will have to produce some concrete results. Now I must focus on preparing for the one-day Everest climb. Without attention to my health and constant training, I won't last too long. Other goals I set for myself are mastering the marathon distance, the ski marathon distance, and ice-climbing techniques. I want to start a company called Extreme Sport. Also, I must be able to climb a 5.11 pitch comfortably; otherwise around here I look pretty funny.

Boulder, Colorado, November 21, 1990.

3

THE YEARS BETWEEN, 1991–93

A natoli climbed Everest in 1991. He was not the only Soviet mountaineer to stretch his legs in the Himalayas. On various expeditions in 1990 and 1991, Anatoli's Kanchenjunga teammates summited the hardest 8,000-meter peaks by new or difficult routes: the South Face of Lhotse, the South Face of Annapurna, the South Face of Manaslu, the East Ridge of Cho Oyu, and the West Wall of Dhaulagiri. Their accomplishments were so impressive that in Kathmandu 1991 was called the "Russian Year in the Himalayas." As her alpinists left their marks in climbing history, the Soviet Union collapsed. The shock waves from that event changed the rules that governed every facet of their existence at once and forever.

In a mountaineering life, tragedy is no stranger. When friends are lost or you watch their painful adjustments to life after frostbite has taken its toll, it is difficult. In the winter of 1990, our team was forced to turn back just below the summit of Pobeda Peak. Six of our expedition members had sustained such severe frostbite that they required helicopter evacuation for medical attention. For many of them, the road to the mountains closed forever that day. Out of the twenty-nine members on the international team of the former Soviet Union who climbed Kanchenjunga, five have died. Nineteen eighty-nine was not so long ago. Nine of my Almaty teammates were on that roster, and three of the best of them remain in the mountains forever. Valeri Khrichtchatyi was buried in an avalanche guiding clients on Khan-Tengri in August of this year. In the autumn of 1990, Grigori Luniakov and Zinur Halitov died attempting a futuristic route up Manaslu.

Anyone who has lost friends while climbing understands how difficult it is to live through their deaths. Confronted with the impact it makes on their loved ones, you are forced to reexamine your passion. Each loss makes it harder to return, once again to take up the paths that lead to the summits. Yet there are those of us who must return. The mountains speak to something deep inside, and the inner longing that answers cannot be ignored.

From the moment we heard that Zinur and Grigori were lost, our team at the Sports Club vowed that our future climbing experiences would keep their spirits and courage alive in our hearts. Our success on Dhaulagiri in the spring of 1991 is a tribute to the influence they had on each of us. The West Wall of Dhaulagiri (8,172 meters) is one of the most technically difficult routes in the Himalayas. There was no fighting or competing for first place during our expedition, and every man on the team climbed to the summit without the assistance of bottled oxygen.

We endured a harrowing descent from the summit, making it back to the shelter of the tents at Camp IV in darkness while a fierce storm rolled up the mountain slopes. Back in our flapping shelters, it was as if a freight train were rushing by two steps beyond the thin walls. Suddenly there was an incredible ringing sound, followed by crackling and hissing. For two hours in what should have been pitch-darkness, the walls of the tent glowed with blue light. In dropping temperatures, chased by a violent wind, the next day we retreated down the mountain. The memory of our friends helped the ten of us work together like a well-oiled machine while we secured that difficult route. It helped us survive the harrowing descent without trauma or tragedy.

In October of 1991, I returned to Nepal as a member of a Russian-American expedition. We were there to challenge the Everest speed-ascent record of twenty-two hours and thirty minutes set by French climber Marc Batard. Vladimir Balyberdin of St. Petersburg was our expedition leader. My American friend Kevin Cooney was my climbing partner. After seventeen days of work, only two Spanish climbers had succeeded in reaching the summit. High winds prevented most people from climbing above Camp III. Though the gales blew strongly, on October 6 our team managed to lash our tents down onto the rocks of the South Col.

As preparation for a later speed ascent, Kevin and I decided to make an easy acclimatization climb on the seventh. He pulled on his old Koflach boots. We left our tent at 8:30 A.M., not taking our ice axes, just our Leki ski poles. Balyberdin climbed with us for a time; he had his movie camera. I did not pay any attention to him, thinking that he intended to do some filming on the Col. Kevin climbed ahead of me for a while. It was easy going and not particularly a struggle. Somewhere around two o'clock in the afternoon, rather unexpectedly, we found ourselves on the South Summit. I went ahead across the ridge below the Hillary Step. At one point I looked back; Kevin was still standing on the South Summit. He waved me to go on.

The wind blew with strong force across the ridge-top, but without enough momentum to push me off the slope. I crawled up the Hillary Step using the remnants of old rope that survived from previous expeditions. Above on a steep incline were the vestiges of steps that the Spanish climbers had cut into the ice the week before. I kept going. Almost by accident, I arrived on the summit at 3 P.M. Was it a coincidence that I stood on top of Everest for the first time one year from the day Zinur Halitov and Grigori Luniakov died on Manaslu? I do not think so. That moment remains clear in my memory and I will never forget it. Their spirits were close, and strangely I sensed that we were together again, there on top of the world.

Those feelings passed. I became aware that Kevin was not visible on the slope below. I hurried down. Around 6 P.M. I climbed into our tent and was relieved to find him waiting for me. Too tight, his old boots had caused numbness in his toes. Sensibly avoiding frostbite, he had turned back at the South Summit. All night I argued with Balyberdin because as leader he had not given me permission to attempt the summit. Kevin and I were just climbing, but my independence caused a rift between "Bal" and I that permanently affected my opportunities to join his expeditions.

At first everyone down in Base Camp insisted that it was impossible I had reached the top of Everest in such high winds and without using supplemental oxygen. Faced with their disbelief, I sheepishly revealed that I had taken a souvenir from the summit-marker poles. I produced the small silver cross that Spaniard Ralph Vidaurre had attached to them when he'd summited the week before. Ralph was delighted with my confession, and it changed the mood of everyone in camp.

In the following days the jet stream dropped lower, producing winds that tore across the South Col at hurricane speeds. Kevin could not wait for conditions to change. His responsibilities at work demanded that he return to Colorado. For two weeks more, I tried to make a speed ascent. Once I climbed from Base Camp to the South Col in a little less than ten hours. My results made me think that breaking Batard's record was a possibility, but the mountain had other plans. Approaching the South Col on a perfectly clear day, I was literally forced to crawl the final meters to the pass. Snow and tiny splinters of ice sand-papered my face. Not one of the tents that ten expeditions had pitched on the Col had escaped destruction. Taking shelter in the least damaged one, I spent a frigid night in a blast that made keeping a gas stove lit impossible. Unable to rehydrate myself with water, I felt my chest become tighter and tighter. For two hours the next morning I struggled to go up, managing to gain only two hundred meters. I gave up. As our team packed up to leave, I made a final attempt to ascend Everest by the West Ridge. Under a clear sky, faced with a medium breeze, I made it to about 8,000 meters. There conditions changed abruptly; the force of the wind became an invisible, impermeable wall. Again I was forced to turn back. I learned from those first experiences with Everest that she decides who gets up.

Our Sports Club's success on Dhaulagiri along with results from other Soviet expeditions was the reason 1991 was called the "Russian Year in the Himalayas." No one would apply such a title of triumph to 1992 and 1993. The Union of Soviet Socialist Republics collapsed in 1991. Before the year was out, former republics like Kazakhstan were independent countries and found themselves in difficult economic situations. This impacted everything in our lives. Especially affected were those areas and interests that had no previously developed commercial potential. For athletes this meant a loss of government support for training in sports that were not Olympics events or those that had not produced world championships.

In all my years of mountaineering, I abandoned my goal before the end only three times—twice climbing Everest and once on Pobeda. Turning back is so difficult when a hundredth or even a thousandth part of the total labor is ahead of you. At the beginning of 1992, after twenty years of preparation, a fraction of what I had dreamed of accomplishing in mountaineering had been achieved, and everything in my life challenged me to quit. Though our success on Dhaulagiri proved our club had many men who were capable of climbing the hardest routes on 8,000-meter peaks without the use of bottled oxygen, all national sponsorship for our expeditions evaporated. My friends and teammates would not talk about climbing anymore; they struggled to earn money literally for bread.

Dreams of the mountains did not leave me alone, and I focused my efforts on finding support for my ambitions in our new economic environment. With my level of experience, I knew I would be a welcome addition to any international team going to the Himalayas—if I could pay my way. All attempts to interest local sponsors failed. Independent businessmen had no understanding of patronage as it is practiced in the West and could not imagine that my efforts might be used in advertising to promote sales. In the summer of 1992, Balyberdin financed an expedition to K2 in Pakistan by charging the

American and French climbers who were included on his permit. Because I had circumvented his authority while climbing Everest, I was not invited. I wrote to mountaineers I knew from other countries, and from time to time I received a response.

On December 23, 1992, a letter arrived from German alpinist Reinmar Joswig. It was an invitation to join a summer expedition led by him and his climbing partner Peter Metzger. Success on three other 8,000-meter peaks in Pakistan had prepared Reinmar to take on the great ambition of his life—Chogori. Known to mountaineers as K2, she is the most alluring and seductively dangerous of all the world's highest mountains. At that time, fewer than ninety individuals had been on the summit of K2, only one of them a German. For me as well, she sang a siren's song. In 1992, seven men had climbed the three highest peaks in the world—Everest, Kanchenjunga, and K2. Success would make me the eighth.

Reinmar and I had become acquainted in Kathmandu, Nepal, in May of 1991. Two months later, I was in the Pamirs with members of Balyberdin's St. Petersburg team camped at 7,000 meters on Communism Peak. We were the first to make it to the highest camp that year, and the following day Balyberdin planned for us to break a new trail through deep snow to the summit. With recent success on 7,134-meter-high Lenin Peak behind us, everyone was in great shape and well acclimated. Below in the comfort of the International Mountaineering Camp Pamir, members of Japanese and South Korean expeditions were patiently waiting for us to make tracks. That afternoon, a lone mountaineer appeared at our campsite loaded down with a big backpack. Immediately I noticed that he moved as though not fatigued by this effort. Fresh from the summit of 7,105-meter-high Korzhenevskaya Peak, Reinmar Joswig was making a rapid solo ascent of Communism Peak. As I helped him set up his tent, a gust of wind blew the outer cover toward the drop-off over the southern wall. Reinmar hurried to recover the tent fly. Familiar with those dangerous slopes, I went after him, offering him my rope and a belay.

He joined us as we set out for the summit the next morning. For us that was a training run for the fall speed ascent of Everest. Reinmar kept up with my fast pace, and we soon left everyone else behind. Clearly, I was in the presence of a strong and experienced mountaineer. In the following days I became just as impressed with his modesty and good character. The letter from him in December of 1992 opened a crack in the door that I had thought closed forever. Remembering Reinmar from the Pamirs, I knew it would be an honor to climb with him again. I immediately agreed to join his expedition. Only my financial situation could stop me.

My job as a ski coach was eliminated early in 1992. Though it had produced national champions, the program did nothing for the collective farm's profits. My basic survival depended on a $20-a-month Master of Sports stipend and a $30 paycheck from the Army Sports Club. Everyone else in my country found himself in the same situation. Salaries were frozen at the old levels. Inflation was rampant. Unemployment was high. There was no hope of earning enough to pay my way to K2. Government sponsorship for our sport had stopped, and all my efforts generated no interest in the private sector. Financial difficulties lay like a stone in my soul, which distracted me from my regular routine of training.

If there is a mountaineer who can climb the highest peaks the way I do without preparation, I envy that man. For twenty years I have strictly adhered to a self-devised formula of exercise and rest, always seeking to proportion my level of readiness to the level of the approaching goal. More than once my program of conditioning had allowed me to perform in critical situations when temperatures were unbelievably cold and my body was deprived of liquids for as much as twenty hours. In those times my survival depended on my endurance. On K2, I expected to face the most extreme conditions of my career.

I live with the knowledge that because of my height and weight, my body requires more time to adjust to altitude than that of a smaller person. On expeditions, prolonged time above five thousand meters exhausts the human body. Physical conditioning actually deteriorates. Without preliminary acclimatization, you risk finding yourself in the stupid situation where your body has adjusted to the altitude, but you have no physical strength to make it to the top. To maintain a basic level of adjustment to altitude and to keep up endurance, my routine training includes rapid ascents on 3,000-to-4,000-meter-high peaks all year. Going at a speed that keeps my pulse high prepares my body for the oxygen fasting one encounters at high altitude.

As well, before the sustained intense effort required to climb above eighty-five hundred meters, it is obligatory to allow the body to rest completely. If you come to a mountain with the body's immune response weakened by the stress of overtraining, you are more susceptible to exacerbation of chronic problems or to sickness caused by bacteria or a virus. Illness can progress rapidly at high elevations, lowering the body's work potential. Weakness can make climbing impossible. At very high altitude, the effects of illness can cause a sudden drop in energy and you can die.

Twenty years of sports experience imprinted in every cell of my body exactly what I needed to be doing to be ready for K2. The obstacles to my preparation were aggravating day-to-day problems resulting from the turmoil in Kazakhstan. Shelves in the stores were empty. Whole days were wasted searching for food. Suddenly all basic services were privatized. Eight hours standing in line resolved one tiny problem only if you happened to have the appropriate documentation with endless stamps from endless bureaucrats in your hand. Otherwise the next day you started over. It was insanely frustrating. Living costs skyrocketed, inflation made money worthless, and wages did not change. My thoughts were always occupied with the training that would keep me alive on K2. Exercise had become as important to me as food and water; without it I had no psychological strength to deal with the pettiness of my situation. As the discipline on which I based my life was broken, I became depressed.

A miraculous invitation from an old friend, San Francisco architect Jack Robbins, liberated me from the problems in Almaty. Magnanimously he offered to pay my expenses to America if I would join him in a May climb up Mount McKinley. He suggested I make plans to arrive in April so that we could train together to prepare for the expedition. Jack and I had shared our love of travel, training, and climbing on other occasions. I had met him on the slopes of Mount Shasta in 1990; at that time we were both preparing for McKinley. In the summer of 1992 I had worked as his guide and coach on the 4,000-meter peaks near Talgar and on 7,000-meter-high Khan-Tengri. I well knew that for Jack a successful ascent of McKinley was as important as succeeding on Everest had been to me. It would fulfill a dream of personal achievement; as a coach, his goal inspired me. K2 was pushed into the background.

Thanks to him, I found myself in Berkeley, and I could escape the worldly problems that had distracted me from training in Almaty. Together we ran for hours through the eucalyptus forest or along the seashore. We climbed Mount Shasta and spent the night out at four thousand meters to begin our acclimatization for McKinley. His strength and endurance improved. Because of Jack and our training, I recovered the psychological stability and inner peace that had eluded me at home. Over our three-year relationship I had come to value his calmness and good sense. Age and a unique personality make him wiser about many things. In the spring of 1993, during a disturbing time for me emotionally, he helped me cope with the way my world was changing.

In America, my efforts to find commercial sponsors for the K2 expedition were futile. There, big companies commit their support well in advance of any project. April was too late to ask for funding for a summer expedition. The day before my departure for Alaska, I called to advise Reinmar of my situation. He said my participation in the expedition had become critical. One of his team had dropped out due to a serious respiratory illness, and another for personal reasons. Without me the team was not strong enough to take on K2. Reinmar offered to pay for my share of the expedition cost. He said I should meet him at his home in Bremen, Germany, before the middle of June. Jack and I flew to Anchorage the next day. My financial relief regarding K2 was not complete. There would be other expenses. As things stood, I did not have enough money to get to Islamabad and back to Almaty.

Two weeks passed as we worked our way to the summit of McKinley up the the West Buttress route. That adventure is another story; I will say things went remarkably well. The park rangers remembered me as "No Problem." It was satisfying work. At seventy, I think Jack is the oldest man to climb the highest peak in North America. Celebrating our success with dinner in an Anchorage restaurant that offered a big salad bar, I had enough experience by then with American buffets not to leave the restaurant hungry. Warmly saying good-bye, Jack headed to his home in the fairy-tale woodlands of northern California. I boarded the plane to Moscow satisfied that I was prepared to face an 8,000-meter peak. Ahead of me there was still time for a good rest before the K2 expedition began.

4

CHOGORI, THE SIREN'S SONG, SUMMER 1993

I arrived in Moscow on May 28. The cumbersomely ineffective bureaucracy seemed to be the only thing left operating normally from the Soviet era. After spending a week resolving the numerous problems associated with my passport and obtaining visas for the trip, I took a train to Bremen. The ticket cost a little more than $100. That was a relief. I had $500 in my pocket. I changed trains in Warsaw, and leaving behind the last outlines of hills or mountains, I watched perfectly flat North Sea coastland fly past the window for hours. On June 13, I arrived in a charming German town. Crowded, spotlessly clean streets were full of people going about their business on bicycles. The monument in the Bremen town square honored fabled animal musicians, not war heroes.

The time that had passed since our previous meeting had not changed Reinmar Joswig. Though fifty years old, his physique would have caused envy in someone thirty. In Bremen he religiously avoided any kind of motorized transportation, preferring to ride his bike from place to place. A dedication to fitness had allowed him to make it to the top of several 8,000-meter peaks: Gasherbrum I, Broad Peak, and Nanga Parbat. Many of our expedition's logistical details fell on Reinmar's shoulders. He managed them all with typical German precision. In the final days before our departure, I helped pack the equipment that had not been shipped earlier with our main baggage. Undisturbed by a thousand last-minute details that would have driven me crazy, Reinmar found the time to train every day.

His climbing partner on Nanga Parbat and longtime friend Peter Metzger was our expedition coleader. After meeting Peter, I was confident that our leadership was strong and wholesome. The personalities of these two good men complemented each other: Metzger was charismatic and possessed boundless energy, while Reinmar had a quiet strength and calmness that was reassuring.

On June 18 we took a train to the Frankfurt airport. There we were joined by the fourth member of our group. Though lacking his friends' depth of experience on 8,000-meter peaks, fifty-four-year-old Ernst Eberhardt's success on a hard, high peak in India's Himachal Pradesh had inspired him to try K2. I found Ernst easy to talk with; he had a wonderful full beard that gave him a genial look. His mild manner and patience proved to be blessings, helping to solve the many problems that confronted us during our sojourn in Pakistan.

After a six-hour flight, the four of us stepped off the plane into the sweltering heat of the Islamabad night. Foul-smelling city air fell on us like a blanket. When we claimed our baggage, Ernst's pack containing all his climbing gear was missing. Mishaps would not end there; they were only beginning.

We settled into the Holiday, a pretty good hotel in Rawalpindi, the old city next to Islamabad. The next morning our expedition agent, Ashrif Aman, welcomed us with more bad news. He had been unable to notify our government liaison officer that Reinmar had changed our arrival date. We were stuck. Foreign expeditions are forbidden to travel in the sensitive border regions around K2 without an army officer to report on expedition progress and assist in solving problems with the local citizens. Peter and Reinmar spent the next four days at the Ministry of Tourism lobbying for a new officer.

I laid out my financial situation for Ashrif. Being a mountaineer (he was the first Pakistani to summit K2), he was sympathetic. He convinced me the most interesting way for me to return to Almaty was overland through the Hunza region and Sinkiang. Land transportation was cheap. The Chinese controlled Sinkiang, so I spent my time in their consulate trying to obtain a transit visa for my trip home to Kazakhstan. Ernst made daily visits to the airport until he recovered his backpack and equipment.

Andy Locke, the last member of our expedition, joined us. At the last moment Reinmar had included this pleasant, muscular Australian policeman on our permit. At thirty, he was the youngest person on the team. I had become acquainted with Andy during my time at Everest Base Camp in 1991. He arrived in Rawalpindi straight from his second unsuccessful attempt to climb Mount Everest. Though he was tired, several nights at the South Col had given him the advantage of excellent acclimatization. As events unfolded, we had plenty of time to rest before there was any work to do.

After five days in Rawalpindi, we breathed a sigh of relief when an official at the Ministry of Tourism assigned us a new officer, only to be disappointed that he could not arrive in the capital until June 26. With that problem partially resolved, none of us had any desire to wait in the city suffering the heat. Peter volunteered to stay to meet the officer.

His sacrifice liberated the rest our party to fly to Skardu, the last refuge of civilization on the trail to K2. There the countryside and traditional Moslem culture was reminiscent of the pleasant villages in Tajikistan in the southwestern Pamirs where I had done a lot of climbing. Eternal snows on an embrace of high peaks made the air clean and cool. Our roomy accommodations at the Sehr Motel were simple and comfortable. Peter called to confirm that he and our new officer would arrive on June 28.

We settled down and made the best of the delay. The next portion of the journey was by jeep over a rough dirt track to the village of Askole. There everything would be loaded on the backs of porters for the trip to Base Camp. All supplies and equipment had to be repacked into 25-kilogram loads for the porters. Thanks to Reinmar and Peter's lists of what, where, and how much to put into each load, we finished that job quickly in Skardu.

During our stay, a helicopter arrived, evacuating from K2 Base Camp a doctor and two Slovenian climbers who had bad frostbite. Their black, shriveled feet appeared all too familiar; it was clear to me that most of their toes would have to be amputated. These men had reputations as excellent mountaineers, so their predicament increased my motivation to stay in shape. Each morning I ran for an hour along the banks of the Indus River, which flowed by the edge of town. In the evenings, I climbed to the rock ridges of the nearest mountains. Reinmar continued his training routine as well. The delay did not tell on our physical readiness, but our vacation would haunt us in other ways throughout the expedition.

Toyota jeeps loaded down with us and all our supplies left Skardu for Askole on the twenty-ninth. Bad weather had caused all the flights from Islamabad to be canceled. Peter and the new officer raced to catch up with us by car. Finally joining us in Askole, the officer assembled sixty-seven porters. Each man was assigned a load and a ration of food, and at last we set off on the trail to Base Camp. Given our earlier experiences, things went pretty smoothly on the trek. Enjoying the hot, sunny weather, our small army traveled seven days through the mystical countryside. It is impossible to do justice with words to the grandeur of the mountains along Baltoro Glacier. Nothing compares to that place; the stone towers and rocks are mysterious and wonderful. By day six we arrived where two great glacial rivers, the Godwin Austen and the Upper Baltoro, flowed together. As we camped at Concordia, the imposing pyramid of K2 dominated the view and our imaginations.

Following the Godwin Austen glacier another eight miles, we arrived at the site that would serve as home for the next six weeks. Though most of expeditions camped on the glacier had been working for several weeks before we arrived, only two groups had managed to climb higher than Camp II.

In two days of sunny weather when we were setting up camp,

three members of a Canadian-American team summited. Tragedy did not pass them by; one of the Canadians fell to his death descending the slopes above the snow-burdened bottleneck couloir. The members of the Slovenian team were descending from the summit. In addition to the men who had suffered frostbite, they lost one member of their group to complications from cerebral edema. A Dutch team aided by expensive high-altitude porters and a well-equipped Swedish group had gotten no farther than camp at 6,500 meters. With satellite communication to their homeland, the Swedes had the advantage of accurate weather information for the area. Three friends from Great Britain, Victor Saunders, Julie Clyma, and Roger Payne, had established their first camp. Like us, all those expeditions were climbing K2 via the Abruzzi route. My American friend Dan Mazur was leading a big team of international climbers attempting the West Ridge. Other, smaller groups were trying harder routes. About one hundred mountaineers were camped below K2 with us. Its history had nothing to recall like that. The permit fee in 1994 was going to cost three times more than what we had paid; that was the reason for the invasion.

We spent July 6 and 7 setting up a kitchen and dining area and sorting out supplies. Separating gas, equipment, and food into high-camp loads occupied my time, but I made a special effort to locate Dan Mazur in the maze of tents around us. For almost a month in the fall of 1991, Dan and I had lived together on the Khumbu Glacier in Nepal. High-altitude mountaineers are a small group. Our friendships are formed under unusual circumstances. It seems there are no foreigners among us. Men and women are judged not for what they have or where they come from, but who they are in hard circumstances. We meet in remote camps, a community of individuals with strange, difficult ambitions and a peculiar appetite for mountaineering life. For me the opportunity to reacquaint with old friends is important. The positive emotions I experience in these encounters give me an unusual charge of strength and energy.

Eager to get started, on July 8 we were up at 2 A.M. We left camp at three-thirty after eating breakfast. On our backs were the supplies we needed to set up Camp I. We crossed the glacier in two hours, following a trail well marked by members of previous expeditions. Like the other teams on our route, we climbed to Camp I having been spared the effort of fixing line on the steep section above the glacier. We had the Slovenians and the Americans and the Canadians to thank for that.

Peter and Andy climbed ahead of me. When Peter stopped to make radio contact with our Base Camp, I went ahead, trading places with Andy. Working in the lead is slow and tiring. Every step you must kneel into the loose snow above you to compress it, so there will be some traction for your crampons when you step up. That day the snow was not too deep and we shared the work. At about nine-thirty we arrived on a flat snow-plain where the other expeditions had set up their first high-altitude camp. All the level areas were occupied. After locating a suitable gentle slope, we worked together digging out tent platforms. Ice underlay the fresh snow, and the work was tiresome. The weather steadily deteriorated until we were working in horizontally blowing snow. Julie Clyma and Roger Payne, who were acclimatizing in their tents at Camp I, decided to head down. Rapidly securing our supplies, we followed them back to Base Camp. The weather got much worse before it got better.

In the night, a heavy accumulation of new snow and the force of the gusting wind collapsed the roof of our kitchen. From 5 until 10 A.M. we worked rebuilding it. Snow fell continuously for four more days. That delay weighed heavily on Peter's and Reinmar's nerves. The clock was ticking; we had a limited time to accomplish our goal. Reinmar was scheduled to leave for Germany on August 18. Because of his work, that date could not be changed. Confined to our tents, we passed days restlessly inactive. Occasionally, the monotony was broken by a visit from climbers on other expeditions. Hospitality would prompt us to move to more comfortable surroundings in the mess tent. For a time the delay would be forgotten in the diversion of our stories and conversations.

At eleven in the morning on the thirteenth, the weather improved. Carrying a load of supplies, we decided to forge a new trail to the beginning of the fixed rope. The glacier was covered in deep new snow that lay like icing on a treacherous cake. No trace of the many crevasses marked the smooth surface; our progress had to be slow and deliberate. I worked first, testing the snow, cautiously probing with my ski poles to reassure myself that the next weighted step would not be into a frozen abyss.

We returned to camp about dinnertime and accepted an invitation to dinner from the Canadian-American team. Though three members of their expedition, Phil Powers, Dan Culver, and Jim Haberl, had summited, there was no mood of victory or celebration in their tents. Dan Culver had paid for the summit with his life. He was remembered fondly by Phil Powers and his other teammates. In conversations that night we listened to the questions mountaineers ask in such times: "Do we need to return to the summits above the clouds?" " Is this risk of life necessary?" We said good-night to those companionable men. A jar of honey and a part of the grief over the death of their friend were the gifts we took back to our tents. Each of us had new feelings and a clear awareness that danger awaited us as well, somewhere at the top.

At 3:30 A.M. we were at the breakfast table, after which we shouldered heavy loads of supplies for our high camps and crossed the glacier on our newly broken trail. Ascending the next steep section where before we enjoyed the fixed rope was difficult. Sinking with a heavy pack through waist-deep snow, the leader had to wade forward, compress a new step, liberate the frozen, buried rope, and pull it up to the surface. By noon we had made it up to Camp I and set up two tents. The weather was excellent, clear and calm, and our spirits were high.

After lunch and a short rest, I asked Peter and Reinmar if I could carry an eight-kilogram load with two tents up to 6,700 meters. They gave me permission, though they were mystified why after such a long, hard day I wanted to go higher. I was aware that my capacity for work would drop dramatically for the next two days while my body adjusted to a higher elevation. My rationale was that if I could accomplish the work in good spirits that afternoon, I should not delay until the next day when the same job would feel much more difficult. Thanks to the time on McKinley, carrying a regular load to 6,500 meters had not bothered me. Our many days of forced inactivity left me feeling I had rested enough for a month.

I set out from camp at four o'clock, enjoying a hard crust on the névé snow that made climbing easy. In two hours I reached a band of steep, yellow rocks. Phil Powers had advised me that above those yellow rocks at 6,800 meters we would find the best location for Camp II. I secured my load in a protected place, and one-half hour later I was back in camp. My teammates had eaten and were comfortably resting in their sleeping bags. I drank some tea and ate a little food. Sleep came quickly without problem.

After years of self-analysis, I know that the ability to fall asleep after hard work is an indication that my body is properly adjusting to the altitude. Difficulty falling asleep indicates that I must reduce the stress on my body and slow down the rate of my ascent. In general, I am so accustomed to exercise that I cannot sleep if I do not work hard enough during the day. Though the process is different for each individual, I think that if you maintain a normal pulse rate and can rehabilitate by sleeping well, you should work until you feel a pleasant tiredness, even at high altitude. Then the body accepts rest as a joy.

Of course, this rule does not apply to anyone who is ill in the mountains. It is crucial for an athlete and especially a mountaineer to listen to his body, to feel it intuitively. Though it is possible to overcome fatigue with inner motivation in the early stages of an expedition, too much work is unnatural and can affect resilience. Serious fatigue can go unnoticed by someone who is physically fit. No dramatic effect from overwork will be appreciated until it is too late. I know from personal experience that fatigue subtly accumulates in the body, only to manifest at the most stressful moments, usually up high. Insidiously it can leave you without strength and the ability to perform. In mountaineering, much that happens and many decisions depend on external factors over which we have no control, such as the weather and the conditions on the route. The most important individual responsibility on an expedition is balancing personal needs so you maintain your strength and health while still performing in accord with the group's desires and objectives.

The next morning after a leisurely breakfast we left our tents at nine o'clock. True to my intuition, my load felt heavier and I could not maintain my previous day's speed. The weather was no help. We unloaded our supplies at Camp II in the kind of gusting wind that comes before a squall. That afternoon the trip down to Camp I took an hour instead of thirty minutes. Everyone was moving slower.

I arrived at the tents ahead of my friends. Ernst and I began fixing dinner. Not feeling well, he had turned back halfway to Camp II. At his age it was natural for him to require a longer period to adjust to increases in elevation. Andy reported that he was not experiencing problems with the new altitude, not surprising since he had recently camped at eight thousand meters on Everest. When they arrived, looking really fit, Reinmar and Peter said they felt well. They were not novices and knew what to expect of their bodies, thanks to a good foundation of experience at high altitude. Judging from the huge supply of food we had carried up, I could see that they had no problems with digestion.

Appetite at high altitude is an individual thing. For me it is generally best to consume as little as possible, and then only those foods that are metabolized quickly. That night I tried to joke with Reinmar, saying that if we ate half the store of provisions we had carried up, our bodies would be so occupied digesting that we would have no ambition to make it to the summit. That was taken as a criticism. Because of nuances in languages, it was easy for us to misunderstand one another in subtle ways. We used English to communicate, which, except for Andy, was not anyone's native tongue. Reinmar was comfortable speaking it, but my English is far from good. The effort we each had to make to understand one another created a fatigue of sorts.

The sixteenth greeted us with miserable weather. I made hot chocolate for breakfast. Certain we were going down, I wanted to hold out for flat-bread chapatis and eggs at Base Camp. Reinmar and Peter were ready to carry up another load of supplies to Camp II. I thought we would be better off waiting out the bad weather in Base Camp. At the lower elevation our bodies could recuperate from the previous days of hard work. When the weather improved and we were rested, a big supply carry to Camp II would be easier. Then, after one night sleeping at Camp II, we would be acclimated well enough to go up the next increment of elevation. Offhand, I remarked that if we exhausted ourselves carrying loads high in bad weather, we could be compromising our ability to climb when the weather improved.

Reinmar had a short answer to that: "If you are feeling tired, then you should go down and rest, but the team is going up."

I did not think I felt any weaker that anyone else, so I gave up trying to make my point of view understood. I broke trail for them in fresh falling snow. Behind me, Reinmar and Peter were slow; the days of work without respite had affected their pace. My intuition and experience were telling me we needed time for rehabilitation after carrying so much weight to 6,800 meters.

Despite my concerns, I sympathized with their point of view. Peter and Reinmar had committed great effort and energy to organizing the expedition for all of us. Certainly I had contributed nothing in those areas. The bad weather ate up many of our days. It would have been unfair if after so much work they did not have time for an assault on the summit. Reinmar's departure deadline hung over us and influenced all our decisions. Willingly, I cooperated with them. They were my leaders and were responsible for our climbing plan. I wanted to work for them and for our success.

Initially, I presented a completely different acclimatization strategy for their consideration. Appreciating the problems that the delays in Islamabad and the weather had cost our expedition, I suggested we focus on achieving a good acclimatization. I thought we should make a schedule of trips to allow our bodies to adapt to each new level of altitude before beginning to carry up the heavy supplies. I suggested we should carry minimum food and equipment to Camp I, spend the night, and go on to Camp II at 6,800 meters, sleep one night, and descend to rest at Base Camp. Then subsequent trips to 6,800 meters carrying weight would be easier for our bodies. We could ferry up summit-day supplies to Camp II before going on with minimum supplies to acclimate at 7,300 for a night, come down again, and move the loads up to 7,300 when we went up for the final acclimatization trip to 7,900 meters. That way we would have preliminary acclimatization at the level of our last camp, and we could climb lightly loaded to 7,300 meters on the summit bid.

I did not invent this scheme. It was tested and proven by many men on tens of Soviet expeditions to 7,000- and 8,000-meter-high peaks. From my first steps as a mountaineer in the Almaty club, our experienced coaches taught me that formula.* It had worked for me on every expedition. Our experience proved that multiple nights at progressively higher altitudes without descending for the body to recuperate was a less effective method. Actually, that kind of advance diminished the body's ability to perform work. In prolonged oxygen-deprived circumstances, working to capacity, lactic acid and other waste products build up in the muscles, which produces weakness and fatigue. Sleeping and eating at high altitude, one cannot replenish the body's energy stores or eliminate waste. Digesting complex food at high altitude, the body actually spends energy, and many foods cannot be digested in that atmosphere. A fit body is naturally resilient and responds to rest at lower altitude.

Properly acclimatized, like me, Peter, Reinmar, and Andy were

---

*The heart of the Soviet school's scheme for climbing high was a pattern of acclimatization and rehabilitation. A plan was developed relevant to the height of the peak and the speed those climbing could travel at different elevations. Speed of ascent depended on the physical condition of the climbers, adaptation to altitude (acclimatization), and the conditions on the route. Everyone knew his personal variable, but in general the higher you go, the slower you go. After proper acclimatization and carrying a load of twenty kilograms, I can ascend 300 vertical meters an hour on normal terrain up to 7,000 meters. Between 7,000 and 8,000 meters carrying ten to fifteen kilograms, I gain 200 vertical meters an hour. Above 8,000 meters my rate of ascent with minimal weight is 100 vertical meters an hour. Generally, I can go down twice as fast as I can go up on the same terrain.

The altitude of the last camp and last elevation for acclimatization on an 8,000-meter peak is derived by a simple formula. Subtract the vertical height one can ascend and descend in ten hours from the mountain's summit height. You make trips to acclimatize at 500-to-1,000-meter intervals up to that height. Each acclimatization trip is two to four days long, depending on the altitude to be achieved. Following each trip there is a two-to-five-day rest period. The rest period depends on the time spent on the previous trip.

able to climb one hundred meters an hour above 7,500 meters. The summit of K2 is 8,611 meters high; I outlined a schedule that would have prepared our bodies to work ten hours above 7,900 meters on summit day. There was no guarantee that in adhering to my schedule we could summit. In the forbidden zone, fate and luck play their hand. But the commitment of time and effort to adequate acclimatization improves personal performance and decreases the odds of developing acute mountain sickness. Proper acclimatization is the most important variable of safety an individual can affect when climbing at altitude. Ignoring that responsibility, a climber raises the risk to himself and his team.

Reinmar listened to all I had to say, as well as I could explain it, and made a good-natured response to my ideas and concerns. I understood from his gentleness that he did not want to offend me. He conceded my plan might be correct if we were attempting a "sports climb," but countered that our group had variable physical conditions and we were climbing the normal Abruzzi route. For our purpose he felt that the demanding acclimatization would not work, that it might even be dangerous, exhausting us before the summit bid.

My friends' good judgment had brought them success on Nanga Parbat, Broad Peak, and Gasherbrum, all about 8,100 meters high. My reservations were based on my experiences climbing Everest and Kanchenjunga. K2 is 8,611 meters high, and performing above 8,500 meters, especially without bottled oxygen, is different from climbing lower 8,000-meter peaks. I did not feel it was my place to argue about our tactics because I was just a member of the expedition, not the leader. Also I respected that the Russian scheme was not the only way that high mountains were successfully climbed.

Peter and Reinmar had confidence in their plan. During the summit bid we were going to acclimatize to 7,300 meters and to 7,900 meters as we ascended. Now I am certain, given the turn of events, that my concerns were well-founded. Any climb higher than 8,500 meters without the use of supplemental oxygen is a major athletic undertaking, and there are rules you cannot break in the mountains. That day I had no wish to see my reservations validated by the high price we paid. My hope was that we would make it to the top and back to Base Camp without tragedy.

On the sixteenth we made our deposit at 6,800 meters and returned to Camp I exhausted. The weather left us wishing for better. Peter gave Andy and me permission to descend to Base Camp. Our absence would spare the food supplies we had struggled to carry up. To avoid the problems of crossing the glacier at dusk, Reinmar and Peter chose to stay the night at Camp I. Going down, we met Ernst coming up with a load from Base Camp. We told him Peter and Reinmar planned to descend the next day. Finally feeling good, Ernst wanted to spend the night at an elevation higher than Base Camp and went up.

To my surprise our descent took only two hours. The temperature on the glacier was so much warmer than above, we were able to remove our outer layers of Gore-Tex clothing. Back at Base Camp, Andy and I headed straight to our mess tent. Our Pakistani cook, Rastam, cooked up a stack of delicious chapatis. We ate with the gusto of men who had been on high-altitude rations for several days. Our evening radio contact with Reinmar and Peter confirmed that Ernst had arrived with his load. Weather permitting, they decided to ferry it to Camp II the next day. We were instructed to bring more supplies to Camp I.

Snow was falling heavily when we woke on the seventeenth. With pleasure Andy and I rolled over and went back to sleep. By late morning, like a broom, a sudden wind swept away the clouds. About 11 A.M. we learned by radio that Peter, Reinmar, and Ernst were starting for Camp II with supplies. Since it was late, Andy and I decided to rest a day and carry double loads up the following morning. Anxious to spend my first night at 6,800 meters, if the weather did not confound my plan, I thought our rest would make it possible for us to climb directly to Camp II in one day.

Toward evening, men and women emerged from their tents, escaping from another day of tedious confinement. We said our farewells at the Canadian-American camp. The porters for their expedition had arrived, and their equipment was being dismantled for transport down the glacier. The next morning, Phil Powers, the genial mountaineer from Wyoming, and his friends departed for civilization. Behind them they left a sad remembrance of their experience. A plaque engraved with the name of Dan Culver was fixed to the rocks in a place below Base Camp—the site of the memorial cairn for all climbers who die on the slopes of K2.

Under a clear sky Andy and I got an early start from Base Camp. Alone on the route, our silent progress was suddenly interrupted by Rastam's shouts. He came running after us to deliver my forgotten thermos. After the day's rest, even with a double load of supplies, I moved easily in the knee-deep snow, breaking trail and pulling the ropes up to the surface. I imagined many climbers would follow us, happy not to be trapped in their tents. Due to the continuous storms, many teams who had arrived as early as May had only reached 6,800 meters. After ten days of work our team could expect to spend the night at that elevation.

About eight-thirty I joined my German friends for breakfast at Camp I. After the previous day's hard work, they weren't moving very quickly. With the double load I had carried, I had no pangs of guilt about my contribution to our effort. I felt strong; my only problem was a cough caused by breathing the dry, thin air. Thanks to Rastam I had my preferred remedy—mint tea. About ten o'clock Peter, Reinmar, and Ernst were ready to go. Andy arrived; stomach problems had slowed him down. Carrying about fifteen kilograms of group equipment and five kilograms of my personal gear, I set off and was soon ahead of Reinmar and Ernst, catching and passing Peter below the yellow rocks. He looked stronger than his comrades and was feeling quite good at that elevation. I used a jumar on the fixed rope to climb up a steep section of rock and arrived on a snowy ridge.

Camp II was located in an inconvenient place on the ridge completely exposed to the prevailing winds. Flapping flags, the shredded remains of many tents littered the area, their debris a testimony to the hurricane-force winds that ripped across this slope and the trouble those tents had caused their owners. I began to cut ice bricks from the snow as I cleared level platforms in the slope. Peter, Reinmar, and Ernst arrived later and immediately began to help me. Andy, not feeling well, had turned back to spend the night at Camp I. By radio he said that he would join us the following day. Peter and Ernst set up our three-man dome tent. Carefully, Reinmar and I secured my two-man North Face in the lee of an ice-block wall. The evening weather was beautiful and the air was still. Far to the south, the ridges of the mountains were painted with the splendid reds and purples of sunset. After making ourselves comfortable in our sleeping bags, we cooked a wonderful supper. That night I had no complaints about the delicacies we had hauled up the mountain.

Though I slept soundly through the night, the next morning I felt the increase in altitude for the first time. I had no appetite. My teammates were none too joyful either. The multiple nights above 6,000 meters and the hard work were telling on them. That morning we discussed a plan for setting up the next camp. I suggested that we ascend carrying minimal equipment and supplies and spend a night at 7,300 meters for acclimatization at the new elevation. Peter and Reinmar were totally opposed to my idea. They decided we would transport heavy loads of gas, food, and equipment, which would be needed in the future, and that we would return to Camp II for that night. The next day we were supposed to carry another load up and overnight at the new elevation.

I tried to reason with them, explaining why I thought it was important to spend one night without the stress of heavy work at the new elevation. Also, the ropes on the steep section ahead of us were the unstable remnants from old expeditions, and descending tired later in the day along this precipitous terrain without the benefit of a well-secured trail was an added risk. I lobbied for the night of acclimatization at 7,300 meters because I thought it was necessary for my German friends, more so than for Andy and me, who had spent the spring climbing high. I knew this safety precaution would improve our performance later on. Given the energy level that morning, I seriously doubted we would be in form to make another carry to Camp III the next day. My plan was dismissed out of hand. Peter and Reinmar pedantically insisted I return with them to Camp II after our carry. They had a confidence in their physical resilience and energy stores I could only admire.

As we waited for Andy to arrive, we sorted the loads for our last two camps. Ernst felt unwell in the night; he was tired. After bringing up the load he had left below the yellow band the day before, he decided to descend to Camp I to spend the night. In my professional assessment, Ernst was adjusting fairly well by taking interim days of rest. Many times I had seen older mountaineers in the Soviet Union succeed on peaks higher than eight thousand meters by taking more time to acclimate.

I left camp following Peter and Andy up the fixed rope. Reinmar came behind me. By his pace, I could tell he was fatigued. Reinmar, with his strong soul, looked fully ten years younger than his fifty years. Twenty- and thirty-year-old men would envy his physical condition. Though fluent in German, English, and French, he was not a man of many words. His inner strength and his rational mind impressed me. When climbing, he was disciplined, motivated, and always good-tempered. Whenever I found myself ahead breaking trail, Reinmar was close to me, ever ready to exchange leads, to help me, even if he was tired. Though sometimes we found it difficult to comprehend what the other was saying, mainly due to my poor command of English, Reinmar and I always reached a common understanding. I never heard any tone of reproof from him, even if he was not happy with me. If things were not going according to plan, he would simply spread his arms and say in a way that sounded like English, "Yeah, yeah."

We had interesting discussions about the political problems that had beset our countries since the Second World War. Germany and Russia share a common history, and not much of it was good. Because of men like Reinmar, I learned it was possible for Russians and Germans to respect one another despite the dark experiences of our recent past. Reinmar's determination had taken him to the top of many mountains. I watched him moving surely toward his goal, the summit of K2. He deserved to succeed. He had earned that victory.

The summit was within his physical and mental grasp, but so many things in our expedition worked against him. We had lost valuable time in Islamabad and were haunted by bad weather, and there were personal details, which depend on fate and luck, the significances of which are magnified by the circumstances up high.

At the beginning of the steep part of the route to Camp III, I went ahead of Peter and Andy. The weather was weird. Tiny snowflakes were blowing around, and occasional gusts of wind were strong enough to push a man with a heavy load off-balance. When the sun broke though, the wind calmed and our windproof Gore-Tex suits were instantly hot and stuffy. The rocks became less steep and I searched for the location of the third high-altitude camp. After a section of rocks, we came to an icy slope with a veneer of deep, dry snow. I sank up to my knees. The dry powder flowed like a river from my steps down the steep slopes. There was no traction between my crampons and the snow. It was so bad that, two hundred meters below, Reinmar, moving persistently, had trouble ascending, though I had just compressed the snow with my weight.

Across a crest of ice that dropped away abruptly to rocks, I emerged onto a steep, snowy slope. The wind calmed down, the sun came out, and the snow stopped falling. I moved up, pulling out pieces of old fixed line from under a thick covering of snow. I came to a huge waterproof bag; it belonged to two Swedish climbers. Somewhere under the new snow was the cave Phil Powers had told me about. The Canadian-American team had built it for their Camp III. I did not stop to look for this landmark. Two hundred meters higher there was a flat place; an obvious route lay ahead of me through the new snowdrifts that had piled up on the bergschrund. I decided that establishing a camp on the flat area would require half the effort needed to dig out a platform on the windy slope where I was standing. It was 2 P.M. I plunged ahead, soon sinking up to my chest in powder. It was impossible to extricate the fixed rope. I worked with my hands and elbows in a swimming motion, shoveling the loose snow aside and ramming it into walls with my shoulders. Then I brought up my knee and searched for a spot that would support my next step up. Reinmar followed the trench I had created and caught up with me plowing through the snow. I explained my rationale for moving ahead. He agreed it was a good idea. Fifty meters away just behind the bergschrund, I could see wind-hardened névé, which would provide perfect traction and stable support for walking. Completely exhausted by this hellish work, we stopped for a drink of hot tea. I was so tired that I could no longer lift my backpack. Reinmar went ahead of me and worked for about fifteen minutes before exhaustion forced him to stop. Peter arrived at the level of the Swedish dry bag. I saw him try to move up in the trench we had made. Quickly, he gave up, deposited his load, and began his descent.

I gathered the last of my strength and switched places with Reinmar. With clenched teeth I swam through the final meters of bottomless powder that overlay the ice crevasses of the bergschrund. Finally after forty minutes more work, my crampons found traction in hard snow below. As I moved forward, the depth of powder decreased to two feet, then to the top of my plastic boots. On the level ground ahead I saw the abandoned remnants of a camp—a Russian Primus stove, a few abandoned oxygen bottles, and an orange shovel with the name Ed Viesturs written clearly on the back. I had found the site used by members of the 1992 Russian expedition led by Vladimir Balyberdin.

Ed Viesturs and two other American climbers, Scott Fischer and Charlie Mace, had been on that expedition. Ed Viesturs I knew and respected as a strong mountaineer. I had first met him in Kathmandu when the Americans and the Russians were celebrating their ascents on Kanchenjunga in 1989. We had succeeded on different sides, as usual. After that our paths crossed many times, on Lenin Peak, once in the Caucasus, and again in 1991 after our ascent of Dhaulagiri and his success on Everest. With an impressive ascent of K2, Ed Viesturs became the seventh person in the history of mountaineering to climb the three highest peaks in the world. It was my turn to add my name to the short list. Judging by the determination of my German friends that day, I felt the opportunity would not be lost.

About five in the afternoon Reinmar and I dropped our load of supplies and gear at the hard-won site for Camp III. We started down. The weather became pleasant toward evening; the wind that had worried us all day ceased, and the air was still during our descent. Reinmar was ahead of me until he decided to rest for a moment. I passed him at the beginning of the steep portion of the route where the fixed lines began. It was difficult to say which of us was more exhausted, Reinmar after four nights and days steadily working above six thousand meters or me after struggling all day long through the terrible snow. After rappelling down the first section of rope, I turned to locate my friend; he was moving down steadily as well. After I saw him past the worst section, I turned to continue my descent. The route below us all the way to the tents was protected with fixed line and was not so difficult.

Peter and Andy were fortifying their tent when I arrived at Camp II. I removed my crampons and climbed into my tent. I fired up the Primus stove and melted a pot of water from the snow I had prepared before leaving that morning. Drained by my day's efforts, I drank the water and sank into sleep, comforted by the warmth of my sleeping bag. Shouts awakened me. Judging from Peter's and Andy's voices, I knew something unexpected had happened, and that it must concern Reinmar.

Rushing out of the tent, I found Andy standing next to Reinmar, who was covered in blood. Fifty meters above the camp, he had unclipped from the fixed line at a juncture of rope. He had relaxed his guard too early. Believing the snow was stable névé, he had misstepped his crampons onto ice and slipped. Collision with a ridge of rocks that jutted out of the snow was all that had kept Reinmar from falling over the rocky south wall into bottomless space. A head wound was bleeding profusely, and he had cuts over his face. He said he felt that he hit his head and chest pretty hard.

We were concerned about a concussion, and because of his pain when breathing, it seemed likely he had broken ribs. All his extremities were functioning fine, and only time would reveal if he had serious internal injuries. Reinmar settled into Peter and Andy's big tent, where we cleaned and bandaged his wounds. I boiled water all night long and carried it to their tent thinking because of the head injury we needed to rehydrate him. The night was terribly cold. I did not sleep until just before dawn.

July 20 I awoke tired and groggy from the night's ordeal, but I immediately began preparing tea. We decided it was best to descend to Base Camp. It took us a long time to get ourselves ready. We helped Reinmar into his clothes and harness and at about 10 A.M. started down. Andy went first, Reinmar next, belayed on Peter's rope. After securing the tents, I left camp with my backpack full of Reinmar's extra belongings. I caught up with my friends at Camp I.

Many climbers were ascending the fixed line and settling into their tents while we enjoyed a good lunch and drank more tea. Ernst, who had been informed of the accident by radio, had prepared everything for us. The weather had stabilized and was perfect for working on the route. We warmed ourselves in the sun, enjoying the food and tea. Reinmar was upset when I told him that I had his personal gear. Embarrassed or uncertain of his plans, he insisted he could carry his things. I did not say so, of course, but I thought the climb was over for him. When he'd left the higher camp, I believe he, too, harbored serious doubts that continuing was possible. At Camp I with only side pain to remind him of the accident, giving up on the insidiously dangerous peak was no longer a certainty.

Under the blazing sun, we began a lethargic descent from Camp I. Heavy, wet snow stuck in our crampons and our boots got heavier. Tired bodies were forced to work a little harder. As we finished negotiating the last section of fixed rope, fortune smiled on us from the face of a cute, young British doctor. Thoughtfully she had hiked across the glacier to help us. From the first sight of her, our fatigue disappeared. Suddenly we were laughing and chatting amiably. Sitting on the rocks, we drank tea and watched as she cleaned and examined Reinmar's wounds. She led us back to the British camp, where she skillfully put six stitches in his scalp. Although she confirmed our suspicion that he had a broken rib, his other injuries were superficial. Reassured by her diagnosis, Reinmar would go back up the mountain.

We slept late the next morning, and no one was in a hurry for breakfast. The day was sunny, without wind. One could only envy those men who were working up higher in such perfect weather. After eating, I stripped down to my underwear to spend fifteen minutes sunbathing on a cot. My stomach was full and the warmth of the sun was intoxicating. I fell asleep instantly and came to my senses three hours later. The result was a vivid red sunburn, which became so painful that it kept me from sleeping that night.

On July 22 the weather changed and another storm enveloped the mountain. Tired climbers from the other expeditions returned from their high-altitude camps. I heard the clank of their equipment and the rhythm of their tired steps as they passed our tents. The day evaporated; we visited other camps or entertained friends in our mess tent. Dan Mazur and I had time to catch up on the events in our lives since 1991.

Reinmar felt better. Again I watched him put aside the adversities that fate had dealt him. Perhaps it was that ascent that makes me superstitious. How does a man escape his destiny? Now as I look back and analyze events, I am certain that if we had made a proper acclimatization, we could have avoided the tragedy that awaited us. Every setback and difficulty conspired to keep pushing us up the mountain. Each difficulty forged a link in the chain of events that would cost my friends their lives.

That night we sat in the mess tent discussing our tactics. We had news from the Swedes that a window of good weather would begin on the twenty-eighth. Calm conditions were predicted to last for about forty-eight hours, then a major storm would follow. We decided to leave Base Camp on the twenty-fourth for Camp I, move to Camp III by the twenty-sixth, establish Camp IV at 7,900 meters on the twenty-seventh, and go for the summit early on the morning of July 28. We had one or two days of leeway, but if success eluded us during that window of opportunity, there would be no time for a second chance.

When asked for my opinion, I said we did not have adequate acclimatization to 7,300 meters, much less 7,900 meters. I cautioned

Reinmar and Peter that our bodies were ill-prepared for those heights, that an attempt on the summit would be dangerous. As a team, I felt we would run out of power at or near the top, but that it would be difficult to turn around so close to our goal. The descent could be treacherous. But I added that I was ready to go with their decision. They were my leaders. Peter and Reinmar insisted they had never experienced difficulty above eight thousand meters. I pointed out that the last five hundred meters on K2 should not be compared to the difficulty of other mountains. Still, if they were going, I was ready to accept the risk. The discussion ended on that stark note, and we did not come back to the topic. By unanimous consensus, we were going up.

To provide a diversion from the bad weather, Reinmar and Peter sent out invitations to members of all the other expeditions to join us on the twenty-third for the "Baltoro Rock Olympics." Wet, falling snow did not deter one hundred climbers of every nationality from abandoning the comfort of their tents to participate. The entry requirement was a team song and introductions. The main event required marksmen to knock a small rock off a bigger one from one hundred paces. There was no end of ammunition in the endless store of rubble around us. I do not recall which team won; the opportunity to laugh and talk was more important. Socializing went on late into the night. For a day, humor and friendship relieved us of the burden of our ambitions. Reinmar's organizational skills and Peter's unfailing energy and enthusiasm presented us with those gifts.

On July 24, Peter, Ernst, and Reinmar climbed to Camp I: the Canadian-American team had started out this way—slow, with a night at the lower camp. They had hoped an easy day would compensate for the long one that came at the end. Andy left at five in the afternoon, so the climb to Camp II would not be as long and hard for him. For me it would take seven hours to reach II. Traveling light, I left Base Camp on the twenty-fifth at five-thirty in the morning. Two members of the Swedish expedition, Rafael Jensen and Daniel Bidner, followed in my tracks. I arrived at Camp I as my friends were finishing breakfast. There I brewed tea and rested awhile before setting out with Andy. Reinmar was in no hurry to move; it appeared to me that his ribs were bothering him. He did not move with the same ease he had in the days before his fall. What could I have said to him? How could I have helped him? In those situations, each person makes his own decision to go up or to end the risk and go down. I watched Reinmar begin to ascend, just as sure, but slower on the ropes. There was still time for him to change his mind.

I passed Andy and Ernst and arrived at Camp II with Peter only to find the big dome tent broken and torn by the wind in the last storm. Another adversity; they fell on us one after the other until they no longer surprised me. Peter's down suit and sleeping bag had blown out of the tent. Unable to conceal his emotions, he said the climb was over for him. Fate seemed to be giving him the opportunity to abandon the effort. He began to descend. Sitting there alone, I felt relief in my soul. Deep in my heart, I believed that without proper acclimatization our attempt was too risky. I gathered the remaining things from the broken tent and put them aside in a place protected from the wind. Then I climbed into my tent, set up my stove, and began melting snow into water for tea.

Later I heard the voices of my teammates, Peter's voice as well. I understood from their conversation that Ernst had given his down suit and sleeping bag to Peter. Ernst was giving up the summit attempt. This was wise of him, because in our situation, given his age and without better acclimatization, he had little chance of succeeding.

We set up the three-man tent we had stored for Camp IV. Then we lit up the stoves, cooked dinner, and quickly settled in for the night. Later we heard the two Swedish climbers arrive. They elected to follow our plan of assault. Like us, Daniel and Rafael found their tent broken. They radioed Base Camp and asked permission of the British team to use their tent. Roger Payne, the leader of that expedition, kindly agreed.

After breakfast on the twenty-sixth, as Reinmar and I dressed to leave for Camp III, a foul wind began to blow. I thought the force of the blast would sweep away the tents and us as well. I was silently grateful for the snow wall that we had built days before, which afforded the only protection from the gale. The sun was shining through the clouds that flew over us, but no one started out. We contacted Base Camp for a weather report and learned the window of good weather was predicted to move in on the twenty-ninth. We had to wait. The storm was relentless and blew with hurricane force all day and all through the night. The Swedes, like us, endured the gale in their sleeping bags protected by the thin walls of a buffeted tent.

When we awoke on the twenty-seventh, it seemed that the tempest had passed. Reinmar and I broke down my hard-tested North Face tent and packed our backpacks. Loathe to move from their shelter, Peter and Andy watched us and the weather. Like the Swedes, they were not in a hurry to leave that refuge.

As if lying in wait, the wind increased as Reinmar and I started out. Weighing the effort it would take for me to reconstruct the tent against the effort of climbing, I chose the latter. It was possible to balance my body against the direct pressure of the gale; I leaned over into the slope and moved up, secured by my jumar on the fixed line. Everything necessary for the night was in my backpack. Our instructions were that if anyone ascended to Camp III that day, they should wait for the team there. I needed no further permission. Seeking relief from the wind, I stopped in a crack, pressed against the rocks, and looked down. Below me, Reinmar was climbing. Andy moved into the squall, but gave up and rejoined Peter, who prudently observed our efforts from the tent. In that moment huddled against the rocks, I felt the wind begin to abate.

It took four more hours of climbing to arrive at the loads we had dropped for Camp III. I selected a place for the tent in the lee of an ice wall above the site of the old Russian camp. I shoveled away snow, making a hard, flat surface for the tent. Reinmar arrived about two hours later. He informed me that Peter and Andy had decided to wait at Camp II until the next day.

I felt pretty well during the night, but the next morning I was much less energetic. That was normal for the first night at 7,400 meters. After the sun hit the tent, I stirred from my sleeping bag and slowly prepared water for tea. The air was still. Protected from the wind by the ice wall, the sun-warmed atmosphere in the tent reached tropical comfort. The heat and altitude made me feel sluggish, and I had no appetite. I knew that I was better off moving around to stimulate circulation. So after eating some dried fruit and drinking tea, I decided to dig a snow cave to compensate for our lost tent, knowing it would save Peter and Andy some effort when they arrived. Reinmar watched for a while. Despite complaining of pain in his ribs, he ate a hearty breakfast. I advised him against working with the shovel. The weather appeared to be clearing, and wind had decreased. Reinmar went down to the load dropped previously by Peter and brought it up to camp. After five hours of work, a cave big enough for three people was finished. Reinmar decided to settle into the comfortable space with me. We moved our things from the tent, freeing a place for Peter and Andy who finally arrived later that evening.

After breakfast on the twenty-ninth we loaded our packs in clear, calm weather and started out for our assault camp. Last to leave, I packed up the food in the cave and covered the entrance with the dry bag we had found, securing the cave for use on our descent. Above me Peter and Andy moved up really well, and Reinmar was ascending easily. The route was in perfect condition: the hard névé snow was easy for climbing. I felt worn-out from the digging the day before and caught up with the group only after they'd stopped to rest before a steep section. Above the rest spot we could see the terrain flatten out, and we knew that there we would find where previous expeditions had made their assault camps. There were two routes to the flatter ground: up a steep, icy slope or around through the deep snow. We chose the second alternative. I climbed about one hundred meters and passed Andy and Peter. For another hour I took the lead, breaking trail in the deep snow up to the gentler slope. The weather was perfect: the sky was cloudless, the wind mild. Mercifully, the forecast of good weather proved true.

The remains of a tent and some equipment abandoned by the Slovenian expedition littered the site of Camp IV. The summit was clearly visible, and from that perspective the final distance did not look too difficult. In one hour we were in our tents, two men in each. We prepared dinner and climbed into down sleeping bags.

From the security of our tents, the clank of equipment was heard as the Swedes approached camp. Like us, they had minimal acclimatization: Rafael and Daniel had spent only one night at 6,800 meters. In favor of light loads, they carried only a tent, thinking they would sleep without bags and leave for the summit just after midnight. They counted on the warmth of their excellent down suits and state-of-the-art gear to protect them. I wondered if that was enough to compensate for the lack of acclimatization. I surrendered a down sleeping bag to them that I had found abandoned in the tangled equipment remains around camp. The night was bitterly cold.

On July 30 Reinmar and I woke up to five centimeters of hoarfrost on the inside walls of our tent, a lace of ice condensation from our breath in the night. Peter and Andy departed for the summit about 3 A.M. Reinmar and I waited for better visibility. I moved sluggishly and had a poor appetite—the negative effects of altitude. Though Reinmar said he felt okay, I believe he had the same symptoms that I experienced. He managed to eat more breakfast than I could choke down. I was only thirsty and forced myself to eat some muesli. Judging by Andy and Peter's early departure, I thought they felt better than we did.

We packed up, and each of us put forty meters of rope into our backpacks. The Slovenian and American-Canadian groups had reported they had not used fixed line above this camp. It was later in the season, and storms had continuously swept the route. One man had fallen above us, and we wanted to avoid that. We would fix line on the infamous "bottleneck," providing some security for our descent.

At 4 A.M. Reinmar and I left camp. Our crampons found good traction in the névé-covered slope. The cold penetrated my Gore-Tex jacket and down clothes and freshened my step. I was more energetic, though I was aware that my speed was slower than normal. With the dawn light, we could see Peter and Andy ahead of us. After moving for one hour, I noticed the distance to the summit did not appear to change. Distance in the mountains can be deceptive; the perspective from Camp IV was misleading. Ascending, I understood that the summit of K2 was a long way off.

About ten-thirty, I caught up with Peter and Andy at the bottleneck. There the slope became much steeper. Peter asked for the rope and two ice-screws, and I pulled them out of my pack. We decided to traverse to the left. The sunlight caused a stifling heat. At high altitude, nights are as cold as deep space, and the sun has an intensity that parches the skin; its heat robs one of ambition. The air was motionless. We had dressed for the morning cold, and in the blazing sun we became hot and stuffy in our clothes. On any other day that would have been perfect, but at that altitude the heat made us sluggish. Our speed was catastrophically slow. Seven hours of climbing for Reinmar and me, and eight hours for Peter and Andy, had brought us only one-third of the distance to the summit! Reinmar was two hundred meters below, but catching up to us since we had stopped.

Andy and Peter stripped off and stored their down gear. I sat on my backpack secured to the fixed line, musing on our plan while sipping tea. My throat was dry. It felt dehydrated from the effort of breathing. Periodically, I moistened my throat with small amounts of mint tea to relieve my discomfort. Ascending to the assault camp the day before had made my chest hurt, and the pain had become more noticeable. I was certain we should fix the rope on the bottleneck and descend to rest in our tents for the night. I thought we could make another attempt on the summit early the next morning.

Peter, Andy, and I discussed how to cross the insidious bottleneck. Fresh, knee-deep snow was on a steep slope, but when testing the snow, one hit a thin, brittle crust of hard ice that broke away in layers and slid down the mountain. The powder underneath did not compress into reliable steps. I suggested we wait for Reinmar. Rafael and Daniel were following close behind him. I thought it would be safer for us to negotiate the traverse together. Andy was standing secured to a well-fixed ice-screw.

Near me an abandoned ice ax lay among the rocks and ice. I picked it up. After testing the snow conditions on the section ahead of us, I thought I would need it. Ignoring my warnings, Peter moved up and across the slope, trampling down steps in the rotten snow. He fixed one section of line, moving cautiously but without protection. I thought of Phil Powers and recalled his summit-day recollections. Only a little higher on that ridge, Dan Culver had fallen while descending. More than twenty days had passed since they were in our position; the snow conditions and temperature were now different. Gazing at the section ahead of Peter, I thought that area looked quite treacherous, and I knew that we needed to fix it with rope. Late in the day the sun-melted snow would turn to solid ice. I looked at the sheer rock walls of the south face; it would be impossible to stop if you started to fall in that place.

Reinmar joined me and wanted to know what our plan was. I asked for his forty meters of rope. Leaving my backpack with my down jacket, my thermos, and my extra gloves attached securely to the end of the fixed rope below the bottleneck, I went up along the line, caught up to Peter, and went ahead to secure the next section. As I suspected, under the unconsolidated snow was hard ice. My crampons scratched it. I adjusted to that condition by relying more on my ice axes. My fortuitous acquisition of the second ax now provided a measure of safety as I ascended: kicking my crampons into the ice with all my strength, driving in the two ice tools, one after the other, and moving up a step. Every ten meters I stopped to rest, breathing hard. Belayed by Peter, slowly but surely I moved up and to the left, fastening the rope along the slope with ice-screws. Finishing the job left us so short of breath we were unable to speak. We looked at one another and asked only with our eyes, "What next?" The air passed whistling and wheezing through our dry throats. My watch said 2 P.M. Reinmar and Andy were sitting on their packs at the bottom of the fixed line talking to Rafael, who in the interim of our work had caught up with us. Peter called down to tell them the route was secured.

As we rested, trying to catch our breath, I asked, "What are we going to do about the time?"

Peter replied that a little higher up the slope would flatten out and from there the summit was close. I could see he was tired but feeling well. The nearness of our goal was energizing him. I was worn-out by the effort of fixing the rope. I told him that I had left my backpack with my warm clothes at the beginning of the fixed line, and that I was tired. "It will be better to go down to the tents and try again tomorrow," I said. "We can start earlier than we did today, and using our work on the lines, we will move faster. The summit will not take so long."

Peter would have none of it. "Anatoli, the weather may be stormy tomorrow; today is our last chance. We must endure a little."

True, the weather was finally in our favor, but our pace frightened me. Never on any previous ascent had I felt so weak. But I knew Peter might be right. The next day I might not feel stronger, and the weather was supposed to get worse. Some intuition told me we should not go up. I sensed danger waiting for us at the top of the mountain. It was not exactly fear, but some kind of alertness possessed me. I felt as if we were crossing the border of what is allowed and what was forbidden—as though we were going into foreign territory. Peter and I did not argue. We spoke quietly. That venerable fifty-year-old man with his beautiful black mustache went on ahead to continue up, and I was left on the snow slope leaning over my ice ax, struggling to keep my equilibrium.

I felt empty inside, probably because I was so tired. At that altitude inner emotions and moods change at a different speed: both movement and thinking slow down. I watched as Reinmar and Andy ascended the fixed line, moving in slow motion like characters in a film. I could feel the emptiness in me slowly being replaced by a feeling like anger. It was not anger at Peter, but at this whole situation, and at myself. At that moment, I was without self-esteem or pride. My brain was asking, "Why is it so important to go to the summit, what is the meaningfulness of our effort?" Perhaps some inner instinct of self-preservation was working, prevailing over my ambition. I cannot tell even now what changed in me as I watched Peter moving off. I can only recall that this jumble of emotions generated new energy in me . . . some force that challenged me to move.

Perhaps this energy had been passed to me from Peter, because he was a man who could inspire people in that way. First I followed after him like a robot. Then I experienced the same feeling one has during a marathon, when older people pass you by. That does not make you angry, you do not wish to get even with them in a bad way. It makes you turn inside to see what is wrong with yourself. The example that Peter set was like a push, and some internal engine that had been out of order in me started to work, producing energy.

When I caught up with him, he let me go in front without saying a word. He had probably known that his example would influence me in such a way. This man had a shining virtue and a boundless energy that were infectious. He put himself to a task honorably and inspired others by his standards. His social grace allowed him to tackle problems easily, and he knew how to influence people and lead them. If the situation was difficult for him, he never showed it. Such inner strength in a human being always generates respect.

After the fixed line, we crossed another hundred meters of steep ice and snow; then finally the slope became flatter and it was easier to move. The crust of snow was hard. Occasionally a slab would slide out from under my step, skittering toward the abyss that was the drop over the South Wall of K2. That was a warning to us not to relax too soon.

We moved that way, with Peter ten meters behind me, for two more hours. Then again, totally worn-out, I sat down in the snow. Peter approached me, took out his thermos, and poured a drink of hot tea. Without a single word he offered the cup to me. The hot drink passed down my dry throat, and the energy of that gesture slowly penetrated my tired muscles. The summit appeared to be no more than fifteen minutes away. I gathered all my energy and all my soul into one bundle and moved toward the peak. It was terribly difficult. In the late-afternoon shadow an invigorating coolness settled on the southeast slope. I was unable to think. I felt only a primitive awareness to go forward.

During my years of training as a ski racer, and then as a mountaineer, I had learned how to wring out the last of my energy for a finish. But this is dangerous in mountaineering, because the summit is not the finish of your competition with a great mountain. To survive you must be able to get down from the forbidden zone. There is no pausing in this place, no possibility to recover. If you have spent all reserves of power, and you are required by circumstance to fight for your life, you reach into a dry well. That moment, on K2, I was in just such a condition. I could think of nothing. The summit before me became the finish line. That was bad.

Perhaps Peter, Andy, and Reinmar, and those two Swedish mountaineers, felt exactly the same way. Maybe they were not thinking beyond the finish line—about the descent. I do not know. Instead of fifteen minutes, I climbed for exactly one hour more before I reached the summit. When I crossed that imaginary line, I did not feel joy or satisfaction at my achievement. I did not care that I was standing on the summit of the second-highest mountain on earth. The only pleasant thought that came to me was that the tortured effort of placing my feet one higher than the other was over.

I could see the whole length of the glacier running from K2 to Concordia. Across the glacier, opposite me, the top of massive Broad Peak was lit by the last rays of the sun. There was no strength to admire the colors of the sunset as I half-sat, half-lay on the snowy slope in a dreamlike state. I felt like a squeezed lemon. As soon as the sun slipped beyond the ridge, the stifling warm air was replaced by a cold that instantly penetrated my gloves and boots. Like a robot I removed my camera from the chest pocket of my bib and took photos of the surrounding mountains. I was unaware of the time passing, but Peter came up sometime before 6 P.M. Andy arrived right behind him. Everyone was tired and slow. I cannot remember what we talked about while taking photos of one another on the summit. I put my camera away and became aware of the cold in my hands and feet. My old Koflach boots were the ones the Soviet team had been issued for Kanchenjunga. Looking down, thinking of the long descent ahead, I wished I were wearing the One Sport boots that had protected me on the last two expeditions. Those I had sold to pay bills.

Peter and I left the summit simultaneously. Andy waited for Rafael, who was climbing the presummit ridge. I could not see Reinmar. About two hundred meters lower, we met him moving slowly and steadily; he was two hours climbing distance from the summit. I stopped ten meters away on easy ground and asked how he was feeling. I looked at my watch. It was six-thirty, with only ten to fifteen minutes more light in the day. Reinmar did not answer my question. When Peter came up, they discussed the situation in German. I thought that Reinmar would turn back, knowing that in the dying light, it would be safer for him to negotiate the dangerous section above the bottleneck with us. Though I wanted him to descend, at that moment it would not have been right for me to intrude; only he could make the decision. Even Peter did not have the right or authority to order his friend to turn around. Now I think it most likely that he could not consider the dire possibilities hidden in his choice. He was determined to go to the summit. K2 was the goal of all his years of climbing in the Karakoram. Daniel was behind him, two hundred meters lower. Slower than Reinmar, he would need more time to reach the summit. Peter removed Ernst's down jacket and a headlamp from his pack and gave them to Reinmar, who continued up the slope, while Peter and I went down.

I still wonder if I could have helped in that situation. My clothing for the cold was in a backpack at the end of the fixed line. As darkness was falling, I knew I had about one hour before my hands and feet would begin freezing. Descent for me would then become impossible. If I did not move and get to my clothing, I would shortly be in a fatal situation. How could I have changed the chain of events? I do not know the answer even now. I continued my descent, using the two ice tools. As on the climb to the summit, when there was only one thought in my mind, I could not contemplate the possibilities hidden in our situation. I had to focus on my every move to descend without losing my balance or misjudging the conditions of the snow under my boots. If I fell, I would not be able to stop myself. The darkness obscured our trail and made judging the relief difficult. I turned to face the slope and descended down randomly.

At one point, intuition alone inspired me to move fifty meters to the right. There I felt a ridge of hard ice and snow. I drove my ice axes into the slope and stepped down, kicking into the snow and ice with my crampons. At times, snow fell on me from Peter's steps above. In places of poor traction, big chunks of the névé snow slipped from under my feet, falling into the black emptiness. I arrived at the beginning of our fixed line, clipped a carabiner onto the security of the rope, and descended. I was working on autopilot; there were no thoughts. It had been fifteen hours since I'd left our camp. It would be more than an hour in total darkness before I could hope to reach the tents. I was at the end of my strength and on the brink of failure.

Ten meters before the end of the fixed rope, a crampon came off my boot. I lost balance and fell to the anchor point at the end of the rope, crashing into my backpack. Removing my gloves to replace the crampon, my fingers froze numb while I struggled with the metal. Unsuccessfully I tried to warm them against my body, then continued down the route below the bottleneck in the dark, moonless night. I had no sensation in my toes or my fingers. The cold penetrated my body, and my heart did not have the energy to pump my thickened blood into my feet and hands. Almost every ten meters the crampon came off my boot.

In one such moment I fell again and slid slowly down the slope. Automatically I turned onto my stomach and with my entire strength drove the ice tools into the snow. By some miracle I stopped. That extra ice ax, a gift from some unknown climber, had been like an invisible hand of help, assisting me all day. After that fall, I lost my orientation to the route. I was unhurt but more alert. There was no visibility. I had no headlamp. I fastened my crampon on my boot once more and moved randomly down. When the slope started to flatten, I chose a direction. Luckily it proved to be right. I fell again

Anatoli skate-skiing on the expansive south Ilynichk Glacier near the
International Mountaineering Camp Khan-Tengri in Kirgizstan during the
summer of 1987. *(Collection of Anatoli Boukreev, photo by Vladimir Yakushkin)*

Members of the 1989 Soviet Union International Expedition sorting supplies and equipment near Taplejung, Nepal, before beginning the trek to Kanchenjunga Base Camp. *(Collection of Anatoli Boukreev)*

In the autumn of 1989, a route up Mount Elbrus in the Caucasus Mountains was the site of the first international high-altitude speed competitions in the Soviet Union. Anatoli's victory in that competition resulted in an invitation to the United States. *(Collection of Anatoli Boukreev)*

FACING PAGE, BOTTOM: A team of the Soviet Union's strongest climbers accomplished a history-making traverse of the four 8,400-meter-plus summits of the Kanchenjunga Massif. Coaches and members in Kathmandu, Nepal, in May 1989. Climbers, back row *(left to right)*: Evgeny Klinetzy, Vladimir Balyberdin, Anatoli Boukreev, Vasili Elagin, Vasili Senatorov, Grigori Luniakov, Vladimir Karataev, Leonid Troschinenko, Mikhail Turkevich, Alexander Gloushkovski, Mikhail Mojaev, Sergei Bogomolov, Victor Pastukh, Sergei Bershov, Vladimir Suviga, Vladimir Koroteev, Serge Arsentiev, Alexander Pogorelov; climbers in the middle, *(left to right)*: Valeri Khrichtchatyi, Zinur Halitov, Victor Dediy, Rinat Khaibullin; climbers, bottom row *(left to right)*: Alexander Sheinov, assistant leader Nikolai Tchorny, Kazbec Valiev, expedition leader Edward Myslovski, coach Valentine Ivanov, coach Sergei Efimov, Evgeny Vinogradski, Vladimir Voskoboinkov. *(Collection of Anatoli Boukreev)*

Ledge camp on the Cassin Ridge, Mount McKinley, Alaska. Respected American mountaineer Michael Covington was Anatoli's mentor during an ascent of this difficult route in April and May of 1990. *(Collection of Anatoli Boukreev)*

Anatoli worked as Covington's assistant, then returned to the mountain for a record-setting ten-and-one-half-hour speed ascent to the summit via Mount McKinley's West Rib. *(Collection of Anatoli Boukreev)*

In the spring of 1991, Kazakh Army Sports Club team members pioneered a new route to the summit of Dhaulagiri. Anatoli photographed his climbing partners, Rinat Khaibullin and Andre Seleshev, securing a crucial portion of the route up the sheer rock face of the West Wall. *(Collection of Anatoli Boukreev)*

In the autumn of 1991, Anatoli and his longtime friend and climbing partner Kevin Cooney were members of Vladimir Balyberdin's Russian-American Expedition to Mount Everest. *(Photo courtesy of Kevin Cooney)*

FACING PAGE, TOP: Anatoli crossing a crevasse in the Khumbu Ice Fall en route to Camp I. *(Photo courtesy of Kevin Cooney)*

FACING PAGE, BOTTOM: On October 17, 1991, ascending alone below the Hillary Step, Anatoli makes his way toward his first successful summit of the world's highest peak. *(Photo courtesy of Kevin Cooney)*

RIGHT: Sherpa children posing with Anatoli on the trekking route to Mount Everest, Khumbu Region, Nepal. Fall 1991. *(Collection of Anatoli Boukreev)*

In the spring of 1993, Anatoli was pleased to act as a personal guide for his friend, seventy-year-old Jack Robbins, during an ascent of Alaska's Mount McKinley. Robbins is seen here approaching his goal. Kazakh Army Sports Club climber Rinat Khaibullin is waiting on the summit. "Anatoli knew everything there was to know about mountains, and he knew that you could never know enough."—JACK ROBBINS *(Collection of Anatoli Boukreev)*

German climber Reinmar Joswig invited Anatoli to join his 1993 German Expedition to K2. Located in the Karakoram Range on the border between China and Pakistan, K2 is considered by many mountaineers to be the most difficult of the world's 8,000-meter peaks. *(Collection of Anatoli Boukreev)*

In Askole, Pakistan, porters are supplied with their meat rations before leaving for K2 Base Camp. June 1993. *(Collection of Anatoli Boukreev)*

During an arduous seven-day trek, expedition supplies are transported through the dramatic spires and towers that line the Baltoro. Summer 1993. *(Collection of Anatoli Boukreev)*

ABOVE: 1993 German K2 Expedition members. *Left to right:* Reinmar Joswig, Ernst Eberhardt, Peter Metzger, and Andy Locke seen here resting below Camp I. *(Collection of Anatoli Boukreev)*

RIGHT: A British medical officer examines Reinmar Joswig's broken ribs. *(Collection of Anatoli Boukreev)*

Exhaustion marking their faces, Anatoli and Peter Metzger stand on the hard-won summit of K2. *(Collection of Anatoli Boukreev)*

On their K2 summit assault, Anatoli's teammates ascended between ice walls lining a portion of the Abruzzi route between Camp III and Camp IV. *(Collection of Anatoli Boukreev)*

After the expedition, Anatoli returned to his home in Almaty, Kazakhstan, overland through the Hunza region of Pakistan. After crossing high mountain passes into the far western edge of the Sinkiang region of China, he encountered herds of rare wild ass and yak grazing on the high plains. *(Collection of Anatoli Boukreev)*

After pioneering the route to the crest of Makalu for Condor Adventures team members, on April 29, Anatoli and climbing partner Bernardo Guarachi posed for this portrait at an approximate elevation of 8,460 meters, near the base of Makalu's first summit tower. *(Collection of Anatoli Boukreev)*

FACING PAGE: In the spring of 1994, Condor Adventures owner Thor Kieser invited Anatoli to join a commercial expedition headed for the Himalaya. Behind Anatoli, Makalu rises in a halo of clouds. *(Collection of Anatoli Boukreev)*

RIGHT: Anatoli descending at 8,400 meters, where storm clouds obscure visibility on Makalu's elusive summit. April 29, 1994. *(Collection of Anatoli Boukreev)*

In the spring of 1995, Anatoli was in Tibet, pleased to be employed on the north side of Mount Everest by Himalayan Guides, Henry Todd's international expedition company. The memorial marker for George Mallory overlooks the tents of Base Camp on the Rongbuk Glacier; Everest rises in the background. *(Collection of Anatoli Boukreev)*

Anatoli joined Kazakh mountaineers in their return to Himalayan climbing for a winter ascent of Manaslu in November 1995. This photo taken from advanced Base Camp shows team members in the background ascending along the route to Camp I. *(Collection of Anatoli Boukreev)*

FACING PAGE, TOP: Manaslu sunset and the tents of Camp II. Winter ascent, 1995. *(Collection of Anatoli Boukreev)*

FACING PAGE, BOTTOM: Avalanche run-out on the glacier at the base of Manaslu. Winter 1995. *(Collection of Anatoli Boukreev)*

Anatoli at 6,500 meters on Manaslu. The difficult winter ascent culminated a
year of climbing, which he felt put him in the best athletic form of his life.
(Collection of Anatoli Boukreev)

and again, clumsy with fatigue, but the slope near the tents was less steep, and it was not difficult to arrest my falls. At last I made out the dark silhouettes of the tents. When I could finally see them, they were fifteen meters away.

I staggered to the tent with one crampon on my boot. With effort, I liberated myself from my equipment. After falling into the tent, I found my headlamp and turned it on, so the tent would be a reference point for those who were coming down the mountain. It was 8:30 P.M. when I lit my stove and put the pot of compressed snow on the burner to melt. That was all I could manage to do. I could feel nothing inside my plastic boots, but I had no strength to do anything to warm my feet. The heat of the stove raised the temperature in the tent. I dozed off cradling the pot in my hands while attempting to thaw out my frozen fingers. Hot water spilled on me; it burned my hand and startled me to my senses. I checked my watch; I had slept forty minutes.

Only after I had warmed up by drinking the hot water did my mind go beyond the primitive needs of my survival. Then I focused on the critical situation forming on the mountain. Obviously, something had happened to Peter; he should have arrived. Like me, he was not well equipped for cold or darkness. Three hours had passed since I'd last seen him two hundred meters above the beginning of the fixed line. I thought, even with the down jacket, Reinmar did not have enough warm clothing. Andy was better off with his down suit. The Swedish mountaineers were dressed really well and could survive the night out. But with what kind of aftermath? My thoughts were interrupted by steps outside the tent. It was Andy.

He had seen nothing of Peter during his descent. If Peter had made it to the fixed rope, he should have been in camp by now. If Andy had not see him, he might have fallen, as I had, on the relief below the fixed line. It would be impossible to find a person on that slope in the moonless night. I understood that brutal fact clearly. Outside events were unfolding chaotically. My mind told me to go out, to look for Peter, to help someone, but I had no strength at all. What could I have done in those hours but add one more name to the list of victims? Andy and I did not discuss going back up the mountain. Exhausted, we had no options. I did not sleep, but spent the night semiconscious, aware only of the cold.

At 4 A.M. I looked out of the tent. The relief of the slope was still unclear. I saw a slow-moving red dot. Who was it? Dressed in red, it could only be one of the Swedish climbers. When Rafael came up to the tent, tears were streaming down his cheeks. Tears of grief . . . his friend had been lost. Daniel had developed altitude sickness, cerebral edema; he had become disoriented and fallen while descending. Rafael had no news of Peter or Reinmar. He believed they had descended ahead of him to the safety of the tents.

I did not cry. Slowly I reckoned with what had happened. I did not want to accept Peter's and Reinmar's deaths. I wanted to change something in the situation, to find some peg on which to construct a scenario for their survival. I could find nothing that gave me hope. Finally it was clear to me that they were dead. For two hours I sat staring at the tracks we had made in the snow on the way to the summit the day before. The mountain was lit harshly by the sun, and in the shade it was cold blue. K2 looked like a monster. I suggested to Andy that we should go up. He shrugged his shoulders as if he could not understand. In reality, I had no strength to go up. Around 11 A.M. Andy and Rafael started down the mountain. I spent three more hours in camp, just sitting, looking at the mountain, as if hypnotized.

I left camp at 2 P.M. and caught up with Rafael and Andy. They were talking to the British mountaineer Victor Saunders. He offered to help Rafael down to the snow cave below Camp III where the other members of Rafael's expedition were waiting. Andy and I stayed in the cave I had built, and on August 1 we descended to Base Camp. That day the wind came up again and destroyed all the tents at Camp II.

Writing this now, there is no joy in my achievement. I only look at life and value it a little differently. It is easy to lose in the mountains if you step over the border of what is possible. Where are those borders? For four months since my return, I have searched my soul for answers. Why were Rafael, Andy, and I allowed to come down alive, after crossing into that no-man's-land, the forbidden zone? Why was the door of return closed to Daniel, Peter, and Reinmar? I feel my participation in these events acutely. What more could I have done that day to help my friends? Is it wrong that I lived, that I did not die with them?

5

MAKALU, SPRING 1994

The bus trip home to *Almaty from Pakistan telescoped Anatoli through a thousand years of time and lifestyles. Intriguing aspects of the modestly durable cultures in Hunza and Sinkiang provided some distraction from his somber ruminations.*

News of his success on the second-highest mountain in the world was received indifferently by officials in the Kazakh Ministry of Sports. Reconciling his exponentially expanding worldview with the narrow mind-set of people at home became increasingly difficult. In September of 1993, frustrated by the lack of opportunity in Almaty, he scraped together the means to return to America.

While resting in the haven of Jack Robbins's Berkeley home, he wrote a ninety-page history of the K2 expedition. Though it did little to assuage his sadness over the deaths of Reinmar Joswig and Peter Metzger, writing allowed Anatoli to reflect on the order of events and to examine the choices that had led to the tragedy. Later that fall he moved on to Boulder, Colorado, to visit friends and to take advantage of an opportunity to earn money. The champion ski-coach-cum-mountaineering-master accepted the work that was offered. Wry humor concealed the humiliation that Anatoli, a proud man, felt using his tal-

ents for mixing cement. He was not the only Soviet climber who found refuge in the West.

After marrying American adventurist Fran Destifano, Serge Arsentiev, Anatoli's Kanchenjunga climbing partner, settled in the mountains of Colorado. Besides having been a member of the prestigious Combined Team, Serge has been the first Soviet to summit Everest without the use of supplemental oxygen. Anatoli credited him as being one of the strongest climbers their old school had produced. Before the Soviet Union had deconstructed, the Leningrad native had worked as a high-level satellite communications engineer.

In the summer of 1993, Anatoli reconnected with Serge and his new wife, Fran, who were visiting in Almaty. Serge told Anatoli he was making his own adjustments to life in America as a carpenter in Telluride, Colorado. Hearing that Buka wanted a place to stay for the winter, Fran Arsentiev had offered to rent him a room in her home. Anatoli remembered that the appealing alpine location was reminiscent of the taiga around Mountain Gardener. During his stay he found that many of the small-town citizens were accomplished counterculture athletes.

Fran had plans to put Anatoli to work as a summer guide for her new business, Trek around the World. Combining her organizational skill with that of top-level Soviet athletes, she aimed to provide the first adventure-travel packages to the mountains in the former Soviet republics. She remembered, "Anatoli was an intensely private man, with a religious dedication to training."

He credited their relationship and that time in her home with teaching him the ropes of survival in America. Anatoli's English was still rudimentary and his business acumen naively "collective." The cost of living in America required some mental gymnastics for a parsimonious athlete. One month's rent in Telluride ($500) would have paid his apartment expenses in Almaty for one year. Russian-style, his blunt frustrations were candidly expressed to only a few friends. Serge's mild-mannered equanimity helped Anatoli round some sharp corners during that season of adjustment. The neighbors who dropped in at Fran's often found the two mountaineering giants making bread with all the attention normally reserved for a science experiment. (Anatoli openly wondered why the richest country in the world produced the "weak" bread for sale in our markets.) He earned the money to pay his bills clearing snow off *the steeply pitched roofs in Telluride. His $5-an-hour wages did not go much further than that. Shoveling, he remembered, did not become a favorite form of exercise, but there were enough days off for skiing on the high backcountry trails to keep him fit and acclimated to three thousand meters.*

Tolya became a well-liked, familiar figure in town. A reporter from the local newspaper printed an interview with him that detailed his K2 experience. The account caught the attention of the owner of a Colorado company, Condor Adventures. International mountain guide and entrepreneur Thor Kieser made Anatoli an offer that provided him with a natural next step in his career.

Yet another Himalayan expedition is behind me. The name of the first citizen from the Kazakhstan Republic to climb the fifth-highest mountain in the world is written in Elizabeth Hawley's record books. Few Soviet mountaineers find ways to climb an 8,000-meter peak these days. Our nation has fractured into independent countries that can boast only of having the lowest workers' wages in the world. Three years of rampant inflation makes money worthless. Over the same period, permit fees and expedition costs for climbing the highest peaks in the Himalayas have increased so much that even my foreign friends complain that they are prohibitive.

Twice during my last expedition I was on top of Makalu. Standing there, I felt that I represented all Soviet mountaineers of my generation, men parted from their dreams forever by the financial chaos that plagues our lives. These great climbers can not afford to think of mountaineering. Literally, they struggle to earn the money to pay for bread to eat. I refuse to forget the honor bestowed on me by the Soviet Union or that my ability was perfected in the most outstanding school of mountaineering in the world. When we destroyed the old system of government, we said good-bye to traditions that had taken years for us to build. In sports, the arts and sciences, knowledge was passed from generation to generation. I was one of those who benefited from our national commitment to perfecting human excellence.

These days when I return to Almaty from my expeditions, I see that the achievements of our Sports Club are not valued or appreciated the way they were in the past. Our best climbers spend every moment resolving petty everyday problems that have nothing to do with their hard-won expertise. The insulting predicament devalues the enormous work done by my generation pioneering new routes in the Himalayas. It slanders the courage and commitment of those who taught us, whose experience paved our way to those great peaks. The growing social indifference renders meaningless the lives of men and women who paid the ultimate price and remain forever in the mountains.

My accomplishments are connected directly to the efforts of all those who helped create the high standards of Russian alpinism. Step by step with courage, discipline, and commitment they redefined the limits of human potential. With my life I endeavor not to discredit those standards, only to improve them. Painfully, I wonder, "Who will follow in my footsteps?" Having neither personal prosperity nor stable social conditions, my peers throughout the former republics have abandoned sport climbing. Young people are denied the support that we were given, for without mentors there is no proper framework for experiential growth.

An impressive tradition of high-altitude alpinism developed in the Central Asia Army Sports Club under the supervision of our honored trainer and coach, Irvand Tikhonovich Illinski. He contributed a lot to our development; he gave a lot to me especially. Despite the changes, Illinski and a few of our club members attempt to preserve the philosophy of our school, sharing their time and skills teaching young climbers. Now we must find the way to climb with money; the time when commitment, readiness, and ambition were enough is over. Now to climb in the Himalayas or Karakoram I pay my own way.

After this expedition I found myself in an especially critical financial situation. It has taken ten days of living in the cheapest hotel room in Kathmandu, every day selling more pieces of my personal equipment, to raise the money for my ticket home to Almaty. I count it as a blessing that I came back from Makalu with my weight above normal, thanks only to the huge supply of food provided by the American company that had the expedition permit. Compared to what is available on the shelves at home, at our remote Base Camp I feasted on first-class meals. We even had beer. My American friends thought the selection was meager. During the expedition they each lost a couple of kilograms; one person lost five kilograms. When I look in the mirror, only my face seems thinner. That I attribute to mental strain and the effects of prolonged time at high altitude.

Actually, I enjoyed the way my employer, Thor Kieser, organized this expedition. Though Makalu is formidable and our route was tricky, no incidents marred our experience. Thor's company, Condor Adventures, specializes in guided excursions in the mountains of South America. Now he has dreams of expanding his business to the Himalayas. In the past, only well-prepared, cohesive teams had tried to climb Makalu. This was the first commercial expedition. We had an international team: ten Americans, an Englishman, a Bolivian native, and myself, Russian by birth, Kazakh by fate. Lately my allegiance to a homeland goes to the mountains: the Rockies, Tien Shan, Pamirs, Karakoram, or the Himalayas.

Thor screened his clients well; most of the group members were familiar to him from a previous expedition to Gasherbrum II. Several men were guides or had experience on harder 8,000-meter peaks. No one required a personal guide, but team members needed strong leadership to support their ambitions. In America the school of mountaineering has evolved in a different direction from ours. It has produced many expert rock climbers with advanced technical skills. In the United States, only a few alpinists have gained my level of experience climbing high without using supplemental oxygen. The 481 meters that Makalu rises above the 8,000-meter mark has a critical impact on athletic ability. Without previous experience it is impossible for a human to work well in those conditions. Americans respect and know how to value professionalism. Thor invited me to join the expedition because he wanted the benefits of my strength and expertise. My presence gave the other team members a psychological advantage.

The basic price per person was $9,600. For clients who had previously worked as mountain guides or climbed hard peaks, that price was discounted several thousand dollars. In exchange for my share of the cost, I agreed to be responsible for all the technical work on the route. That deal did not cover any of my travel expenses or equipment. Even that sum of money was problematic for me in my current situation. Officially, Thor introduced me to the team as his assistant. In reality, I assumed an enjoyable role, that of climbing leader and expert consultant for everyone. Climbing first, I selected our route and secured rope along the more dangerous sections. I picked the location of camps and set them up. It was interesting work, even for me.

The physical burden of my job increased when all but one of our participants developed mild mountain sickness at the elevation of Camp I (6,500 meters). Only Bernardo Guarachi, a native of the Andes, adapted to increases in altitude without problems. The weight of equipment and supplies we hauled up the mountain represented a considerable amount of work for only two men. Though Bernardo is the first native of the South American Andes to climb an 8,000-meter peak, at that time his experience was limited to the lowest and easiest of the giants. His lack of technical mountaineering skills meant that he could only belay me in the critical places. To provide adequate protection up the sixty-degree slopes of the six-hundred-meter-long ice couloir below Makalu La, by myself I fixed twenty successive sections of climbing rope. The continuous stress of working in front exhausted me psychologically. Unfortunately, my partner did not speak English, and I do not speak Spanish, so some days passed and not a word was spoken between us.

We supplied the second camp at the elevation of 7,400 meters on Makalu La. A short climb higher, about one kilometer below the summit, Bernardo and I encountered the remains of a climber. His frozen body rested casually on the snow slope. Tattered, faded clothing fluttered in the breeze. Wind and time had eroded his features. Like a climbing partner from the past, death's face was there to remind us of the dangers and difficulties overcome by the pioneers who had broken the 8000-meter barrier before us. This man had a powerful psychological effect on my American friends.

Our last camp was set at 7,800 meters. On April 29, Bernardo and I were free to pave a way up the final meters to the top. Above a dangerous icefall, we came to the peak's final bastion. Above 8,400 meters the relief was obscured by a milky fog. The steepness of the last ice and talus slope required that we use rope and place pitons for security. Then we explored the top along a corridor between abrupt crags. The first native of South America and the first Russian climbed what we judged to be the highest tower on the summit of Makalu. By that effort we joined ninety-two climbers who had claimed that honor before us. Our route repeated the line first completed by the French in 1955. It is far harder than the normal route to the top of Everest, which four hundred men and women have negotiated. We descended to Base Camp full of satisfaction and proud of our good news. Bernardo headed back to Kathmandu.

Ten days passed before the remaining members of our team were able to put themselves within striking distance of the top. On May 9 four climbers set out from Camp III. At an elevation of 8,200 meters the Englishman, Alan McPherson, turned back. Thor and my good friend Neal Beidleman ascended the last section of fixed ropes, but they gave up 120 vertical meters shy of their goal. With his effort reinforced by a canister of Poisk oxygen, good-natured Steve Bain stole up to the base of the summit's icy tower, though wisely he did not risk surmounting the last meters on the steep crag alone. After a team discussion that compared Bernardo's and my description with the top relief on a clearer day, I learned that Makalu's summit has two towers. The highest one rose up another fifteen meters and was located approximately fifty meters past the one that I had climbed on April 29.

After these efforts, Thor decided to end the expedition. The allotted time on our permit was about to expire, provisions were running low, the beer was gone. Most important, no one had the strength to try again. The tent at Camp III was abandoned. The equipment from Camps I and II was packed and brought down by the retreating climbers. Back in Base Camp, Neal reported that the moment they turned back was the happiest one in his life, so great was his relief that his body would be spared further torment in the inhuman atmosphere. After a few days of rest, like any athlete he regretted his lack of success. Neal had long dreamed of summiting an 8,000-meter peak.

I could sympathize with my friend's depression, because I knew that my fortunes would not likely offer me the opportunity to climb to Makalu again. I suggested that we should make one more effort together, employing a different strategy. While working with Bernardo, I couldn't consider a sports ascent. My first responsibility was to make my presence on the expedition worthwhile for our team. Ten days of inactivity while the others climbed had allowed me to recover some strength. Rested, I had a fresh perspective. Neal listened skeptically to a plan I had formulated that put the summit less than twenty-four hours away. The top was six to ten hours of climbing above Camp III, and I pointed out that we had abandoned a tent there to use as needed for rest or shelter. I was aware that there were drawbacks. What I proposed to him was a climbing supermission. Under optimum circumstances we would have approached the project very differently.

Time above 7,800 meters on the previous summit bid had provided Neal's body with an adequate period for altitude adjustment. Resting for three days at our 5,300-meter-high Base Camp would not let him completely recover from his effort, but I had faith in his reservoir of strength. Of all the athletes I have met in my sporting career, Neal has the best endurance conditioning. Many marathons and hundred-mile races are behind him. I was sure that his failure on the previous assault was due mainly to his lack of experience at high altitude. The endurance required to run marathons is different from the kind you need to climb high mountains. If he agreed to try again, I knew that I could help him climb at a proper pace. After my rest, though not back in peak form, I sensed that I could make an effort that would be only one or two hours off my best time.

Lobbying for one more try, I expressed a personal commitment to Neal's success. It seemed psychologically vital for him; he had turned back on K2 in 1992, and I did not want a second defeat to leave him permanently discouraged about his ability as a high-altitude climber. Also in about a month, many of our mutual friends were gathering to celebrate his marriage. I wanted him to have the success of climbing Makalu to share on that important occasion. My ambition to succeed was fired by the knowledge that the great Mexican climber Carlos Carsolio was attempting to make another mark in mountaineering history with a speed ascent up Lhotse that season.

My arguments did not fully convince Neal. For him, the most acceptable course was to ascend the peak at a normal rate with no attention to records. He acquiesced only because our situation did not allow us the luxury of any other style of climbing. My plan got a cold reception from the rest of the team. They thought I was kidding or crazy and that my idea of negotiating the technical slope below Camp II in the dark was unrealistic.

As Neal and I were preparing to go up, everyone else finished packing so they could leave Base Camp on the fourteenth. After six weeks of penetrating cold and bitter winds, the comforts of civilization exerted a magnetic appeal. At 6:30 P.M. on May 13, Neal and I said our good-byes and headed up the mountain. Members of our send-off party predicted we would not reach the level of Makalu La.

During six weeks of climbing Neal's body had become accustomed to performing in a certain way. For the first ten hours of our ascent he had trouble reorganizing his rhythm to a style that did not allow rest breaks. Above 6,500 meters, if I had taken the lead, his slow pace would have created too much distance between us, so I fell in behind and continuously urged him on. Leading a sustained climb was not new to me. If I had gone too far ahead, I knew Neal's pace would have dropped even more. Given all the energy he had spent on his previous effort, it would have been easy for him to feel sorry for himself on this cold night. I did not want Neal to give up. We were lucky there was no wind to make the bitter cold worse. For eleven hours the thin light from our headlamps pierced the darkness, illuminating steep slopes of ice. At five-thirty A.M., we arrived at Makalu La. The close proximity of the tent at Camp III, the idea of rest and the warmth of a stove, restored Neal's drive. Above 7,400 meters, the route was simpler; I went out ahead, leaving Neal to climb at his own pace. I promised to prepare hot drinks that would provide vital heat and energy for our bodies.

Dawn was fantastic. The performance began in the gray dawn light; I could just make out the giant silhouettes of Lhotse and Everest in the west. Makalu's slope and the beauties of Tibet spread out below. While all else rested in shadow, the distant sun painted the celestial summits of Kanchenjunga an intense orange hue. Not even in Roerich's paintings, which sing of Himalayan beauty, have I seen that color. My delight was cut short by the specter of my former colleague. I wondered if his spirit floated somewhere nearby above the peak. That world of timeless beauty is only home to gods and souls of the dead. Neal and I entered the prohibited zone that is dangerous to all living things.

Reckoning our progress was encouraging. Instead of the ten hours I had projected, it had taken eleven hours to climb to Makalu La, but the ascent to Camp III took only one and one-half hours. That was one hour better than I had projected. At a normal pace, the summit was six hours away. My feelings of strength and confidence ended abruptly when I found our tent at Camp III broken, turned over, and torn by the wind. Obviously little attention had been wasted securing it properly, which neglect now complicated our situation. Soberly assessing our predicament, I knew the shelter was vital to our safe descent. Having spent so much energy and motivation getting to the summit, we would be in a critical state of fatigue coming down. It would be all too easy for us to join our unfortunate friend resting on the slope below. A vital part of reaching the top of a mountain is looking back at it alive from Base Camp. Your effort earns you the opportunity to understand your life more clearly and rejoice in it. Looking at the broken tent, I admitted that the opportunity to set a world's record was only important to me. For Neal, just reaching the summit would constitute a victory. When he arrived about an hour later, I was digging out a new platform that would protect the broken tent from the force of the wind. Two more hours of vital strength and attention went into repairing and securing our shelter. Though we tried to resume our climb, fatigue and the cold dictated some caution, and I decided we had to turn back and spend the night at Camp III.

The next day we made it to the summit. That was it, no record. On top, Neal was as happy as a kid. It is important to me that he returned home to his beloved Amy unharmed, without frostbite and full of his success. The significance of his accomplishment will not be lost in Colorado, where every other person considers himself or herself a mountain climber.

Before me, no Russian had climbed this peak. I cannot say I summited Makalu to be popular—in my country mountaineering is not a popular sport anymore—or because I wanted to feel good before an upcoming marriage. Though that is a serious matter, I have no plans for marriage sooner or later. I understand Neal well; we share many friends and acquaintances in the mountaineering world. From the depths of my heart I rejoice in his success. Sitting in Kathmandu trying to raise money, it has only been possible for me to envy his social situation. I climbed Makalu for myself, and deep down there is some discontent with my results. We were close to the record, our time would not have been bad, between eighteen and nineteen hours, but there is not enough luck in the world to risk pushing someone else to his limit.

After the expedition I encountered some familiar faces in the streets of Kathmandu, friends who are veteran mountaineers from other countries; not so many can afford the sport anymore. One big commercial expedition celebrated success on Everest and Lhotse, with high-paying clients covering all expenses, including salaries for working guides. Only Carlos Carsolio's ambitious efforts are advancing our sport. He made some noteworthy marks in the record books this season by climbing Cho Oyu in nineteen hours and Lhotse in less than twenty-four hours. Success makes it easier for him; his achievements are a source of national pride in Mexico. Sponsors willingly finance his projects; now he can afford to undertake mountaineering problems on his own terms. Life looks more complete for

Carlos. He has money and travels with his lovely wife and their new baby.

What else can you do but envy his success in a good way, just as I envy Neal for living in a country where many respected citizens climb or engage in athletic pursuits for no other reason than their own health? It is a pity that athletic endeavor has lost its inspirational appeal for citizens of Kazakhstan. The way things have turned out, I have to wonder if regular people ever understood the price we paid to be the best.

Tonight, Makalu is behind me. What the future holds is unknown. These are my thoughts and impressions. Kathmandu, June 13, 1994.

6

THE MARKETPLACE

During the spring of 1994, a rise in the cost of mountaineering permits in Nepal reduced the number of individuals who could afford to undertake small, private expeditions in the Himalayas. So several new companies were specializing in group expedition services, and at the end of my successful climbing season, I met a new kind of businessman in the streets of Kathmandu. Despite the $50,000 price tag on the permit, the owner of the New Zealand company Adventure Consultants, Rob Hall, had found a way to make an expedition to Everest pay for itself. He was even able to pay salaries to his guides. Only a few days after our return from Makalu, Neal and I were invited to a party that Hall was hosting to celebrate his success. A small group of professional climbers gathered in a restaurant in the city's quaint tourist district. That night there was much genial backslapping and beer drinking, and here I first met Scott Fischer.

Spotting Neal, Scott greeted us with generous congratulations on our Makalu success. The Seattle climber was a sort of hero for Neal, who had come to know him well during the summer of 1992, when they were both attempting to climb K2. Over the years I had heard about a personable American who set himself up for the same sort of physical challenges that interested me. Among Russians, Scott had earned a reputation for valor and persistence on Balyberdin's K2 expedition. His countrymen remarked about the human qualities that made him an inspirational human being as well as the skills that made him an exceptional sport climber, instructor, and guide. In May of 1994, I thought he had as much cause for celebration as we did. While Neal and I were climbing Makalu, Scott had become the first American to summit Lhotse without the use of bottled oxygen; that spring he had also succeeded in climbing Everest.* Neal confided that, like me, he was not a fan of climbing with supplemental oxygen. Personally, I feel unnatural relying on bottled oxygen above eight thousand meters; I worry that, using it, I am disconnected from the actual circumstances of my experience. It is a difficult concept for me to put into words, and that is another story. Climbing two 8,000-meter peaks in succession without oxygen demonstrated an uncommon endurance. Experience inclined me to rank Scott with Ed Viesturs at the top of the scale of Americans in my generation of mountaineers. As humans we are all basically the same, but an individual's nationality leaves a certain mark on his character. From a Russian perspective, Scott was the American archetype. His external appearance alone made him stand out in a crowd: a perfect sportsman's physique and a disarming, benevolent smile gave him a magnetic appeal.

Most of the evening I was engrossed in conversation with well-known Polish climber Richard Pawlowski and his business partner, Scotsman Henry Todd. Richard is a strong climber, and on several ascents he was the partner of one of the world's greatest alpinists, Jerzy Kukuczka. Neal and Scott sat at a table not far away from us. At one moment, I glanced up and Scott's eyes met mine. Intuitively, I sensed that Neal was telling him about our Makalu experience. There was

*Scott Fischer summited Everest for the first time in 1994 and Lhotse in 1990. Anatoli mistakenly understood that Scott had climbed Everest and Lhotse back-to-back in the spring of 1994. Anatoli set out to repeat this feat as a sign of respect for Scott's mountaineering life after his tragic death on Everest in 1996.

recognition in his gaze. At the end of the evening, we parted with warm expressions of mutual respect.

Some days later, when I was seeing our Makalu team off to America, I ran into Scott at the Kathmandu airport. We paused for a moment to wish each other a safe journey home. Though we did not speak of definite plans, we expressed a hope that in the future we could find a project on which to climb together. I gave him my address and phone number, and he gave me his business card. It did not yet say "Mountain Madness," but simply:

Scott Fischer
Rock, Ice, and Mountain Climbing
International Expeditions and Trekking, Skiing, Safaris, Adventuring

I still have the card. That day we did not know what was ahead of us. Our meeting seemed like a chance encounter, not the orchestration of fate. The longer I live, the more certain I am that there are no accidents in life. There are no chance meetings; everything happens according to a plan, regularly and in order.

.   .   .

From the beginning of my occupation as a mountaineer, I found that the more work I took on during an expedition, the more satisfied I was with the outcome. In the early years I was not dedicated to the mountains because I thought I would become a high-altitude guide. In the 1980s, no one imagined that the highest peaks in the world were destinations for any but a few committed mountaineers or that the experience gained climbing them would ever be elevated to high-paying work.

Until 1991, coaching provided me with a satisfactory source of income. With the collapse of the Soviet Union the possibility of meaningful employment at home evaporated. My limited facility with the English language prevented me from finding work in my profession abroad. At that point, I stopped focusing on anything but my desire to summit the world's highest mountains. Fifteen years with the Sports Club in Almaty and my success on some of the high-est 8,000-meter peaks had given me a rare base of high-altitude experience. Because of that, I was invited to join international expeditions. During those undertakings, it was most important to be able to climb well, not to chat, though I sensed the latter would not have hurt.

By 1994 a stormy competition was developing between companies doing business in the Himalayas. After my part in the Makalu expedition, it wasn't surprising that other employment offers followed. When I arrived in Almaty in mid-June, a letter from Thor Kieser was waiting. He offered me a job on an expedition scheduled for the fall of 1994. At the beginning of September, I was back in the Himalayas, employed by Condor Adventures as the climbing leader on a Cho Oyu expedition led by Neal Beidleman.

Rising 8,153 meters astride the border of Tibet and Nepal, Cho Oyu is the eighth-highest peak in the world. Our trek to Base Camp followed an old trade route through the Sherpa village of Namche Bazaar up the Thame Valley. We set up camp in the company of several other expeditions on a glacier just below the 6,000-meter-high Nangpa La pass. Our climbing route crossed the pass and approached the summit on the Tibet side of the mountain. Soon after we arrived, the camp was alive with rumors that Chinese soldiers had an outpost on the route as it passed into Tibet and were turning back climbers from expeditions that had begun in Nepal. Also, day after day a flood of ragged refugees made our kitchen tent the first stop after surviving a desperate journey out of Tibet. Camp was constantly inundated with men, women, and children begging for food; it unnerved everyone. Our team became increasingly tense because the expedition's supplies and gear had to be watched every moment. These circumstances had such a negative effect on the Americans that they decided to abandon the expedition. Neal escorted the team back to Kathmandu and I went trekking.

On September 29 news of a cholera outbreak in India reached the mountain village of Namche Bazaar. That closed the border to traffic from Nepal. With no avenue home, I decided to visit Everest Base Camp. Richard Pawlowski and Henry Todd were climbing

Lhotse. Naively, I harbored some hope of tackling the world's fourth-highest peak under the aegis of their permit. Unfortunately, it was too late to include me on the team roster. The expedition dragged on because the winds up high made the summit unapproachable. Henry, who was short of help, hired me to guide a group of tourists who were scheduled to climb Island Peak with Simon Yates. I made two trips to the top of the 6,000-meter peak in as many days. During that time, I promoted my sports club, and Simon and Henry decided they would take advantage of the excellent climbing opportunities in the Tien Shan the following summer.

⁎ ⁎ ⁎

By December of 1994 I had offers from both Henry Todd and Thor Kieser to work on Everest expeditions that they had scheduled for the spring of 1995. Henry offered me a salary much higher than what Thor could afford to pay me. I liked the way Thor conducted his expeditions, and I did not want to offend him. When I explained my financial situation, he encouraged me to accept the job with Himalayan Guides.

The Chinese sold permits for the Tibet side of Everest in 1995 at a fraction of what the government of Nepal was charging. That made the North Ridge route attractive to many expedition organizers, though it is generally considered more arduous than the South Col route. My second trip to the summit of Everest was unusual and difficult. As climbing leader, I was responsible for the comprehensive problems of our ascent. I acted as a coach for all the clients, set up our camps, supervised the Sherpas, and summited with two members of the team. For the most part, the men on that expedition were high-caliber mountaineers capable of solving for themselves the small moment-to-moment problems of climbing. With my help, the first Welshman, Cardock Jones, the first Dane, Michael Jörgensen, and the first Brazilian, Mozart Kato, took home the honor of climbing the highest mountain in the world to appreciative countrymen. From May 9 to May 17, eight expedition members made it to the top without much difficulty. Fate was not entirely generous. Nicholas Chaapaz, who was one of the strongest climbers on the team, arrived at the highest camp only to be denied the summit by an abrupt, prolonged change in wind velocity. After three days at the highest camp, he was forced to descend without the success he deserved.

After we left Base Camp, another episode of good weather opened the window to the summit. All in all fifty-three people climbed Everest from the north side that season. The number was staggering; it broke a psychological barrier in mountaineering. For those who discounted our good luck with the weather, it sent a message that the top of Everest was a reasonable objective for anyone who had ambitions as an alpinist. The average of my experience left me with a different set of conclusions.

Notes on the Heart of the Matter

A group of Russian climbers, some old friends among them, were neighbors of Anatoli's at Everest Base Camp in 1995. The nights spent in their mess tent stirred up some deep-seated emotions in Anatoli. These excerpts are from the pages of his day journal.

EVEREST BASE CAMP, RONGBUK GLACIER, TIBET,
MAY 10, 1995

In years past Demiyanich trained with me in Almaty. He has burned with the desire to summit some 8,000-meter peak in the Himalayas for a long time. Fate is not favoring him this season on Everest. Again tonight he refused to eat his supper, complaining that he could not stand the generous dose of Nepalese spices that the cook puts into the dishes. Sadly he recalled every detail of the good borsch that his wife, Tatiana, makes for him at home. For a human to appreciate the mundane, habitual features of life, they must lose them for a while. I know this from my own experience. After spending three months in the mountains deprived of things that under normal circumstances I take for granted, I discover that I have another scale of values. Suddenly something unimportant becomes paramount in my thinking. In Demiyanich's case, Tatiana's borscht had assumed mythic properties in his memory; likely it holds the aura of all his domestic comfort. As he spoke about his treasure, I openly envied him. I did not have that soup to remember and he had not climbed 8,000-meter peaks. At that moment in my mind, those two facts became equal. All my mountaintops were leveled to one bowl of Tatiana's borscht.

•　　•　　•

The best years of my life I dedicated to sports and alpinism; the mountains provided me with ways to perfect myself and gave me opportunities that allowed me to expand my understanding of the world. At this moment in history, the high goals I set for myself are of no importance in my country. Suddenly I have no function in the land where I was born and nurtured to be what I am. Sports and the arts have no basis of support in our new free-market economy. Everything has changed; it is hard for me to understand it all, and finding my place in the evolving social order is difficult. Our government has no inclination to revive the traditions that created people like me, and in the private sector there are no jobs that would reward my level of professionalism with a salary I could live on. Along the way my achievements began to attract the attention of foreigners, and abroad there is a demand for my level of professional experience and skill. Now it is easy for me to find work as a mountaineering coach or guide. While my obsession with the mountains supports me financially, my life would be happier if I worked in Kazakhstan, passing on my experience and knowledge to our new generation of climbers. I do not believe fewer individuals have that inclination in my country than they do in other developed countries, but in the former republics of the Soviet Union most interested people cannot afford the luxury of such high-priced active leisure.

Why climb mountains or set yourself up to face the sort of challenges that force you to grow? Does an individual's struggle for self-perfection have any meaning for a whole society? At home, not many individuals can remember why we took this road. Those who do, I miss so much. It is easy to find like-minded individuals in the West who respect what I have done, but I long to feel such acceptance standing on the ground of my motherland. Is it patriotism, this desire to take your strength from the support of friends and dear ones, to be comforted by the knowledge that your individual personality is a unit in something greater? Over the last five years I have lost all sense of belonging to anything bigger than my inner world. I wonder if the goals I have and what I do contribute anything to my culture. Many people at home do not understand me; they believe that I pursue mountaineering because I have found a way to make easy money. Not even friends and family who are closest to me see the price I am paying for my obsession or how that commitment, made long ago, binds me forever. Money can never replace what I lost or gave up when I took up this road.

KATHMANDU, NEPAL, JUNE 8, 1995

Two days ago Demiyanich and I returned from Everest Base Camp. Earlier tonight we strolled through Kathmandu's Thamel sector of colorful, busy streets. Though our company was brightened by the feminine companionship of Moscow businesswoman Natasha Shaginian, my mood was at level zero. Natasha and I became acquainted ten years ago; then she was one of Russia's best female mountaineers. As we spoke about the last expedition, the reverential spark in her eyes implied that I had done something remarkable. Strangely, her exaggerated respect for my accomplishments annoyed me. She made me think of another Natasha, a woman in Almaty; an unhappy cloud hung over our parting. Her attitude toward my records was completely different. Conversations about my achievements irritated her, even if I spoke with close friends. I have never been shy about what I do. I believe a person should be able to share his victories in life with those who are interested.

Looking over at Demiyanich, I had sincere envy in my eyes. Tomorrow he will be going home to his wife, Tatiana. For weeks he has complained about being deprived of her good borscht. If a woman were waiting for me, she would not have to be as good a cook as Tatiana, just sincerely happy that I was coming home. I wondered how it would feel to have someone waiting. How I wanted what my friend had. Finding that seemed more important than climbing Everest for the second time.

Those thoughts caused a painful twist inside me. I left the restaurant, telling my friends I was not hungry. I found the nearest telephone. Kathmandu is full of them; you can call anywhere for a pittance, anywhere but Russia or the republics. Those places cost more, and making the connection is nearly impossible. I handed over my last thousand rupees for three minutes. I wanted to hear Natasha's voice, thinking that I could make amends for the way we had said good-bye.

The relationship did not work out the way we had hoped, though no one is to blame that our two lives did not become one. In the ways of ordinary life, I am not too clever and I am too difficult to deal with. In the last year, Natasha was the person closest to me, but it seems that I don't have the qualities that will make her love me. Abruptly those thoughts were interrupted by her voice on the line.

Jumbled words poured out chaotically, not the way I intended to express them. The last thing I wanted was to make her melancholy or to remind her of unpleasant memories. With all my heart I wish her the happiness that she was unable to find with me. Hopefully, our future encounters will be less painful and our friendship will be something positive for both of us. I don't want to limit her freedom, nor do I demand her loyalty. Who knows what I expected from that conversation. In any event, I expressed no resentment or regret about what had happened between us. At that moment I needed someone dear to me to know that I needed her. Though it is natural for a person who loves to hope there will be positive feelings in return, I pushed such expectations from my mind.

After our conversation I felt better. Though I heard no love in Natasha's voice, I detected a new warmth and enthusiasm. My attention pleased her, and that is enough to make me happy. When I left, she expressed only coldness and indifference to my overtures. Why was she attracted to me initially? Perhaps she was like a drowning person who reaches out to the first one who tries to help. When the infatuation wore off, the recriminations started. "Why did you offer your hand?" "No one asked you to help." It was easier for her to run away from life, to dwell in the past. Now, I hear some sign that her spirit is rekindled. She is interested in what is going on around her. I don't think her attitude toward me will change. She has her own notion of what is good and bad in that regard, but at least she is concerned about the world and how other people feel. So the process has begun, as Mikhail Gorbachev used to say.

Why has she become so important to me in the last six months? From the beginning, our love of sports put our souls on parallel courses of development. I noticed that she treated the mountains as I did, like cathedrals where worship gives you strength and strips off the scale of ordinary life. It seems to me that every encounter in life is predestined. Each brings with it the opportunity to correct some facet of personal development, and these events occur according to an unfathomable rhythm. When I worked as a coach, my faith in the old slogans was enough; it was our responsibility to be strong units in society. Training was creative; sports were games you took seriously, and they prepared you for something more important. Now I struggle on the front lines of existence to satisfy my own idea of meaning; because I am alone, I sense that something is missing. The hardest blows that life delivers come from behind. I have no one to protect me from those leather blows. There is a refuge behind my shoulders for the woman who possesses the strength to be a positive influence, on others as well as me. That will not be an easy job, for I am far from being weak.

Strong character is hidden in Natasha's face; from the beginning I wanted to revive her interest in the world, restore her ambition. Part of me hoped that she was the woman who would end my solitude. Two separate lives would become a whole; unified, our struggle for spiritual development would benefit the world and us. My greatest hopes went unrealized, but the minimum was achieved. The effort that I made to understand Natasha has helped me grow, and I feel that I am a better person because of it. She has become a part of my struggle to understand the world. If I have reawakened her interest in life, then our encounter was not a waste of time. She has begun to fight on her own. For her, a period of stagnation is coming to an end. Hopefully she will reevaluate her psychological burdens, leaving behind those things that have not served her. She has great potential; I want her to find a place in society and work that will allow her to use her strength creatively. If we two can care about one another and help one another as friends, then the world is a better place. One more person struggles for good to prevail over evil. I do not want her to disappear into boundless space. I suppose that is what I tried to communicate tonight.

I am in a different stage on life's journey; my road was clear from the beginning. Loyalty to skiing and mountaineering charted the course of my destiny. No time or energy was wasted searching for a path to self-realization. Travel and the experience of climbing became the author of my development, physically and spiritually. Remembering that helps me detach myself from the thoughts that have run circles in my head for weeks, about my life, about Natasha's life. Though fate brought us together, and we had things in common and both of us tried to make a relationship work, there was no harmony in our union.

"You are living out a prophecy," Demiyanich tells me, "why do you question fate?"

I cannot argue with him; fate put me on this road in the beginning.

7

THE ROADS WE CHOOSE, 1995*

DHAULAGIRI, FALL 1995

The summer of 1995 was spent working for Himalayan Guides in the Tien Shan. Simon Yates, Henry Todd's wife, Peta Waite, and I led the first British expedition to traverse Myramornya Stena. Three of the team went on to summit Khan-Tengri.

That fall I was committed to a Manaslu expedition that was to be our Sports Club's return to Himalayan climbing. Our intention was to tackle a new route on the difficult South Face. In 1990, on one of the last attempts to blaze that futuristic trail, our teammates Grigori Luniakov, Zinur Halitov, and Marat Galiev had died in their pioneering efforts. This climb was conceived as a tribute to those men. The permit had been purchased from the Nepal Ministry of Tourism in 1994. Subsequent organization had been stymied by the club's inability to raise money for the expensive first ascent. When Simon, Peta, and I arrived in Almaty after the Khan-Tengri expedition, I

*A different translation of portions of the Dhaulagiri and Manaslu expedition accounts was published in the 1996 *American Alpine Journal* in an article Anatoli wrote titled "The Roads We Choose," edited by Christian Beckwith and translated by Beth Wald.

learned the Manaslu project had been put on the shelf once again. The Kazakhstan Ministry of Tourism had reneged on its funding commitment. Irvand Illinski had been forced to postpone the expedition until the spring of 1996. This depressing news came about one week before the beginning of the autumn climbing season in Nepal.

It was too late for me to find work on any of the commercial expeditions heading into the Himalayas, but I went to Kathmandu anyway, hoping I might turn up an affordable opportunity to try some peak I had not climbed. Fortuitously I hooked up with a team of Georgian climbers who had a permit for Dhaulagiri; this was their first Himalayan expedition since the collapse of the Soviet Union. I knew these men from sports climbing in the 1980s; they were members of the military sports club in Georgia, coached by one of my old mentors, Lev Sarkisian. My friends did not need my expertise for their undertaking, but they provided me with an interesting personal opportunity. I paid a portion of the permit fee and other expedition costs and shared the work required to establish high camps during our acclimatization. My summit attempt, a solo climb, posed complex physical and tactical problems that were challenging to me as an extreme athlete. Alone, I had to count on my strength and intuition; my chances of success and survival depended on these.

My goal was to climb Dhaulagiri in less than twenty-four hours. I left Base Camp on October 7 at six-thirty in the evening and reached Camp I at 5,700 meters at 9 P.M. After resting for twenty minutes, I moved on. Gusts of wind scoured the site of Camp II. I paused with a group of Austrian mountaineers weathering the blasts in their tents. Ignoring my momentary doubts about the wisdom of continuing, at 2 A.M. I headed toward Camp III. The wind and the night cold slowed my pace significantly. Often I stopped and waited for violent gusts of the icy blast to subside. When I arrived at Camp III at 5:45 A.M., I found a Bulgarian climber warming himself by the gas stove in my tent. He had spent a sleepless night sitting on my Ensolite pad, wrapped in my down jacket. Four Spanish climbers in the neighboring tent had postponed an early-morning summit bid because of the wind. I ate a little food and warmed up drinking tea, resting with the Bulgarian, whose name was Tony. At 8 A.M. I left for the summit. The Spanish climbers came out of their tents to watch my departure; one pointed to the summit and shouted to me, "*No pasarán*," a slogan from the Spanish Civil War in the 1930s.★

Slowly I ascended the ridge, already brilliantly lit by the morning sun, and finally came into the leeward shelter of a steep, snow-covered slope. Camp III was far below, and I climbed on an angle so steep it reminded me of the dangerous presummit section on K2. But the situation was different; I was not so helpless with fatigue or emaciated by the effects of the altitude. My rate of ascent inspired confidence. Given my body's ability to perform, I determined that I would have the strength necessary for the descent. Far below, following my example, Tony and the four Spaniards were moving up the slope. Their pace appeared considerably slower than mine.

On the ridge just below the summit, the wind intensified. Acutely aware of my insignificance, I sensed that I was moving into an enormous void. An impressive panorama of mountains spread around me; only clouds broke the intense blue of the sky. On a ridge overlain with deep snowdrifts, I crossed the final treacherous meters to my goal. A huge snow slab broke off and avalanched away from the grip of my crampons in the icy slope. That rendered any egotistical desire for records insignificant, and the last vestige of pride in my performance disappeared into the abyss with the falling snow. Exhaustion swept over me as I registered that a tenuous grip on ice was all that prevented me from flying down the slope incorporated in the avalanche. Losing all sense of time, I wondered at the power that the mountains exert over us, calling people to push themselves to undergo such tests of courage, strength, and purity.

I don't know how long I stood on the summit, perhaps fifteen minutes, before I looked at my watch at 11:45 A.M. As I turned to descend, the goal that had been my inspiration below had ceased to interest me. I had climbed Dhaulagiri alone in about seventeen hours, but there was no rejoicing in my success. I understood that time was

★*No pasarán* translates as "it is impossible to go there."

not important, that the true significance of my effort lay in my connecting with the mountains. Standing there, I realized that I needed these trials and struggles, that they are important to me. It is with myself that I struggle in this life, not with the mountains. Their greatness and strength is indisputable, only man is in transit, evolving, growing, and the road that we choose to follow in life depends less on the surrounding world than on our spirit—the internal voice that pushes one to seek new challenges.

Getting down was considerably more difficult and dangerous than getting up. Fatigue increased; the sleepless night had left its mark on me. I paused to rest about 12:45 P.M. and watched Tony as he took my trail up the route. He climbed following his own road, and a personal victory awaited him at the end of his journey. Man struggles helplessly at high altitude with inherent physical weakness—one must constantly overcome and conquer a nagging sense of inadequacy. The Spaniards turned around halfway to the summit; apparently, they were not prepared to face the test the mountain held out to them that day.

I did not linger at Camp III, but packed my gear and continued down, fatigue and dehydration slowing my steps. My progress was steady, without stopping. I did not experience the drop in strength that happens when you are a guide and your movement is constrained by responsibility for others. At Camp II, I shared tea with my Georgian friends, passing on information about the route after the assault camp. The next day they would try for the summit, their effort paving the way for other Georgian climbers in the Himalayas.

Darkness fell as I reached the top of the icefall at five thousand meters. Using the beam of my headlamp, I negotiated a way across ominous crevasses, their black mouths plummeting to the bottom of the glacier. When the terrain leveled out, fog shrouded the landscape so densely that all visibility was lost. Somewhere in the vicinity of Base Camp, I heard the sounds of voices, laughter, and music, and they became my guides. It was 7 P.M.

About twenty-four hours had passed since I'd walked out of camp. Under the growing fatigue, my feelings were more than relief that the trial was over, that I had survived. The experience had left me a long way from the end of my life's clearly defined road. I understood that I needed to accomplish more, I had to endure more if I wanted to know what I was capable of as a mountain climber or as a human being. The end of each journey is the beginning of a new one, one that is longer and more difficult.

Autumn Encounter with Scott Fischer

At noon the next day, October 9, I walked to the hot springs in the village of Tatopani on the Annapurna Circuit and spent two days there enjoying the warmth and restorative effects of the baths. I made my way down to the tranquil lakeside village of Pokhara and rested for several more days before returning to Kathmandu on October 19. After a good night's sleep at the Namascar Guest House, I went out for a stroll along a narrow street, daydreaming among the shops and restaurants. Then, from one of the cars jammed into the crowded lane, someone yelled my name. Walking closer, I recognized the faces of friends, mountaineers from Almaty. In a jumble of words I learned that the postponed Manaslu expedition was back on track. They had just arrived in town from the airport and were on their way to a hotel.

During the expedition, I learned the details of how my friends had managed their escape to the freedom of the Himalayas. Expedition leader Kazbec Valiev (chairman of the Kazakhstan Mountaineering Federation and the director of the International Mountaineering Camp Khan-Tengri) had found the theretofore unobtainable part of the money for the expedition. He had changed the team's objective from the South Face of Manaslu to a more accessible route up the North Ridge: it required fewer men and less time and was therefore less expensive. He had invited eight climbers from the Sports Club, mostly those who worked for him at the IMCKT (International Mountaineering Camp Khan-Tengri).

Suddenly, I was faced with the question of whether I was ready to join the members of the expedition. An immediate answer was required. While I was climbing Dhaulagiri, I had not considered the possibility that another mountain would follow, one that was no less dangerous and difficult. It was important to me personally that, after a four-year break with mountaineering, the climbers from Kazakhstan had created an opportunity to climb in the Himalayas. They had accomplished that in spite of economic hardship, political instability, and the indifference of our government to our achievements in sports and mountaineering. I wanted to believe that a rebirth of mountaineering was possible in our country, that our skill and experience would not be lost, dying with us. I feel strongly that the school of Russian mountaineering with its unique perspective and extraordinary successes is part of our cultural heritage. It stands with the Soviet Union's great accomplishments in space exploration, science, and the discipline of Russian ballet.

The men honored by the expedition, Grigori Luniakov and Zinur Halitov, had been my teachers. We had accomplished many excellent climbs together in the Pamirs and Tien Shan in the 1980s; our last effort together had been Kanchenjunga. I had learned much about mountaineering from them. I hope that our club can dedicate future ascents to the great ones from our club who have died while climbing, men like the accomplished Vadim Smirnov and Valeri Khrichtchatyi, as well as the younger, less well-known Marat Galiev, who in his short life lived and breathed the mountains.

Yuri Moiseev and Vladimir Suviga, veterans of West Dhaulagiri and Kanchenjunga, were the only members of the assault team who had experience above eight thousand meters. Since 1991, only I had been able to pursue mountaineering actively without any breaks in training. During that four-year period immense changes had taken place in our country: in economics, in politics, and ultimately in the lives of each person. But individuals do not change much, especially men who climb mountains. What endures is the spirit that drives a human to choose the most difficult and dangerous roads: unexplored paths that are not accessible simply because one has the money to afford them. There are ways to achieve earthly happiness that do not depend on money, and they should not be discounted throughout the civilized world. I was tired physically and psychologically, yet without hesitation I said yes to Kazbec's invitation.

Final preparations kept us in Kathmandu a few days. My friends and I passed our time relaxing, browsing among the craft stalls, and examining the colorful goods on display in the shops in Thamel. One afternoon I was pleasantly surprised to recognize the hooded figure of Scott Fischer leisurely absorbed in his own window-shopping along the busy streets. His appearance was unchanged; only his hair was a bit longer, now pulled back in a ponytail.

Slapping him on the back, I asked, "Scott Fischer, what is new in America? How are you?"

His blue eyes lit up as he said, "Hi, Anatoli! It's good to see a familiar face."

We ducked into the small Tibetan restaurant at the Sherpa Guesthouse, drank a little beer, and caught up on the events in our lives. While I'd worked in the Tien Shan that summer, Scott had climbed Broad Peak (an 8,000-meter peak in Pakistan) and had successfully led several clients to the summit. He said that now there were enough mountaineers to warrant commercial expeditions to the 8,000-meter peaks. Business was picking up for his new company, Mountain Madness. In fact he had flown in from America to purchase a permit for Mount Everest for the spring season of 1996; Neal Beidleman had agreed to be one of his guides.

We spoke about Balyberdin, who had died, shot by someone in St. Petersburg for the money he made driving his car as a cab. A national hero had lain in the morgue for a week before anyone had realized who he was. I told Scott about my work for Himalayan Guides on Everest the previous spring and that I had just finished a sports ascent on Dhaulagiri. He knew I had climbed the peak for the second time, and with a note of surprise Scott remarked that he thought I worked for money; he didn't know I climbed for entertainment.

"Dhaulagiri was so enjoyable that in a week I intend to double my pleasure by attempting Manaslu in winter," I replied.

Scott's laughter stopped when he realized I wasn't joking. He paused, then said that he envied me.

"What are the problems, Scott?" I asked. "Join our team, it is very strong, I am sure we will succeed."

The idea of an ascent on Manaslu appealed to him; it was one of his dreams: no American had ever summited that peak. In all seriousness I encouraged him to come with me. He said he would have to think about it. His decisions about climbing were based on many considerations: his family, business, and money. He was not free, as I was, to do as he pleased. He was in Kathmandu on business and needed to focus on that. Earnestly, Scott spoke about how he enjoyed his work, how he liked interacting with people and opportunities to take them climbing. That way he combined two of the things he loved in life. From that conversation I developed a new level of respect for him. Though I doubted he could say yes to my invitation, I was pleased to offer him the opportunity. We sat for a time enjoying one another's company, then he said that he had a business appointment and asked if we could meet for breakfast the next morning.

I replied, "Yes, of course." I wanted to tell him more about the programs I had developed for expeditions in Kazakhstan, thinking he might see some opportunity in the mountains in my homeland for his new company.

The next morning, we talked over several cups of coffee in the restaurant at the Manang Hotel. I showed him photos of Khan-Tengri (which to me is one of the most beautiful mountains on earth). I saw Scott's eyes light up with appreciation. The Tien Shan was unknown to him and interesting. At heart Scott was an adventurer. Practically, he pointed out that going to Kazakhstan depended on whether he could find clients to pay for the cost of an expedition or trekking there. After working as a guide for American and British companies, I understood this approach to life, to work: the philosophy is to make the things you do pay for themselves.

Our conversation changed to the subject of Everest. Scott asked for my professional opinion as a guide about commercial expeditions. I clarified that I did not work as a guide with Henry Todd's clients but as the climbing leader. I was responsible for two of the less experienced members during their climb to the top. When the other members summited, I was available to assist if a rescue or problems arose, but I did not climb with them.

Scott had heard that fifty-three people had been successful during our season, a fact some professional climbers found unbelievable. He wanted to know how that was possible on a route considered harder than the South Col way. I told him what I thought were the contributing factors. We discussed details of other expedition experiences: organizational styles and outcomes. With Rolf Dujmovits taking clients to K2 and Rob Hall getting people up Everest, I admitted that it looked as if mountaineering was moving in the direction of commercial expeditions. Scott asked me what I thought of the risk on such expeditions. He wanted my opinion as a climber experienced with high altitude.

I approached the subject of our Everest success conservatively. I said that the mountain would clearly always be difficult and dangerous. She demanded caution and respect. Risk and success on Everest depended on the quality and depth of the guides' skills, on timing, and on the experience and physical condition of the clients. High-quality, experienced guides were no guarantee; I shared how close I had come to failing in 1995. At one moment on the spring expedition, I had found myself alone, blinded by a storm, literally crawling on my hands and knees back to Camp II. At high altitude, I pointed out, there was no insurance against abrupt changes in the weather, and no amount of guiding expertise could prevent clients from developing altitude sickness. Everest will always be Everest. In the end she decides who approaches the summit, and effectively that made it a game of chance.

"Guiding Everest is a game of Russian roulette," I said.

Scott sobered at this remark and only echoed, "Russian roulette?"

Out of the blue, Scott offered me a job working for him in the spring of 1996. I had not anticipated this invitation. It seemed impulsive to me. We were just talking. I did not know what to say. My mind was occupied with the coming Manaslu expedition. Actually, I did not immediately understand why Scott needed me to work. It did not make sense to me. I understood well why my cooperation with Himalayan Guides was useful to Henry Todd. He no longer had the services of Richard Pawlowski. Because of that, he had to pay a highly qualified mountaineer who was capable of working above eight thousand meters. Henry is skilled at organization and managing expeditions to 8,000-meter peaks, but he is not a lead climber. As for Scott Fischer, he was as fully capable at high altitude as I was. Why did he want someone like me to work for him? America is full of mountaineers with less experience who would be honored to help him on an expedition, happy to take his orders and carry them out. Frankly, Scott's offer flabbergasted me.

I apologized to him, saying I had accepted a job in the spring with Himalayan Guides. We would be working together on Everest, on parallel expeditions. Scott burst out laughing. He said, "Anatoli, I want you to work only for me. I can see many possibilities for the future in our cooperation."

I told him that while I appreciated the role I had as a lead climber, it was not as interesting or enjoyable to me as ascending peaks unencumbered in my own style. He pointed out practically that the world turned on money, and that I would need to make money guiding to finance my own projects. Scott asked me what Himalayan Guides was paying me. I told him, but I also said that other things about my cooperation with Henry Todd were important to me, such as developing some business at home in the Tien Shan. My agreement to work for Himalayan Guides was not solely based on what Henry was paying me. The work was too dangerous for what I was making. I had invested a lot of time and my own money in getting the program in the Tien Shan going, and I had some reason to think that a partnership with Henry regarding the delivery of Poisk oxygen would eventuate. Russians have a proverb, "Do not change horses in the middle of the stream." I was thrown off-balance by Scott's offer. I do not like to hurry or make decisions quickly, and at that moment I couldn't decide what was right to do.

Scott laughed. He said he was ready to pay someone with my qualifications twice what Himalayan Guides was paying. He said he wanted our "cooperation" to work out. I liked Scott, and more than that, I respected his skill as a climber. Although I was looking for someone of his caliber to be my climbing partner, someone as capable of sports ascents as I was, I felt that I needed time to think about what he offered and about my relationship with Himalayan Guides. I said that if Scott could pay me $5,000 more than his offer, I would probably say yes. Scott was clearly taken back by that: he had already offered me more than most guides make for working on Everest.

Actually, I found it hard to focus on this proposition. My mind was on Manaslu, and the way the conversation had changed had taken me by surprise. Though I could easily see the benefits of working for Scott, and the idea of our climbing together as partners on sports ascents was appealing, I thought changing companies would put me in a difficult situation with Henry Todd. I didn't so much want extra money from Scott as I wanted a way to explain to Henry Todd why I had suddenly given up our relationship. Henry is above all a clever businessman. This was the same situation I had been in when he had offered me more money than Thor Kieser was able to pay. I figured Henry would understand, as Thor had, if I elected to take advantage of an opportunity that was so much better.

As Scott had another meeting at the Ministry of Tourism about his Everest permit, he left the table saying he was ready to pay me what he had offered and that I should think about it. We agreed to meet the next morning at Mike's Breakfast.

The rest of that day I organized gear and supplies for the Manaslu expedition. I went over Scott's invitation in my mind. It began to make sense to me that he wanted the best-quality guides possible for the spring expedition. I knew from our conversation that he understood my level of experience and that he respected my point of view. I thought of what sort of organization I wanted to work for and about the opportunities I hoped to create for myself by doing such dangerous work. Running a smooth mountaineering expedition takes special skill. I felt Scott had the kind of strong, positive personality that experienced mountaineers, clients, and Sherpas could follow. He could provide good leadership on commercial undertakings, and the opportunity to climb purely for sports objectives with someone of his caliber was appealing.

My Almaty friends joined me for breakfast in the garden at Mike's the next morning. After weighing the pros and cons, I decided to accept Scott's offer as it stood. He was late and I surmised that he had decided not to pursue our conversation because of my initial reaction. I felt regret regarding the lost opportunity. About 10 A.M. he arrived, entering the garden, talking and gesturing to his trekking agent, P. B. Thapa. After "Good morning," the first words from Scott's mouth were that he would agree to pay me what I'd asked for to work. Since I had already decided to work for him, the issue was closed. Immediately we began discussing organizational details.

We met several times that day and outlined my responsibilities. Scott wanted to buy lightweight, Kevlar-wrapped oxygen canisters made in Russia for the coming expedition. We agreed I would make those arrangements. He ordered two of the prototype Russian tents we were field-testing on Manaslu, and I was to be responsible for their delivery. We signed a contract. I would be able to explain to Henry Todd why I had left his company for another.

Scott was unable to secure his Everest permit. P. B. Thapa was left to work on those details for him. Scott gave me a deposit for my work in case the expedition was canceled. He had to leave urgently because of other business commitments. We agreed I was to contact him through P. B. Thapa's office as soon as I returned from Manaslu. I said good-bye to him, truly regretting he was not coming with me.

The Winter Ascent of Manaslu

Winter climbing adds a dangerous rigor and hardship to the alpine challenge. This expedition account was prepared for the American Alpine Journal. *Anatoli's writing had a military terseness that he felt was appropriate to the distinctly "Soviet" climbing style. Clearly ringing though this matter-of-fact retelling is his sense of relief and pride. Irvand Illinski reminisced, "Nineteen ninety-five was the year that Anatoli came home."*

Yuri Moiseev and Vladimir Suviga and the younger members of the team left Kathmandu on a bus November 3. They trekked to the village of Somongon, gaining a gradual acclimatization to 4,200 meters. November 18, Kazbec Valiev, our doctor Valentin Makarov, and I met them at the last village on the trek to Manaslu Base Camp. Expedition supplies and equipment were off-loaded from a Russian helicopter owned by Asian Airlines, and we said good-bye to pilot Serge Danilov, who was an old friend from Kazakhstan. After two more days of hiking over snow-covered trails, we set up our base of operations at 4,400 meters.

Younger team members were familiar with expedition routine. Seventy-two hours of combined effort forged the trail to Camp I at 5,500 meters. Reconnoitering the icefall that cascaded from the North Slope and pushing the route through its obstacles took a few more days. Above it on the most level spot available we carved out Camp II. After sleeping one night to gain proper acclimatization, we descended to Base Camp for two days of rest. On the twenty-ninth, our ranks split into two five-man climbing units, and together we headed back up the mountain.

The short winter days dictated an abbreviated work schedule. By 3 P.M. the sun would slip behind the northern ridge and the wind would pick up; then a terrible cold would descend on the mountain. Thin tent walls and our sleeping bags provided the only refuge from the frigid conditions. Night temperatures plunged to minus forty degrees centigrade, and even in the tents it was minus ten. Above the elevation of Camp I a steady wind blew, which was rarely dependent on the time of day. First light found us preparing food and water; by 8 A.M. we left the tents. Like one machine, the two teams worked in harmony, alternating effort on the route. Due to the inherent danger, though each work group separated to its own tent for the night, in the day we worked in close cooperation.

On December 1 on a 6,800-meter-high ridge, next to the wind-blown remains of a previous Japanese expedition, we pitched tents for Camp III. With us we had carried enough extra food, gas, and equipment for the summit assault. For acclimatization, we slept at that elevation one night, then returned to Base Camp for another two-day rest.

On December 5 ten members left for the final assault, climbing directly to Camp II. On the sixth we ascended to the well-stocked tents at Camp III. Though extremely cold, we had some luck with the weather when gusting winds subsided. Despite low temperatures, we climbed rapidly to a large ice plateau beneath the summit at 7,400 meters. Working together, we quickly cut a level platform into the hard névé slope. But before the barrel tents were completely secured, the wind increased, threatening to reach hurricane force. Inside our resilient, hard-tested shelters, it was tolerable, though five men were crammed into a space designed for four. During the night the icy blast pierced the walls, penetrated the insulation of our sleeping bags, and sucked away our bodies' warmth. The temperature inside registered minus twenty degrees centigrade; one could only imagine what it was outside.

We had agreed to try for the summit regardless of conditions. By consensus, the most experienced members worked out our plan. Departure preparations began at 4 A.M.; we wanted to leave at six, keeping the team together. Crowded conditions in the tents made a simultaneous start impossible. At the appointed time, the first two climbers headed up the gradual slope, climbing on hard ice and snow. Around 10 A.M. Yuri Moiseev and twenty-four-year-old Alexander Baimakhanov crossed the last steep, icy ramp that led onto the corniced summit ridge. Shortly behind them I came struggling with my camera, which was refusing to work in the low temperatures. The second group of summiteers, Dima Sobolev, Shafkat Gataullin, and Oleg Malikov, arrived as we abandoned the peak. Demetri Muravoyov and veteran Vladimir Suviga brought up the rear. Arriving in five-to-ten-minute intervals, eight men managed to pull their bodies to the top. During the morning's coldest hours, the threat of frostbite had sent two of the team back to the tents.

It was close to 2 P.M. before the whole team reassembled at the assault camp. Our plan had been to descend as rapidly as possible to Camp II at 6,200 meters. But the lack of rest combined with the altitude, intense cold, and work was more than some could endure. Being the first to arrive at the tents of Camp III, I could see how difficult it was for most of the members to negotiate the final meters of the descent. At 6 P.M. only eight of the group had arrived. The two missing men were Misha Mikhaelov and Dima Grekov; they had been unable to cope with the summit assault. Leaders at Base Camp informed us they were visible sitting on the snow above the rock face, where the descent from the assault camp began. Something had happened to our friends, though before we had left camp neither had complained of poor *samochuvstvie*.* It was evident they did not have enough experience with the extreme altitude to correctly judge their reserves of strength.

Immediately, without rest or drink, young Shafkat Gataullin and I started back up the slope. Darkness obscured visibility; the distance we could make out seemed disturbingly inadequate. Occasionally we turned on our headlamps, ever mindful that the power in the batteries was limited. Finally, after three hours, we saw the two men sitting in the snow; we arrived in time to help them. Misha did not have enough strength to refasten his crampons or to descend the steep ice slope unassisted.

It was a risky, cold descent; we worked late into the night. Through fog and frost we moved toward the help waiting below. Above Camp II our friends came to meet us, carrying hot tea; during that encounter a misstep occurred. Below, the refuge of the tents was a tantalizing sight. Drinking tea, the sick Misha and his friend Dima relaxed their guard and slipped down the snowy slope. A sudden jerk

---

Samochuvstvie is a Russian word that refers to a person's total psycho-physical state of well-being. There is no exact English equivalent.

tore me from my ice ax, which I had secured as the belay point for the climbers. My gloves went flying; we flew twenty meters and came to rest at the midpoint of the belay line. Our fall was arrested by a carabiner, which was providently locked onto the rope. Fifteen minutes later in the tents, I thawed my instantly frozen hands; luckily I escaped with light frostbite. Emergency oxygen that we had stored at Camp III revived the disabled climbers. Thanks to our solidarity and collective action, we avoided a tragedy. Those qualities had made the high-altitude climbers of the former Soviet Union famous during its heyday.

We descended to Base Camp together, arriving on December 9. No one had sustained serious frostbite; amputation would not be required. Thanks to a continuous flow of supplemental oxygen, Misha's condition had improved. Our doctor determined that helicopter evacuation would not be necessary.

The winter ascent of Manaslu was not an ordinary climb. I hope that is only the first of a series of victories for the Kazakh team, that our success will spark a revival of interest in our sport. It would be better if the accumulated knowledge of previous generations of Soviet mountaineers did not die with the fall of the Communist era, better if our experience could carry us farther and higher to other summits in the Himalayas and Karakoram.

I want believe that the roads we choose to follow in life depend less on economic problems, on political battles, on the imperfections of our external world, and more on our internal calling. An inner voice compels us to go into the mountains, to the heights above the clouds, breaking new trails. The fathomless sky and sparkling summits with their grandeur and mystery will always appeal to that part of humanity that loves beauty. This is and will always be their magnetic power. They exist free of the petty vanity and trivial worldly aggravations that cloud our experience of the present moment and shadow our view of the beautiful and eternal.

8

THE END OF AMBITION, 1996

Guide to the Unknown

Guiding experience on mountains above eight thousand meters has a short history. Some think that it can be looked at in the same way you would guide a lower, nontechnical peak. Absolutely, responsibility is the factor those two jobs have in common: responsibility for the lives of the clients and responsibility for conducting a safe ascent and offering timely assistance when necessary. Aid on peaks higher than eight thousand meters cannot be compared with the type of help a guide can guarantee in the Alps, for instance, where you can count on assistance from professional rescuers and special rescue services that are equipped for everything and prepared to arrive quickly. Above eight thousand meters, as a guide you can only count on your own strength and experience to help you avoid irreversible mistakes. Risks are always present in the mountains, and at high altitude the risks are incomparably greater. Climbing as a guide is about three times more difficult and dangerous than going alone. In 1996, my physical and psychological resources were tested as never before. Fortunately, seven months of almost continuous climbing in 1995 had prepared me to endure those challenges.

Mountain Madness, Everest

In the three months after my return from Manaslu, my communications with Scott Fischer were handled through his business partner in Seattle, Karen Dickinson. During that time, which I took to rest, Scott worked, constantly traveling. He led an expedition to Kilimanjaro, taught an ice-climbing clinic in Colorado, and visited Europe to raise money for his Everest expedition. Before leaving Almaty for Kathmandu, I received my first direct communication from him in a fax that contained instructions regarding my role in the early stages of the expedition. My job would be to go in ahead of the main party of clients with our gear and supplies and supervise the setup of our Base Camp on the Khumbu Glacier. On March 22 I met Scott in Kathmandu; that evening we joined trekking agent P. B. Thapa and our two sirdars and reviewed the final details and responsibilities for each person. On the twenty-fifth, Ngima Sherpa and I flew to Syangboche airstrip above Namche Bazaar.

Rain stalled our progress in Namche for forty-eight hours. Once the yaks had arrived and been loaded, the trek to Base Camp took four days. After arriving, I pitched in to help with leveling the glacier rubble for tent sites and the kitchen, enjoying the tranquil, measured life and the physical fatigue after the strenuous exercise. Lopsang, Scott's climbing sirdar, and most of our Sherpas were from settlements near Gauri Shankar in the Rolwaling Valley of Nepal. Lopsang was young, only twenty-five, a three-time Everest summiter (once with Scott); he had been to Seattle and had worked for Mountain Madness on the Broad Peak expedition in the summer of 1995. His youth was worrisome to me, but I was reassured by the presence of Ngima Sherpa from Phakding, whom P. B. Thapa had put in charge of all our Base Camp operations. Notes from Neal Beidleman informed me of our team's progress up the Khumbu Valley. With work almost finished, on April 6 I hiked two hours down and across the glacier to Gorak Shep, where I met our team and reported to Scott. After warmly greeting Neal, who has been my friend since my first visit to America in 1990, I was introduced to the people whom I did not know. Scott outlined my experience. Our meeting was cordial.

With the eye of a coach and trainer, I reviewed our clients' respective climbing histories, age, and outward appearances at five thousand meters. Sandy Pittman had been on Everest before. I was familiar with her list of mountaineering accomplishments; her robust good health at that altitude left me with no doubts about her well-being. Lene Gammelgaard's excellent appearance and positive frame of mind indicated she was ready to be the first Danish woman to summit Everest. But her desire to make a summit bid without the use of supplemental oxygen, combined with her lack of experience, was alarming. The third woman on the expedition, Charlotte Fox, had succeeded in climbing two lower 8,000-meter peaks, Cho Oyu and Broad Peak. She had also summited McKinley, Aconcagua, and all fifty-four 14,000-foot peaks in Colorado. In addition to that sound résumé, in winter she was on the ski patrol in Aspen, working above three thousand meters. Her boyfriend, Tim Madsen, was also on the ski patrol. As well as being a competitive athlete, he had extensive climbing experience in the American and Canadian Rockies. How his body would respond to very high altitude was an unknown. Another well-conditioned athlete, Klev Schoening, had a strong base of mountaineering skill and experience; Kilimanjaro, Aconcagua, and Kango Karpo, a 7,000-meter peak in China, were behind him, as well as many years of climbing in the Cascade Mountains in Washington. He was on the expedition with his uncle Pete Schoening, a sixty-seven-year-old American mountaineering veteran and hero. Pete was the first of his countrymen to climb Gasherbrum and was on the first American expedition to K2. His age provoked a guarded feeling in me, though I sympathized with his ambition to be the oldest man to summit Everest. Dale Kruse had been a regular on Scott Fischer expeditions; his greatest mountaineering achievement was

Barnutse, a straightforward peak near Makalu. His ability to carry himself at very high altitude was unknown. Martin Adams I knew from our Makalu expedition in 1994; his body had adjusted well to 7,400 meters, but on that expedition too many days waiting at the elevation of Camp II had undermined his strength and thwarted his summit attempt.

After meeting our team members, I walked back to Base Camp; along the way I analyzed each person. My initial concerns were that Lene, Tim, and Dale had inadequate exposure to elevations above seven thousand meters. Pete was experienced, but I knew age was a factor that affected the body's ability to acclimate. At five thousand meters, the good form and fighting spirit of our participants were reassuring. For me, final conclusions on their preparation would have to wait until they had recovered from the necessary acclimatization excursions to seven thousand meters. Repeated trips to high elevation make it easier for the human body to adapt to the low oxygen content of the atmosphere; it also gives a climber confidence. Everest is a multiday marathon. The process demands that team members spend enough time high enough to adjust to the elevation increases; the body must compensate for functioning in an unnatural environment. The strength spent during this process is hard to recover even at the elevation of Base Camp. That is why prior conditioning is so important. Scott had to be given his due; this was his first large-scale expedition, and success meant more to him than finding people who were able to write a big check. His sincere desire to create a strong team was evident in the conscientious selection of guides and Sherpas, and the effort he had made to solicit strong members.

During the first few days after the team reached Base Camp, Scott and I outlined a plan for acclimatization excursions and rest days that would let us follow the adaptation of each individual. That year 250 people were climbing Everest, but every expedition lives by its own rhythm, independent of others. A good route had been secured through the Khumbu Icefall by Sherpas from two British expeditions. With our plan in place our expedition slowly gained speed.

Scott and I closely observed the level of training that our team members demonstrated on the first acclimatization trips. We agreed their performance made them look far better than the members of other expeditions. Privately, I noted that the overall level of expertise on the mountain was far lower than it had been on the Tibet side in 1995. The weather, route conditions, and clients' states of mind all instilled some confidence in our success. Our tactics differed quite a bit from those being used by others who were traveling up and down the icefall. That our group was sufficiently prepared technically and physically for self-reliant travel on a completely developed route allowed this. As guides, we were always making global checks on how people were doing and were prepared to render assistance if required.

I can't say I had a fixed notion about the work I faced on the Mountain Madness expedition. For me, some things were significantly more important than others, things that I paid attention to that others did not. For me, the most important responsibility of a high-altitude guide is to ensure the safety of ascent conditions and to try to keep the risk of unforeseen danger to a minimum. Along with the usual dangers you face on a mountain, on a very high mountain you must be alert to the greatest danger, which is the altitude itself. Increasing altitude intensifies the consequence of every action. So the second most important aspect of the job is to monitor the client's acclimatization and physical condition. Only someone with a long record of ascents at very high altitude who is aware of the accommodations his body makes can feel a deviation from the norm. For a person who climbs high for the first time, every sensation in the body feels abnormal; it is difficult for novices to judge how they are adapting.

My inadequate knowledge of English caused some problems. Sometimes I did not fully understand conversations, therefore I was uncomfortable socializing with clients, and it was hard for me to explain the importance of my opinions and advice. These circumstances were new to me, since before I had worked either as a personal guide, managing all details for one person, or as a climbing leader, solving the more comprehensive problems of the assault. Also, it was the first time that Scott and I worked together. I was working for him and we had different experiences both as high-altitude climbers and in our guiding work.

Our progress up to Camp II was smooth: the work was accomplished competently and harmoniously. Tim Madsen's adjustment was slow, which was normal given it was his first time to high altitude. A serious cause for concern was that Pete Schoening, who looked absolutely superb otherwise, was unable to sleep without a continuous flow of oxygen even at the elevation of Base Camp. On April 22, Lopsang's uncle Ngawang became seriously ill while carrying supplies to Camp II at 6,500 meters. Disoriented, he collapsed and required assistance to descend from the mountain. Despite all the efforts of our team doctor, his condition deteriorated. Because of the bad weather during those days, helicopter rescue from Base Camp was impossible. Our Sherpa staff transported Ngawang down to Pheriche, the nearest air-accessible village. In the hope of stabilizing his condition, he was on a continuous flow of supplemental oxygen. Nothing helped. He lapsed into a coma in Pheriche and was flown to Kathmandu for hospitalization. Lopsang went along; that trip compromised his acclimatization. Scott's supply of oxygen canisters dwindled under the weight of those unforeseeable demands.

Our trouble really began with Ngawang's rescue. Team members had acclimated to 6,500 meters, and most of them were ready to begin the acclimatization ascent to Camp III. Our third camp had not been set up or supplied, nor had the route across the steep sections up to the South Col been opened. The manpower we committed to the rescue of Lopsang's uncle left us short of strength. I felt positive about volunteering for the job because I knew that actively acclimatizing to elevations above Camp III was the best way to prepare my body to work well during our summit bid. Ang Dorje, who was Rob Hall's sirdar, and I, with a few Sherpas from the Taiwanese expedition, fixed the rope and anchors on the technical portions of the route up to 7,900 meters. Neal and Scott were left to deal with the problems in Base Camp.

April 28 at Camp III, I rejoined the team's rhythm; some of them were spending their first night at that elevation. Dale Kruse developed acute problems with the altitude. Scott and I assisted him down to Camp II, and then I helped him descend to Base Camp to recover. Our climbing plan called for a long rest period after the clients had been provided with the opportunity to acclimatize at 7,300 meters. After that, I suggested to Scott that everyone should descend to Deboche, a village in the forest at 3,800 meters, where the oxygen-rich atmosphere promotes a more complete physical recovery. How the weeklong rest period was spent was up to the individual. Scott consulted with Rob Hall and decided against encouraging my idea. They felt descending so low increased the risk of members becoming sick with stomach problems in the lodges. On May 1 everything was in place for our summit bid; I was not needed in camp. Scott excused me and allowed me to follow my inclination to rest in Deboche.

Scott and Neal Beidleman made a choice during that time that I did not understand. They attempted to climb Pumori, a 7,000-meter peak in the Everest basin. I respected Scott's and Neal's endurance, but to climb during our rest period struck me as a waste of strength. Later, I learned that Scott had developed an illness in those days and began taking antibiotics. Also I found out that he used a medication called Diamox to improve his acclimatization. While this is a commonly accepted practice among American climbers, I do not climb and take medicine. I think it is better to know exactly how your body is responding; even a slight illness can be exacerbated quickly by high altitude with disastrous results.

During discussion of our plan for the summit assault, I don't recall that Scott and I spent a lot of time talking about the use of supplemental oxygen. Danish climber Lene Gammelgaard's wish to ascend without oxygen created a problem for Scott. I joined that dialogue and persuaded Lene that her ambitions were not practical given her level of acclimatization and limited climbing experience. Scott and I agreed Neal Beidleman should climb using oxygen since it would be his first trip above 8,500 meters. Every team member would use supplemental oxygen continuously above 7,300 meters. Since their responses to very high altitude were unpredictable, we agreed on the necessary precaution of transporting a supply of canisters to the South Col for emergency purposes. The Sherpas would use oxygen when working during the summit assault. Lopsang would go without it, as he had performed well that way on his previous Everest climbs. As for me, I got the impression from the conversation with Scott that he was more confident than I was that I could work without it. Though I had climbed Everest twice without using bottled oxygen, I knew the success of our clients' summit day would depend on my strength and ability to perform. I felt that it was important for me to base my decision on oxygen use on how I was feeling on summit day. I requested that Scott calculate bottles for me into the supply of canisters he would have delivered to the South Col. He agreed; since we were professionals, those were obvious decisions. Analyzing the situation in retrospect, I understand our expensive supply of oxygen had been stretched to the limit by the unforeseen requirements of Pete Schoening and Ngawang Sherpa. If Lopsang and I had climbed on May 10 using oxygen, there would have been no canisters held as a reserve for emergencies.

On May 6 the Mountain Madness team left Base Camp early, following a familiar, well-beaten trail to Camp II. More than two hundred climbers were in various places on the route preparing for their summit bids. For me it was only a four-hour climb to Camp II, so I left Base Camp at noon. Above the icefall, I met Scott, who was descending with Dale Kruse; once again the elevation was incapacitating, and the climb was over for Dale. I asked Scott to allow me to descend with Dale. For personal reasons Scott said no, that he wanted to accompany his old friend down. He would catch up with us the next day, which was scheduled for rest at Camp II.

On the eighth our nine-member team ascended to 7,300 meters. The next day as we prepared to leave Camp III for the South Col, I noticed that Scott appeared tired. His social responsibility may have been one reason for that. Scott had a great ability to communicate with people and comfort them when problems arose. Throughout the expedition he was available for conversation and support. He gave away a lot of energy this way. From my years as a coach, I knew the value and psychological weight of that responsibility. Scott carried a heavy burden with the clients. The power of his character and reputation had inspired people to join the expedition, and most of our group were only satisfied when they had his attention.

Before we left Camp III on the ninth, an arch of wind-driven snow bowed over the mountain above eight thousand meters. In my experience, hellish wind can be a more difficult obstacle than bad weather on Everest: even under a clear sky it can render climbing impossible. Looking up, I doubted we were choosing the right moment to ascend. I expressed my reservations to Scott and Rob Hall. Rob had a different opinion: the sky was clear, he wanted to get his clients into position for the summit assault, then wait for good conditions. He pointed out there was always some wind up higher, which was true. In many cases I did not have the power to influence Scott's decisions. I was respected as a high-altitude climber, but Rob Hall had much more experience successfully guiding a group of clients on Everest. Naturally, in our circumstances his opinions carried more weight than mine did. On several issues Scott had deferred to Rob's advice. That morning, Scott told me we were going to follow Rob's advice regarding the timing of our summit bid. Climbing up, I met Ed Viesturs and David Breashears descending. Ed confirmed the wind was strong at the Col; he, too, felt the conditions were not stable enough to climb higher. On previously successful commercial ascents of Everest, Ed had been Rob's principal guide and consultant. In 1996, Rob made decisions without the benefit of Ed's sound advice.

Knowing it was important for the team to move directly into the shelter of tents when they arrived, I went up ahead of our team to help the Sherpas set up camp. By 5 P.M. we had four tents ready (two for guides and clients and two for our Sherpas); as a precaution against wind damage, one tent was held in reserve. Klev Schoening and Martin Adams arrived. A cloud blew up on the pass and abruptly the wind increased, scattering fine snow. Clearly the weather at that moment precluded thoughts of a summit assault. Conditions were about two times better than those we would face twenty-four hours later. Waiting for the other members of our team to arrive, I discussed the situation with Rob Hall. The roar of the wind was so loud we were forced to communicate with our heads close together, voices shouting.

"What are we going to do?" I asked.

To this he threw up his hands, saying, "If the weather improves, we go tonight; if it does not improve by midnight, we wait twenty-four hours. If it's blowing like this tomorrow night, we go down."

About that time Scott arrived with Sandy Pittman; I passed on Rob Hall's plan and reported on who was where in our tents. Immediately upon joining Martin Adams, Lene Gammelgaard, and Klev Schoening in one of the vibrating shelters, I retreated into the warmth of my sleeping bag and fell asleep, certain that we would not be going anywhere that night. That pessimistic prediction was in error.

About 10 P.M. the noise of the Sherpas preparing food and tea in the neighboring tent woke me. Half-asleep, I sensed that something had changed. The walls were no longer buffeted. The Sherpas used normal tones of voice, not shouting over the howling wind. I remember being impressed and somewhat amazed with Rob Hall's foresight. There was no question: ahead of us was the summit assault.

For some reason, I had no desire to begin that undertaking. Missing was my usual presummit high, when every muscle and nerve is ready for work, ready to face the hard, wearisome struggle. My internal voice was quiet. I wondered how to interpret that. Was it poor *samochuvstvie*, illness, or lack of preparation? I recalled similar internal states on other occasions: times in bad weather when I had had no desire or motivation to venture out, moments when my intuition about some change in conditions had stopped me. But the weather had improved: at that moment it was astonishingly clear, the night sky sparkled, there was no wind. In my search for the cause of my mood, the weather was not a factor that I considered; I knew that, according to Scott's directive, we were going up. Analyzing my physical preparation in light of my general feelings of ambivalence, I wondered if I was getting sick. In the moments before we left camp, the doubts I entertained made me put a mask, regulator, and oxygen bottle in my pack so that I could make my final decision about using it after we had crossed the section of easy climbing up to 8,500 meters. At that point, if I felt fatigued or was unable to work at the rate required to keep up with the team, I wanted to have the oxygen available to use.

Scott and Lopsang were responsible for our supply of canisters as well as assigning our Sherpas' duties. Scott distributed two bottles to each client. In the three bottles allotted for them, each person had an eighteen-hour supply if oxygen was used at a normal flow rate. I was under the impression that all seven of our Sherpas would be working with us, carrying the extra bottles we needed to resupply the team late in the climb. Usually one Sherpa carries the reserve canister for another person. Looking around, it crossed my mind that we did not have enough manpower. Groggy from the short night of sleep, I did not pursue that train of thought.

The severe night air was so cold that it was impossible for me to work without mittens as I filled my thermos with hot tea. Tea was all that I found available for my breakfast. We left camp on schedule about midnight. Rob Hall's team had left camp ahead of us. According to plan, Lopsang and the Sherpas were to go first to fix ropes, while Neal and I would stay in the middle of the main group, monitoring progress. Scott left camp last; this is the normal position for an expedition leader as it enables him to follow the progress of the whole team spread out on the route ahead of him. At daybreak we overtook the Adventure Consultants team. They were resting on a point of the East Ridge at about 8,500 meters, enjoying the perfectly windless morning. Above us was the steepest section of the route. My understanding was that during our rest the Sherpas would go ahead and fix rope on that section so the guides could stay with the team. Up to that point Ang Dorje had been doing the hard work, breaking trail through the new-fallen snow. Lopsang, our sirdar, was slow, not feeling well; he was unable to work in the lead. The other Sherpas were not experienced at technical work and were obviously tired, loaded down with the oxygen. After six hours of climbing, my body felt fine, my pace was stable, and it had been easy for me to keep up with our clients who were using oxygen. Ascending the last vertical meters was not going to be a problem for me. Neal Beidleman reported that he was feeling quite strong using the oxygen, and I indicated that I would not need the canister I was carrying. Perhaps Neal believed that I was too weak to carry that bottle; actually, when I gave the canister to him, I simply thought that he would use it.

He and Ang Dorje started ahead of Rob Hall's team, pulling old ropes from the snow as they went and securing new line in some places. I noticed that the situation on that part of the route had changed since I'd climbed it with Kevin Cooney. Technically it is easy, just steep: in '91 we climbed with ski poles. By 1996 the remains of many old fixed ropes were on the slope. I stayed with our clients; all were moving well without any obvious problems. Between ten and eleven o'clock we reached the South Summit and stopped to rest. From that point, the summit is about one and one-half hours away. Had Scott caught up with us there, he might have turned some of our clients back. But that was not a decision either Neal or I was authorized to make. Most of our group had paid big money for the opportunity they had earned, and Scott Fischer was the only one with the authority to turn a climber around so close to the goal. My role was to help our team succeed. I was there to work, to carry out Scott's orders.

After forty minutes of waiting, I understood that no one intended to extend the route. Ang Dorje was tired; it seemed most reasonable that I take the initiative to fix the line up the Hillary Step so we could keep moving. After consulting with Neal, I got ready to go. He took a rope from one of the Sherpas and belayed me across the ridge before the Step. Crossing, I pulled old ropes up from the snow. I expected that those who came behind me with more rope would correctly secure that section of ridge with a continuous line. It did not take me long to fix the rocky step. Andy Harris, one of Rob Hall's guides, and one of his strongest clients, Jon Krakauer from Seattle, came up right behind me. It was too crowded for all of us to stand in that one place. I moved off ahead, breaking trail in the snow on the steep section of ridge above, thinking it would be faster and easier for those who followed to fix the rope they carried working from an established track in the snow. That is how I became the first person on the route to the summit. I arrived there at 1:07 P.M. A strong, stable wind was blowing, which is the usual phenomenon on Everest. The sky predicted no storm or cataclysm. Ten minutes after I reached the summit, Andy Harris and Jon Krakauer arrived. They took pictures and quickly started down. Neal and our client Martin Adams came up shortly behind them. I focused on how they were doing: neither had problems. Klev Schoening joined us ten minutes later. I told Martin to pick up some rocks from the summit for souvenirs, which he did and then headed down. I checked my watch and saw I had been on top for almost an hour.

I could not see climbers over the crest; I thought our clients must be having problems with the Hillary Step. I decided to go down to that level to see what was happening. Five minutes down from the summit, I met Rob Hall with one of his clients. With his face covered by an oxygen mask, at first I thought he was Scott. I asked him how he was doing. He answered that everything was all right. He thanked me for fixing rope on the Hillary Step. I asked if he needed help. He replied that everything was going well, that his client was only fifteen minutes from the summit.

In a dense group of climbers coming up after Rob, I distinguished the members of my expedition and focused my attention on them. Though there should have been some space between each climber, they were bunched with members of the other teams in a tight group; four of our Sherpas were with four clients. I wondered why they lagged so far behind the first summiters. Worried because we had been climbing thirteen to fourteen hours, I started to have concerns about our oxygen supply. It would take Tim, Sandy, Charlotte, and Lene about thirty minutes to reach the summit at their pace. I understood that there might not be enough oxygen for their descent. Neal Beidleman was waiting to receive them at the summit.

Where was Scott? I had not seen him during the whole assault. Down the ridge, I recognized him talking with Martin Adams at the top of the Hillary Step. He was wearing an oxygen mask; that fact alone did not lead me to assume that he was having health problems or that he was weak. I thought the choice to use oxygen was most reasonable. Scott had worked hard throughout the expedition, and for various reasons he had not been able to gain the level of acclimatization that I had. I went down to him, stopped, and asked how he was feeling. He said he was tired, that coming up had been difficult, though from that encounter and our conversation, I was in no way alerted that his condition was a problem or that it might lead to the tragedy that followed.

At that moment, we had five clients on the summit; counting Scott, there were two guides and five Sherpas to attend them during the descent. Martin was headed down. Two of the group on the summit had not been above the level of Camp II prior to the assault, so their level of acclimatization was a question in my mind. My intuition was telling me the most logical action for all of us was to turn and go down. I knew that when our people ran out of oxygen during their descent, they would experience a sudden drop in strength and ability. Physically assisting anyone at such high elevation is hard if not impossible; the best help in those circumstances is to provide a resupply of oxygen. Talking to Scott, I expressed my desire to descend, to reach the Col quickly so I would be available to bring oxygen and hot drinks up from the assault camp to anyone who was exhausted. I knew that I was strong enough to do that. Scott listened to me; he said descending was the right thing for me to do. He told me to go down.

Consulting with Scott about this plan, I did not think I was choosing the easiest option for myself. It would have been much easier for me to stay with the group, slowly continuing the descent. It is impossible to get lost on the route from the South Summit down to 8,200 meters. The camp on the Col is visible all the way down a trail that descends on the ridge. With ropes fixed along the steep section to speed the descent and ensure safety, the rest of the relief was relatively easy. At 8,200 meters the terrain becomes more flat; there were no fixed ropes on that section, and in poor visibility, it is possible to lose one's way. But at that moment I had no reason to think visibility would disappear. The weather was not a source of concern; it appeared normal for Everest. Afternoon clouds were blown up the mountain by the normal shift in wind, but below the clouds the route was visible. Looking back, I can say the clouds boded nothing good and I should have been more mindful that just as the weather had suddenly improved the night before, it was possible for it to get dramatically worse.

After we'd decided that I was to go down to be available for re-supply or help, Scott went up. Physically I was past my dead point in energy and I felt much better than I had in the morning. Working on second wind, I caught up with Martin and urged him on. I was not concerned about his climbing ability as he was moving well, wisely hurrying because he was using his last bottle of oxygen. I knew he would come down behind me.

I attempted to get ahead of the climbers who would naturally descend at a slower rate behind me. To free the rope for them and to avoid the possibility of being hit by falling rocks they might kick off the slope, I had to be ahead. It is not safe for two or three people to descend using the same rope. At about 8,500 meters I encountered a man who asked if I had seen Rob Hall; he said he was waiting for him. I spoke to the man briefly telling him what I knew.★ I kept going. Having committed to a course of action, I worked like a programmed machine.

In a little more than two hours I reached 8,200 meters; visibility dramatically improved. Actually I thought the weather was getting better. Usually the afternoon clouds blown up the mountain are cleared off the slopes by the late-afternoon winds. I could see our tents. Carefully negotiating the difficult ice slope, I hurried to camp. Arriving between five and five-thirty, I was surprised to meet Pemba, one of our Sherpas. Unbeknownst to me, he had stayed in camp. I was tired and rested for thirty minutes, trying to collect my strength for the work ahead. I rested watching the descent route for climbers, hoping to see them, and hoping I would not have to go out again.

★Anatoli later learned this man was Adventure Consultants client Beck Weathers.

About six o'clock with no one in view, I asked Pemba to find me three canisters of oxygen. Soon after I started from camp across the Col, the wind abruptly increased and visibility decreased because of blowing snow. Putting on a mask and turning on the oxygen to accelerate my ascent, I rushed to reach the beginning of the ropes at 8,200 meters. Rapidly the blizzard became worse. Stopping at 8,150 meters, I found the relief above was completely obscured. I looked back; I could see light flashing from our camp, signals for the descending climbers. Moving in a systematic way, I went up into the whiteout trying to locate the end of the fixed rope. Fogging up with my breath, the oxygen mask impeded my visibility, so I turned off the flow and removed the mask. As I could not see, speed had ceased to be meaningful, and I thought I should save the oxygen for the clients. Despite repeated trips into the storm, I was unable to locate the ropes. At that point the light from my headlamp penetrated the falling darkness only a few feet around me. Carefully I descended the steep ice to the level of the Col. Unsure, lost, I wandered about half an hour before regaining my orientation only when I was able to see the flashes of light from camp.

Clearly the situation was out of my hands: that stark realization provoked a great wave of fatigue. Forced to accept that the most reasonable course of action was to get back to the tents and stand by prepared to help, I knew too well that our clients were in a critical situation. Returning to camp, I noticed that my feet were freezing. To restore the circulation I took off my crampons and boots and moved into the tent to warm them. At that moment Martin Adams arrived. His face was covered with ice and snow. I helped him into the tent, took off his crampons, put him in his sleeping bag and connected him to a bottle of oxygen. Pemba brought tea; he said that he had seen lights close to the tents and that our group should arrive soon. I went out preparing to help them; I thought it was likely that some would have frostbite. Repeatedly for the next two hours as I could stand it, I moved out of the tent into the wind to flash my headlamp and search, thinking that some people were trapped close by.

About 1 A.M. Pemba started shouting. All that time he had maintained the vigil. Snow-covered figures were coming, their masks covered with ice. It was difficult to recognize anyone. Lene arrived first. I took off her crampons and pushed her into the tent with Martin, then I helped Klev, who came in with Neal. After talking with Lene I understood some people were in a bad situation, cut off by the storm across the Col toward the Chinese side. Three of our team were huddled together without strength to move. Two climbers from Rob Hall's expedition had come down with them. Emotional and scared, Lene urged me to hurry. She said Sandy Pittman was frozen and was probably dying. I could not get specific directions out of anyone. After hooking Klev and Lene to oxygen, I went to Neal, thinking that he would have clearer information, but he was frozen and incapable of explaining anything.

I needed canisters of oxygen, one for each of the stranded climbers. To all my questions about where I could find our supply, Pemba just threw up his hands. Finally I understood our supply was finished. I knew it would be impossible for me to assist five people alone. I went to the tents of Rob's expedition, opening doors, asking for help. No one showed any initiative. Rousing the person closest to the door of our Sherpas' tent, I woke Lopsang, our climbing sirdar. He muttered unintelligibly about the need to help Scott. Everyone in the tent slept in unconscious exhaustion, all using bottles of oxygen. I asked Lopsang if he could help me; he could only repeat that I needed to go for Scott, who had told him to send me. So then I understood that Scott was waiting, counting on my strength. Strangely, in our last conversation we had considered that possibility when he had approved my rapid descent to the South Col. Finally, after further questioning of Lene and Klev, it became clear to me that Scott was not with the group of stranded climbers. Then I had choose what I thought Scott would want me to do; my first responsibility was to help the clients who from my understanding were near death. Lopsang said he was sick and unable to go with me. He was enduring the hardest time of his life. It was too dangerous to expect the Sherpas to volunteer when only ten or fifteen meters from the tents one completely lost control of the situation.

One of the Sherpas surrendered his bottle of oxygen, a mask, and a regulator. Following the directions I had, I spent thirty or forty minutes making my way to the edge of the Col where it falls off to the Kangshung Face. Seeing no one, I realized that I needed more information. I found my way back to camp and woke Klev. He said that I needed to go down over the ridge; the people were huddled a little lower than the place I'd turned back. Neal had revived a little and confirmed the information. Struggling in the storm a second time, I found the ridge of rock and began going down. I saw a beam of light; Tim Madsen had turned on his headlamp. Three people were huddled in a tight group. One person was lying motionless on the rocks next to the group: that still figure was Yasuko Namba, Rob Hall's client. I could not see the fifth person anywhere. Putting the mask I carried on Sandy Pittman, I turned on the flow and asked who could move with me. Charlotte Fox agreed to try. I told Tim to take turns using the oxygen with Sandy. He asked me why I was alone. There was no one else to help, I said.

To keep Charlotte from slumping to the ground, I had to hold her arm over my neck and support her body with my other arm. Half dragging her that way, we faced the hurricane-force wind. I had to stop often. It took me forty minutes to cover the four hundred meters to the tents. After removing her crampons I pushed her into the tent with Neal Beidleman. He helped her by sharing the oxygen canister he used, though he was still not feeling well. Again, I went to Rob Hall's tents trying to get someone to go with me for Yasuko. One Sherpa responded to my pleas; he quickly came out of the tent, but seeing the intensity of the storm, he refused, saying he could not risk his life. Who could blame him, when not even the guides were capable of working in those conditions?

I took another bottle of oxygen from one of our Sherpas and headed back over the familiar route. Sandy was more coherent when I arrived. Yasuko, next to them, had not moved and showed no signs of life. I focused on Tim and Sandy. Without another bottle of oxygen it was senseless to think about helping anyone else. It was after four o'clock in the morning. Sandy could not support her own weight. Her feet dragging, I picked her up, half carrying her. Using the second canister of oxygen, Tim was able to move independently, but his pace was slower than ours. He showed great courage, trying not to lag behind. His strength was amazing considering this was his first time at high altitude and he had poor acclimatization. We struggled about thirty minutes and made it to the tents. I helped Sandy and Tim out of their equipment. I asked Pemba to bring everyone hot tea.

Then I understood I was unable to do more. My strength was exhausted. I crawled into my tent. How long had I been without sleep and food? I felt no fear inside or any other emotion, probably because of my insane fatigue. Maybe this made it easier for me to analyze our situation, even in those last hours. If I had been able to use oxygen during the rescue, perhaps I might have been able to maintain my strength. That was impossible. I needed every bottle I could find to help our clients. Though physically devastated, I was vividly aware that Scott had problems. Spending the night in such storm conditions without any way to replenish his energy, without oxygen and the protection of a tent, would definitely cause frostbite. At that moment, I tried not to think the worst. Scott was much stronger than the other guides or our clients. I thought he would endure. Every hour was important to him. While I was taking tea from Pemba, I asked him to wake two of our Sherpas, any of them who could work. I told him to find oxygen canisters, find one extra for Scott, make a thermos of hot drink, and send two men immediately. It was twilight, the clouds had lifted, the snow had stopped, and visibility had returned up to the level of about 8,400 meters. For some reason I hoped that Lopsang had recovered enough by resting in the night that he would be able to ascend to Scott. Drained of all strength, I climbed into my sleeping bag, shivering. Finally I slept.

Two hours later I woke when Pemba brought hot tea again. My first question was "Has anyone gone up to Scott?"

From his silence I knew the answer could only be no. Again I asked him to pass on my request to the Sherpas; we needed the most rested to go without delay to meet Scott with oxygen and hot drink.

Neal had recovered somewhat. I could hear him moving in the tent nearby. Our focus now was to get the clients down from the Col. Within an hour everyone in our tent was prepared to descend. Klev Schoening asked me accompany him. He had problems with one eye and also some minor frostbite. Reasonably I tried to reassure him that one of our Sherpas would be able to assist him adequately. The situation with Scott was still unclear, and someone besides the Sherpas needed to be available to respond to his needs.

Though everyone was stressed and distraught, no one in the group at camp had suffered any serious injury. I knew with the help of the Sherpas they would descend rapidly on the fixed rope. Once off the Col the weather would improve, and that decrease in elevation would immediately make a difference in how they felt and performed. I consulted Neal, who was silently and quickly collecting his things. Charlotte, Sandy, and Tim were prepared to leave. I told them that I wanted to remain in the camp. Out of the tent door, I saw two of our Sherpas at around eight thousand meters, heading up to Scott. A little higher climbed two Sherpas from the Taiwanese expedition of Makalu Gau, and even higher we could see two men from the Adventure Consultants team rushing to rescue Rob Hall.

I went to the kitchen and asked Pemba who had gone up for us. He said the father of Lopsang and Tashi Sherpa. From their distance above camp I estimated they had left after my second order about 8 A.M. Within fifteen minutes the clients began to descend, aided by three Sherpas. Lopsang and Tshering Sherpa remained. Lopsang informed me he was still sick, offering me no more information. He could only glower at me; obviously he blamed me for not going to help Scott. He did not understand what the night with the clients had cost me.

I advised Lopsang to notify me of any news that came from above. Still exhausted, I crawled into the shelter of my tent, but I could not sleep. Two or three hours later I heard the voices of Pete Athans and Todd Burleson as they arrived from Camp III. They had radio contact with the camps below and shared information with me regarding what was going on up the mountain. Rob Hall was fighting for his life on the South Summit. Trapped trying to save Doug Hansen, during the night Rob had suffered severe frostbite. Doug Hansen had slipped descending the Hillary Step and disappeared. Rob was unable to descend by himself. He waited for the help of his Sherpas, who left at 6 A.M. and were then struggling in the hurricane-force wind that continued to blow higher up. There was no news of Scott or the others who were missing. Pete, Todd, and I knew of many cases where experienced climbers forced to bivouac in the cold at high altitudes had survived, suffering manageable frostbite. We counted on that possibility for Scott Fischer, who we knew was a strong man.

During this time we watched a group of people descend on the route, hoping that it was Scott with the aid of the Sherpas. Taiwanese climber Makalu Gau arrived in camp about 2 P.M. His Sherpas had left an hour earlier than ours and had been able to rouse him to consciousness with oxygen and hot liquids. Scott had been left next to where Makalu had been at about 8,300 meters. Arriving later, our Sherpas tried to rouse Scott but were unable to bring him to consciousness: he had a pulse and was breathing but was unable to swallow the liquid they offered. They secured a mask to his face and turned up the flow of oxygen before descending.

After hearing that news, I consulted with doctors at Base Camp, who advised me of a slim possibility that Scott might regain consciousness. I prepared to go up the mountain. I had directions about medicines that might help and packed them, along with a thermos and three bottles of oxygen. Lopsang's father had taken two full bottles from Ed Viesturs's supply. Tashi and Lopsang's father were not optimistic about Scott's condition. I asked Pete Athans and Todd Burleson if they would go with me. They said climbing at night in unstable weather was irrational. Pete said this with tears in his eyes. I answered simply that Scott still had a chance for survival, maybe one in a thousand. I had to do something. In those circumstances the chance of Scott's surviving was incomparably smaller than the chance of my dying. For me it was impossible to think that Scott, breathing oxygen, might come out of a coma needing help and die waiting for me.

I left camp about 3 P.M. One hundred meters from the tents, I encountered a person wandering slowly across the Col. At first I thought this was Scott. I thought miraculously the oxygen had revived him or that I was hallucinating. By that time all those unaccounted for were known to be dead. Moving slowly with arms extended in front of his body, I saw a frozen face overcome by the pain of survival. His shaking, lifeless arms were carried as though they did not belong to him anymore.

I asked, "Who are you?"

He answered, "This is my last time. I never want to do this again."

It was Beck Weathers. The phenomenon of his courage and endurance urged me up the mountain; his survival fueled the hope that my friend also had a chance to come back to life. I called Todd Burleson and Pete Athans and helped Weathers back toward the camp where I delivered him to their care. Late in the afternoon, I headed up to Scott, turning on the flow of oxygen to speed my ascent.

After two hours of climbing, I arrived at the place where I expected to find him. Scanning the relief, I saw a shadow that did not look like the outline of rocks. Quickly I recognized Scott's clothing and went to his motionless body. His down snowsuit had been unfastened; one naked hand was presented as if he were giving a signal of his location and asking for help. I lifted his mask and looked into his face. I found no signs of life—no breathing, no pulse—but I could see that his passing had been recent. Scott Fischer had put up a hard fight for his life. Only at that moment could I believe that he had succumbed to the mountain. There was nothing I could do. I covered the top of his body with his pack; I thought to protect his face from the ravages of the birds that scavenge the slopes in good weather. I wrapped his body in rope. In a kind of daze I stayed doing these things for about a half hour. Then I became aware that the wind was gaining strength and it was snowing again. It came to me that I had to go down, that darkness was falling.

After forty-eight hours of stress and tension I worked like a robot, moving in nervous tension. As I descended, the wind increased to the same paralyzing speed as the night before. At the end of the fixed ropes, darkness and blowing snow limited my visibility to two meters. After the end of the fixed ropes I moved to the left to avoid the steep ice and the cracks in the snowfields. Descending in the small halo created by the light of my headlamp, I came to the slightly sloping, almost horizontal part of the pass. To survive I had to thread a path between the drop-off on the Kangshung Face and the west slopes, crossing to the other end of the vast oblivion that was the South Col. I turned right, orienting myself by the wind. No light signals came from the tents this night. My headlamp illuminated a wall of milky darkness. Orientation lost, I moved for an unknown time not knowing where I was. Soon I could not estimate distance. I sensed that I was close to the southwest face; afraid of the abyss, I turned back and tried to retrace a direction keeping the wind at my back. In those moments, I felt that someone was close to me and that presence calmed me. Turning into the wind, I struggled on, and after a time I discovered that beneath my boots the rocks and ice were strewn with metallic garbage and discarded oxygen canisters. I knew the tents were somewhere nearby, but where? I moved out from a point and returned, trying to explore a circle, making the radius wider each trip. My bearings were lost in the snowy blizzard. The battery in my headlamp died. I crawled in the darkness, engulfed in the howling noise of the blizzard. Then apart from the sounds of the wind, I heard a long human scream. Moaning and crying continued. I tried to orient myself to this sound. I was close to the end; a tortured human cry was a beacon. Only when my gloves touched the fabric that enclosed the moaning climber did I understand that I had found our camp. I groped along the ground for my tent and moved in out of the storm, crawling into my sleeping bag. I drank the tea from the thermos I was carrying. With a flashlight I checked my watch. It was midnight: five hours of wandering in the blizzard, more than seven hours since I'd left camp to find Scott. Later I would understand I had Beck Weathers to thank for my life. It was his voice crying out in the night.

At six the next morning, Tashi woke me with tea; he and the other Sherpas were going down. I slept a couple more hours. When I emerged from the tent, I met with Pete Athans and Todd Burleson. They were preparing to descend with the severely frostbitten Beck Weathers. Friends from the Himalayan Guides expedition, Michael Jörgensen and Brigitte Muir, gave me something to drink in their tent. I had to rest; it was difficult for me to move. Two hours later I felt able to pack up my gear. Our camp was abandoned in disarray. I dismantled the tents, thinking the equipment belonged to Scott's company and I should be responsible for it. I collected small things Scott had left that I felt would have sentimental value for his family: his knife and his ice ax. I imagined that Scott had carried these things on many expeditions. Absently, I picked up a few personal items that belonged to our clients to return to them.

Leaving camp about 4 P.M., I took photos of the storm raging on the crest of the mountain. Suddenly I had the impulse to go to the place where I had found our clients during the blizzard. I wanted to pay final respects to Yasuko Namba. I felt deeply that she might have survived if I could have given her the attention I gave Sandy. Why did I not put more focus on her? Had the notion of commercialism so shackled my brain that I could not look beyond the responsibility to those who had paid Scott and therefore me for assistance? That question will remain with me forever.

Making my way down to Camp II slowly, in the darkness at about 8 P.M. I crept into my tent. The next day, May 14, I descended to Base Camp. Exhausted and empty emotionally, I could not shake the thought of Scott waiting for me. He had counted on my strength when he'd lost consciousness. In that twilight of sleep, freezing, he stopped fighting for life. The last of my strength had been spent fulfilling what I thought was my duty, but in my eyes that was no comfort. If oxygen had been brought to Scott even one hour earlier, the situation might have been changed in his favor. In the early hours of morning when he needed me, I could do nothing for my leader. I had nothing to pay the great mountain for Scott Fischer's life.

Lhotse

When I returned to Base Camp, I experienced a turbulent flood of conflicting emotions. Coping with Scott's death and my adrenaline-soaked nerves and muscles left me restlessly exhausted. Concern for my physical state prompted our expedition doctor, Ingrid, and Neal to try to help me, but the medicines they gave me triggered an allergic reaction. My emotions released in a torrent during the memorial service, but there was no psychological relief in weeping.

Neal assumed the responsibilities of expedition leader. At the memorial I spoke with him about climbing Lhotse. He and Ngima, our camp sirdar, were occupied with the details of getting our climbers and gear to Kathmandu. In early March, Scott had put my name and that of several interested clients on a Lhotse permit and paid for our share of the cost. The impulse that compelled me to climb after such a tragedy may be impossible for some people to understand. It may seem a vain and ambitious act. It is difficult to explain. Mountains are my life. At the time I remembered the standard that Scott had set for all of us when he'd climbed Lhotse and Everest back-to-back. Repeating his achievement, demanding of myself the price in effort he had once paid, was a way I could express my respect for him as a mountaineer. I wanted to say farewell to him that way. Neal told me to go; he understood.

Tired and a little crazy, I left Base Camp on the night of May 16 at 8:30 P.M. By midnight, I reached Camp II, where I rested an hour and drank some tea before heading up to Camp III. The dark, enormous slope blended into the night sky, and the boundaries between earth and heaven disappeared. Anxiety binding me to the tragedy was pulled out of me and released into space. The night gifted me with strength and tranquillity. The emotions that bound me to the earthly world slipped away. Weathering the cold, at 4 A.M. I arrived at a tent where I expected to find my friend the Danish climber Michael Jörgensen. I drank tea, closed my eyes, and slept like a stone for four hours. Leaving at 8 A.M. I saw evidence of strong winds ripping across the South Col; snow was brushstroked up toward the sun rising over the peaks. The sky was clear. The weather was good enough. It, the altitude, and technical difficulties on the route were my adversaries.

Gusting wind noticeably impeded my rate of ascent above the 8,000-meter mark. The effects of the previous days' work told on my performance. I stopped to stash my small backpack at the beginning of the steep couloir that leads to Lhotse's summit. Into the roomy pockets of my down suit I stuffed essentials—a headlamp, a flask of water, and a thermos of tea. My heavy Nikkormat camera hung around my neck. Alone, without belay, leaning over my ice ax, I climbed the acute angle of the couloir. In the narrow neck I fixed twenty meters of 8-mm climbing rope. Down-climbing that section in darkness would be more dangerous than ascending. The rope protection would speed my descent. I emptied the flask of water, leaving it as well, thinking to spare myself the effort of carrying more weight. The snowy couloir became wider and ended with a shallow gully. A metal stake for anchoring rope protruded from the snow at the top. Climbing the last meters, I left the protection of the steep walls. The wind buffeted me, trying to rip me off the mountain. I dug my crampons into the snowy névé slope and leaned low over my ax to maintain my balance. Terrible hurricane-force gusts deviled my progress. I took the left route up the last slope and reached the summit at 5:45 P.M., slightly more than twenty-one hours after leaving Base Camp.

Through breaks in the clouds, when the wind permitted, I looked over at our route to the summit of Mount Everest. Somewhere on the rock shelf about 8,300 meters was the body of Scott Fischer. His spirit is now in the sky somewhere higher. Everest's sum mit is a springboard for those who dream of rising above earthly concerns to examine their lives, expecting the height of this mountain to provide a vantage point that allows them to understand themselves better, hoping that when they descend, something will have changed inside.

There is no simple answer to what went through the minds of Scott Fischer and Rob Hall as they waited for help that never came. Perhaps they were able to understand something essential about themselves, about our drive to get to these summits. My thoughts during the last few ascents have evolved. When climbing the last meters or even stopping on the summit's snowy ledge, my understanding of the meaning of the achievement has changed. My sense of joy in the accomplishment and my satisfaction with being on the top is overshadowed by the wonder that one could make such an effort for the transitory reasons of human vanity. It is as though, arriving at the top, something has been forgotten or lost, and without that it is impossible for me to understand why I am standing there. A great emptiness fills me, and I experience tranquillity, knowing that when I go down, the world will be easier for me.

On the Lhotse summit, gazing at the route from the South Col to the highest point on the planet, it was important for me to believe that our ascent, achieved at such enormous cost and effort, had some lasting meaning. Something should change in the lives of those who aspire to climb to the summits covered with snow and rock. A human can be transformed by the effort that it takes to breathe the atmosphere above the clouds.

The wind intensified. Loss of ambition accelerated my desire to descend into the windless space. Reasons that down below had seemed so important had evaporated. Off the summit's rocky point, I reached the protected slope of the couloir and relaxed. Abruptly, the hurricane wind ceased; my surroundings became perfectly still. Had the wind understood that its efforts to push me into the abyss were useless? The summit of Everest was absolutely calm in the clear evening air; blameless, every reality was quieted by the advancing coldness of the darkening sky. I was amazed by the overwhelming tranquillity of that moment. My consciousness relaxed, tension left me, and exhaustion rolled over my body and through my muscles.

As I descended one of the steep sections in the couloir, my crampon slipped off its rocky support. I lost my balance and flew down the slope. With the strength in my arms and legs spent climbing up, I could not arrest my fall with my ice ax. Gaining speed, I slid fifteen meters down the incline. Some force stopped my flight. My crampons stuck solidly into the névé on a shelf no wider than my feet. Where did the strength come from that allowed me to hold my ground after the sudden stop? Below me, my trajectory dropped several hundred meters into a rocky funnel where there would have been no possibility of arresting my fall.

I felt no fear, nor did adrenaline give power to my movements. I wondered, "What kept me from dying this time?" As though every bit of strength had been used to make the stop, slowly I made a downward traverse to better footing. Absolute darkness enveloped me at the base of the couloir. I was wrung out physically as never before in my life. In the place I remembered leaving my backpack, I searched the ground, primitively coveting the bivouac sack, stove, and food it contained. Again I lost my balance, slipped off a steep, rocky shelf, and came to rest on a gentle slope of snow. As I fell, my down suit caught on a rock. The weak beam of my headlamp illuminated the finest-quality down feathers floating into the night air as I watched dispassionately. My excellent down suit! Analyzing myself carefully after the fall, I gave up looking for the pack; it might have been just a few steps away. I reached the fixed ropes at 7,600 meters and slowly continued my descent.

Sometime late in the night I arrived at Camp III. There was no wind; the sky held a blanket of enormous, bright stars. The same perfect sky had covered us one week before as we started out for the summit of Everest. My friend Michael Jörgensen, the Danish climber who had been with me on Everest in 1995, was waiting for me in the tent. I drank a cup of tea and slept.

I woke late the next day. There was no strength to follow the impulse to retrieve my backpack from above. I hardly had the power to make the short descent to shelter at Camp II, where I crawled into a sleeping bag in a sun-warmed tent, drank some tea, and slept until the next morning. My physical exhaustion caused me no concern. It was a relief that I was calm inside and that the oblivion of sleep came to me as a pleasure. The sad reality of Everest had drifted away and did not weigh on my brain and consciousness. My nerves relaxed and my heart became lighter, as if I had paid debts that had oppressed me for a long time. Physical labor had healed my suffering soul.

On May 19 I made my way down to Base Camp. No trace of the Mountain Madness expedition remained on the glacier. I borrowed a backpack from Michael and stuffed it full of my high-altitude equipment. After tea in the Himalayan Guides mess tent and reassuring friends that I was okay, about 6 P.M. I set out for the village of Namche Bazaar. Under a canopy of stars, I walked slowly down the Khumbu Valley, arriving at my destination, the Himalayan Lodge, early in the morning. Abruptly, I abandoned my cup of tea in Mingma's kitchen when I heard the distinctive sound of a helicopter flying up the valley to Syangboche airstrip. Shouldering a heavy pack, I rushed up the hill to the airstrip. I found our team preparing to board the waiting helicopter. I felt as if I were running to catch a moving train, and that train was called Life.

Return to Civilization

AMERICA AND THE SUMMER OF 1996

The morning of May 20, 1996, the Russian-made helicopter gained altitude, leaving the village of Namche Bazaar far below. The highest mountain in the world was put behind us. Other expeditions continued their assaults. Taking advantage of a period of excellent weather, several climbers, Ed Viesturs among them, achieved success without incident. The South African climber Bruce Harod was defeated and died during his descent. For us existence on the border between and life and death was over. Charlotte Fox limped slightly, bandages covering the frostbite blisters on her toes; Tim Madsen and Lene Gammelgaard had light damage to their fingers. Klev, Martin, and Sandy looked only tired and thinner. In the ensuing days, the frostbite on my nose and fingers caused the skin to blacken and peel, but there was no threat of amputation from the minor injuries we'd sustained.

The reality of the experience could recede and be sent to the shelves of memory. Details of the stormy night were a vague dream that those who had endured, frozen and oxygen-deprived, would try to make coherent later. Pieced-together fragments of personal memory would become the facts of the total reality. At that moment we were all looking forward, absorbed with our return to the real world, to the familiar world and atmosphere, which demanded no periods of acclimatization for human survival.

Civilization with its warmth and comfort was waiting for us in Kathmandu at the Yak and Yeti Hotel. Also waiting were members of the international press. It seemed the whole world knew about the tragedy on Everest, and mountaineering had become an interesting subject to the uninitiated. Reporters with television cameras met us at the airport. Lene Gammelgaard had a delegation of ten people sent from her homeland to record her return. In the face of the world's continuing wrecks, wars, catastrophes, and disasters, if not for the tragic aspect of our expedition, our return would have generated little public interest. Destruction and death fascinate the general public, especially those ordinary people who try hard to guarantee themselves a comfortable existence. They avoid at all cost risking the loss of happiness, health, and life.

In those first days members of our team were delighted with the small pleasures of civilization: the sun shining on the blueness of the water, the luxurious green of the cozy garden at the hotel, the variety of food, the sauna. For us the world was painted in more vivid colors and nothing was taken for granted. We lived in the moment, in that brief no-man's-land of return, not yet involved with the television, the telephone, the stress of work and small family problems.

In time the hustle and bustle of everyday life would make each of us forget that ordinary life held the possibility of such intense delight.

What drives an individual to climb mountains, to attempt the unnecessary, to risk life? What compels one to habitually abandon familiar comfort for such uncertainty? How can I explain this? Who has gone far away, experiencing the pain of separation, and not known the joy of homecoming? Who has thought life was lost and not rejoiced in the opportunity for a second chance? When the sense of wonder is dulled by the petty demands of civilization, I am pulled back to the mountains and their environment of primary contrast: stars of exceptional brilliance, great white snowfields, and the indigo sky melting to black in the death zone. The grandiose mountains and the blue glaciers strip the scales from a faded life and generate the same sense of awe and wonder that the sun's warmth, the greenness of the plants, and the blue water inspired during the first few days of our return to civilization.

Neal and I bid farewell to the other members of the expedition and stayed on in Kathmandu for two more days. On his shoulders Neal carried the brunt of responsibility for solving the numerous organizational problems that remained: settling accounts with the Sherpas for their work, completing the official paperwork with the Ministry of Tourism and HimTreks, the local agent in Nepal for Mountain Madness. I helped finish up this business as far as my limited knowledge of English would allow. I needed a visa, as on May 24 we were flying to America. I had been invited to attend Scott Fischer's memorial in Seattle.

The only legacy of the Communist era that survives in our countries is an archaic bureaucracy. Because the ambassador was out of town, the staff at the Russian embassy were paralyzed by my request for additional pages to be officially attached to my full passport. Kindly David Schenested, the American consular officer, circumvented the problem by giving me a U.S. visa.

With the business in Nepal finished, Neal and I passed through customs and relaxed in our seats on the plane that would take us to

Bangkok. After overnighting there, the next day we would fly to Los Angeles. A few minutes before our take-off time, an airline worker requested I accompany him to the exit. Neal and I gave one another puzzled looks. I joked out loud that Interpol was probably interested in my narcotics business, and I guessed my work was coming to an end. When I asked the airline official why my departure was being delayed, he said a friend wanted to see me immediately. "Friends?" I joked in a serious tone. "I do not have any friends or business partners in Nepal, everyone is already in the hands of Interpol."

Two television reporters with a cameraman were waiting for me at the exit; they asked me insignificant questions about my *samochuvstvie,* my future plans, and what had been the most meaningful part of the Everest experience for me. I had never experienced such attention from the media, not even after the most successful and difficult of my ascents in the Himalayas. This kept the plane waiting for fifteen minutes. When I returned, going down the aisle, I joked that the authorities did not have enough evidence to detain me. Neal and I drank a fair amount of Stolichnaya vodka and finally relaxed. We slept the sleep of those who are exhausted throughout the long flights to America.

On five previous visits to that country, my goal had been to get to know a different culture or to climb; this time I was going to pay my respects to the memory of a great American alpinist, Scott Fischer. I had no strength. I felt empty, tired physically and psychologically. Unpleasant dreams disturbed my sleep. I was caught in nightmares of struggle at high altitude, fatigued to the brink of collapse, rescuing endless numbers of people. The dreams did not end with my arrival in America; the scenario repeated itself night after night with ever-changing players. The two weeks before the memorial I spent recovering in Lynda Wylie's Santa Fe, New Mexico, home. My body and mind were so fatigued that I slept fifteen to twenty hours a day. Waking exhausted, I would eat, lie down, and fall back to sleep, coming to disoriented, startled by the ringing telephone. Reporters found me, even in America. The Everest story was a sensation.

On June 7 Linda and I flew to Seattle, where we stayed in the home of Jane Bromet, Scott Fischer's publicist. Before the memorial we were occupied trying to correct transcripts of a telephone interview with a reporter from *Men's Journal,* a popular American magazine. There was great interest in the Everest event both by professional mountaineers and those who are far from our world. I tried to answer the questions posed by interviewers and my friends. Should I have avoided those conversations? For those who were truly interested in high-altitude mountaineering, it was important to know the facts of what had happened. For myself I needed to understand the reasons for the critical situation I had endured. I had no reason to keep silent and understood perfectly well the importance of the information I possessed. Previous experience climbing above eight thousand meters made my perspective different, but retelling the incident intensified my dreams and increased my psychological fatigue.

At the memorial service in Seattle, I met Scott Fischer's family and friends. They were kind to me and I appreciated their words of gratitude for my efforts. His parents, sisters, and wife carried the heavy weight of suffering. There were familiar faces: most of our Mountain Madness team attended, and I met Henry Todd, who had flown in from Anchorage to attend the memorial. Moved by that outpouring of respect for Scott Fischer's mountaineering life, I felt the springs of inspiration winding up inside me, momentarily creating a mental readiness to struggle for a higher level of achievement.

Though the life has gone from Scott Fischer's body, in some ways he will always live: his ideas and his energy continue to exist in the common whirlpool of events. The American school of climbing will go in its own direction. Without doubt Scott Fischer made contributions to its development, both in his work as a guide and in his first American ascent of Lhotse. In a few years it may come to pass that only his close friends and family will remember him, but I hope that those good qualities he exemplified, those characteristics that surrounded him like a halo, are retained in the development of American mountaineering.

Scott was a strong man, able to keep all negative emotions deep inside him. In his relations with others and with the mountains, he was always more a romantic than a businessman. Providing guided adventure, he opened new worlds to others. In the short time we worked together on Everest, his ideas and way of thinking, that benevolence and strong spirit, gave a new impetus to my development as a mountaineer and as a person. His love of life and magnanimous nature awoke something in me. I want to preserve those feelings. I hope in the most difficult times, Scott Fischer will be my partner and that he will influence my way of thinking. I felt him with me during the storm while I was rescuing our clients. He was there as well on Lhotse, when I climbed in his memory. Looking back, I think that some unexplainable strength helped to accomplish that ascent, strength somehow linked to Scott Fischer and the power of his spirit.

I hope that our season on Everest has a positive influence on the psychology of those who entertain the idea of climbing that mountain. For strong people, it is a worthy task and an extreme test of the human spirit. Those who want to climb must not only be ready to pay with money; they must be physically and morally prepared for the ordeal of high altitude. Only in this way can they avoid the price of a higher penalty: their own lives or the lives of their guides. Each member of our team paid in full for the lessons he or she learned about preparation and experience. Somewhere we stepped over the permissible limit. It is easy to do this relying on bottled oxygen and the strength of others. Of course, if there had not been a storm, then everything would have been different. But random acts of nature conform to unidentifiable rules that we do not yet understand.

In Seattle there was no opportunity to sleep the fifteen to twenty hours a day that I was resting in Santa Fe. My energy and inspiration did not last; again my internal disequilibrium reached a critical level. I did not have the emotional strength to be with people day after day. I have a lot of friends in this country, and usually I am happy to see them; but this time I did not feel like meeting them. I flew to San Francisco, my body and muscles still unbelievably fatigued. I had only enough strength to write my thoughts, committing this story to paper, and to run in the hills with my friend Jack Robbins. Meanwhile, the dreams continued. I would awaken weak, possessed with ravenous hunger. I was devastated inside and indifferent to life. I traveled to Boulder and then back to Santa Fe. Thank God the dreams finally ended.

Friends called from all over the world asking about getting together or wanting to know my climbing plans for the coming year. This attention was comforting, but I was in no hurry to answer. I responded uncertainly to invitations to K2 and Everest. Aware of my fatigue and my slow recovery, I turned down an opportunity to take part in a Gasherbrum expedition with Dan Mazur. Answering questions and analyzing the situation, I arrived at several conclusions. I knew I wanted to return to the Himalayas and do something in a sports style. It would be difficult no doubt, but that prospect did not frighten me.

My mental state improved in proportion to my body's recuperation, and after six weeks I began to train again. My head began to fill with ideas: Annapurna in winter, a spring traverse of Everest and Lhotse in alpine style, a summer return to K2 on Messner's Magic Line. Everything would depend on my finances and on my technical and physical readiness. I confess that I was afraid of guiding work. Responsibility for another person is far harder than the most demanding sports ascent on any route. One must accept responsibility for so many contingencies over which there is no personal control. The most dangerous variable is the lack of proper preparation in those you are bound to assist. Assuming responsibility in that case slowly but surely eats away at your physical and psychological energy. Perhaps even the strongest personalities—men such as Scott Fischer and Rob Hall—did not have enough of this kind of energy. No one can guarantee success to people who are only ready to pay money to climb to the top of the planet. Anyone with that ambition should begin by ascending a number of 7,000-meter peaks and then easier 8,000-meter peaks. With adequate background experience and luck with the weather, it is possible for a climber to summit Mount Everest without particular risk to his life or the life of the guide.

Why do trials such as the one we endured on Everest fascinate people? Do people go to the mountains to be tested? Indeed, for someone who did not end up in a storm but enjoyed good weather, who followed a well-established trail and climbed fixed ropes, slept in comfortable camps and relied on a steady supply of oxygen carried by Sherpas, ascending Everest would pose no particular difficulty. During this same season, along the very same route, a number of climbers who were not in any physical shape comparable to mine achieved my basic results: they reached the summit of Everest and survived. To this fact you can only throw up your hands and say, "*C'est la vie.*" Always, some are more lucky in life. When you climb a mountain at high altitude, if you are counting on luck, you are playing *hussar*—Russian roulette as you call it in the West. Mercenaries employed by the czar, who in their boredom engaged in all manner of strange amusements, invented that game. One out of every ten people who has tried to climb Everest has died.

You must always be prepared for the worst variant during an ascent at high altitude, and this is especially true of Everest. Sometimes situations develop that cannot be predicted or controlled, despite the best experience and preparation. The variabilities of weather and individual responses increase proportionally with elevation. The likelihood of survival decreases in bad weather or if a climber has underlying health problems. I am incredulous when I hear guides say they have never lost a client climbing Everest, as if expertise alone could prevent this. Unfortunately there is no guarantee against loss of life at high elevation, neither for an experienced guide nor for a novice who pays exorbitant sums of money and climbs with the support of guides and a number of Sherpas. The probability of dying in a storm at eight thousand meters is about the same for both these individuals. A sad example of this is the outcome of the cold night Scott Fischer and Makalu Gau endured on May 10.

Scott's high-altitude experience far surpassed that of Makalu Gau, but Gau survived the night though both of them had climbed the same route using supplemental oxygen. You can only guess why one was luckier than the other. Yet one marked difference between these two men was that as expedition leader and guide, Scott carried an incomparably higher burden of responsibility. Makalu was nurturing his own ambition. I will say with certainty, a guide who carries the psychological responsibility for clients has about two times the risk of dying as an ordinary mountaineer on the same undertaking. My observation is confirmed by the tortured experience of professionals struggling to the last minute for the life of a fatally weakened client. I do not believe that if a client is dying at high altitude, then a guide should also die. Before anyone goes to the mountain, both clients and guides must squarely face the grim risk inherent in their undertaking and the well-documented limits to effective "assistance" at high altitude.

Yes, I feel lucky that I did not die working three days and three nights on or above the South Col in extreme conditions with my fate tied to that of inexperienced climbers. There was no time for me to analyze the situation, no energy for clear thinking; decisions were made hastily, fatal exhaustion always accumulating in the background. Some moments, I felt like a robot with many programs in my head. Relying on experience, I picked the most acceptable program. In such circumstances a mistake could have cost my life or the lives of people for whom I was taking responsibility. I was aware of this reality most keenly the night I returned from Scott's body in the blizzard. I had enough strength to descend and wander blindly for four hours on the Col before locating our tents, but how would the next guided expedition turn out?

All through that summer, members of the popular American press and professional mountaineers analyzed the events on Everest. Unfortunately, my opinions about the reasons for our loss were not correctly understood. Perhaps this is because these reasons are found in each of us. They are the roots of our civilization. Rob Hall and Scott Fischer were the best examples of high-altitude guides on Everest, and they did not break any existing rules. Civilization with its values came to the high mountains. Commerce and business reached the highest point on the planet. Sadly, none of us could escape this. The realm above eight thousand meters is a world unto itself with rules inherent only to itself. The right to go there is not available for a price. You can pay for a guide's experience, experience he has accumulated during decades of work, but to use it correctly and to survive when the situation becomes critical at eight thousand meters depends on the strength of the individual. In the worst case a guide is only able to die, having assumed impossible responsibility for a client's survival.

Neither the writers or publishers, who had no understanding of reality at high altitude, nor professional mountaineers who had dedicated their lives to climbing, wanted to acknowledge that simple truth. I do not know how a person climbing above eight thousand meters for the first time can hope to assimilate the experience a guide has acquired over decades. The lack of experience will be acutely telling if that person is caught in deteriorating weather. Only by luck, randomly wandering in zero visibility, did I not fall off an 8,000-meter-high cliff or into a crevasse. My clients' luck was that I had enough strength in reserve to help them survive. Rob Hall and his clients were not so lucky.

In America my actions were misinterpreted and my descent from the summit was condemned, though regarding that action I had first consulted with Rob Hall and then with Scott Fischer. Neither of them disagreed with my decision to descend quickly to be ready to resupply our flagging clients. At that moment and throughout the expedition no one could have suspected me of being a coward or weak or choosing the easiest job for myself. I can look in anyone's eyes and say I did the best I knew how to do for our team.

Basically I spent the summer engaged in stormy discussions and arguments stirred up by the slant put on events by the publicity in America. My critics were either people who did not have a professional understanding of the situation or those professionals who had not endured such circumstances. They thought I should have used supplemental oxygen during the ascent. For most people that issue became the trump card in evaluating my work. Although I felt no guilt, I wanted to defend my professional honor. I agreed to write my recollections for a book about our expedition. I have nothing

During the spring 1996 Mountain Madness expedition, Anatoli's third
successful ascent of Mount Everest would take a great toll in suffering, testing
his physical and emotional resources as never before. "Everest will always be
Everest," he said. He captured this view of the great peak's South Col and
summit from the slopes of Lhotse. *(Collection of Anatoli Boukreev)*

Sherpani Ang Sona offering tea at P. K. Sherpa's Khumbu Lodge. Anatoli spent the night in his favorite lodge in Namche Bazaar during his trek to Everest Base Camp. March 1996. *(Collection of Anatoli Boukreev)*

ABOVE: 1996 Mountain Madness team members: Front row *(left to right)*: Scott Fischer, Charlotte Fox; middle row *(left to right)*: Neal Beidleman, Sandy Hill Pittman, Martin Adams, and Lene Gammelgaard, sirdar Ngima Sherpa, Sherpa support staff; back row *(left to right)*: Dale Kruse, Klev Schoening, Anatoli, Pete Schoening, and Tim Madsen. *(Collection of Anatoli Boukreev)*

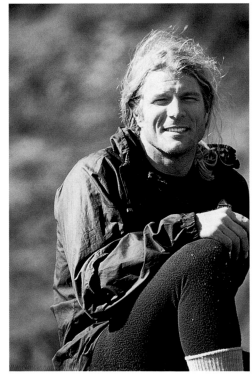

Scott Fischer, Mountain Madness owner and expedition leader, during the trek to Everest Base Camp. March 1996. *(Photo © Jane Bromet)*

Pumori's summit wreathed in clouds rises behind Mountain Madness climbers on the route between Camp I and Camp II on Mount Everest. Spring 1996.
(Collection of Anatoli Boukreev)

Anatoli at the South Col on May 12 after his attempted rescue of Scott Fischer. *(Photo © Brigitte Muir)*

After the Mountain Madness expedition, Anatoli flew to America to attend the memorial service for Scott Fischer. Friend Jane Bromet captured a familiar gentleness in his face in this portrait taken in her kitchen in Seattle in June 1996. *(Photo © Jane Bromet)*

In America, a summer of controversy made Anatoli long for the "peaks that prop up the Tibetan sky." Seen here in September, he waves from a marker on Tibet's Tingeri plain with Cho Oyu rising behind him. (*Collection of Anatoli Boukreev*)

FACING PAGE: The summit of Cho Oyu and Anatoli at Camp I, 6,500 meters. (*Collection of Anatoli Boukreev*)

BELOW: After a self-supported alpine ascent of Cho Oyu, Anatoli moved on to climb Shisha Pangma, the only one of the world's 8,000-meter peaks located totally in Tibet. (*Collection of Anatoli Boukreev*)

The first traverse of the Lhotse-Everest massif was Anatoli's sports objective for his spring climbing season in 1997. The Lhotse-Everest massif seen from the summit of Pumori: Lhotse is the central peak; Everest is left on the skyline. Prior to attempting the traverse, as tactical leader and coach he summited Everest with members of the First Indonesian Everest Expedition. *(Photo © Dr. Gregory Anton Gordon)*

FACING PAGE, TOP: Buddhist prayer flags whipping in the wind at Everest Base Camp, March 1997, as a local Lama blesses the efforts of members of the 1997 Indonesian Everest Expedition. *(Collection of Anatoli Boukreev)*

FACING PAGE, BOTTOM: After their successful summit attempt, Anatoli made the decision to night-over his beleaguered Indonesian team at 8,500 meters below the summit of Everest. They camped on a small aerie with dramatic views; this photo of the camp was taken the morning of April 27, 1997. Makalu is seen behind, floating in a sea of clouds. *(Collection of Anatoli Boukreev)*

Broad Peak, Pakistan. June 1997. *(Collection of Anatoli Boukreev)*

Gasherbrum II. *(Collection of Anatoli Boukreev)*

1997 speed ascent of Gasherbrum II. Self–portrait on the summit. *(Collection of Anatoli Boukreev)*

Anatoli at Gasherbrum II
Base Camp. July 1997.
(Photo © Bob Ader)

In July 1997, Anatoli
joined an expedition
led by old friend Gary
Neptune of Boulder,
Colorado, for the
opportunity to climb
Gasherbrum II in Pakistan.
Gary photographed
Anatoli descending to
Base Camp after his
nine-and-one-half-hour
ascent of the 8,047-meter-
high summit. *(Photo ©
Gary Neptune)*

The South Face of Annapurna glows in the setting sun, December 1997. After conversations with Vladimir Bashkirov in September 1996, Anatoli set his mind on an alpine ascent of a new route up this face. *(Collection of Anatoli Boukreev)*

When he and teammates Simone Moro and Dima Sobolev arrived at Base Camp in early December 1997, their progress was stymied by a series of storms that dumped a record snowfall on the Himalaya. *(Collection of Anatoli Boukreev)*

Anatoli abandoned the steep South Face route because of avalanche danger. He decided to approach the mountain's top from the Western Ridge via Annapurna Fang, ascending to the ridge at the low point above Simone Moro. Using snow caves for camp, they would traverse right along the wind-hardened ridge to the summit of Annapurna I. *(Collection of Anatoli Boukreev)*

After completely stocking Camp I at 5,500 meters with food and gas, Dima Sobolev, Anatoli, and Simone Moro descended to Gandruk on December 17 for a "Russian" rest. Simone and Anatoli spent two days soaking in the local hot springs. *(Collection of Anatoli Boukreev)*

The bracing effects of a glacial plunge in the Modi Kola River put a smile on Tolya's face. December 18, 1997. *(Collection of Anatoli Boukreev)*

Anatoli waves from below Camp I; behind him, the colors of the sunset fade above the heart of Annapurna Sanctuary. December 22, 1997. *(Collection of Anatoli Boukreev)*

derogatory to say about Rob Hall and Scott Fischer. They are men I truly respect, whose courage and valor I will always admire. Neither did I have any desire to impugn the opinions of my opponents: each had his own point of view of the events based on his level of experience. However, I was disappointed in the people whom I knew who kept silent. I had counted on their support.

By the middle of August the pressure of these arguments became an intolerable weight. I felt defenseless and was psychologically exhausted by the accusations. I knew the best medicine for me would be hard physical labor. I needed to breathe the oxygen-depleted air surrounding the giants that prop up the Tibetan sky.

Cho Oyu

I was able to put the situation in America behind me at the beginning of the autumn climbing season in the Himalayas. By mid-September I was back in Nepal, with my name included on a joint Kazakh-Japanese permit for Cho Oyu. I also paid to join a group of strong Russians led by Vladimir Bashkirov who were going to climb Shisha Pangma. Their plans were the same as mine: to do back-to-back ascents of the two 8,000-meter peaks in Tibet. The experienced Russians had been working on the first mountain since the end of August. Jeeps were scheduled to arrive at the Cho Oyu trailhead on September 30 to transport them to Shisha Pangma. I knew there was not much time for me to catch up with the Russians, who, I surmised as I was leaving Kathmandu, were probably well-acclimatized and close to making a summit bid.

I had spent most of the summer in Santa Fe, New Mexico, living at 2,500 meters. To maintain a degree of acclimatization, my weekly training program included a long speed ascent to 3,200 meters. Obviously, that did not prepare me for the elevation gain that was ahead of me. In the past when I had had breaks from high altitude of more than two months, my body had required gradual acclimatization for more than ten days. To catch up with the Russian team, I would have to push myself to acclimatize in a more condensed time frame. I wondered if that was physically possible.

Although I'd paid my portions of the permit cost and yak transportation on both expeditions, to save money I was not going to use the facilities of either team at Base Camp. Climbing alone without the help of Sherpas or other teammates would make my work several times harder. I could not actually call what I intended to do a "solo ascent" because other expeditions would be working simultaneously on the common route, but I was committed to relying on my own resources to accomplish my goal. As a sportsman, it would have been much more interesting for me to attempt a new route. But those kinds of expeditions are difficult to join, and they are always more expensive. Without partners who will share expedition costs, an individual must have $30,000 to finance a first ascent. Commerce is a creation of civilization, and the high mountains are now commercial concerns with high prices. Fed up with those constraints, I was interested in spending as little money as possible and climbing the mountains independent of outside help.

At 5 P.M. on September 17, I pulled my gear out of the Land Cruiser parked below Tingri Mountain at the end of the dirt track where climbers begin the trek to Cho Oyu. The elevation was 5,100 meters. My personal gear—down suit, plastic boots, tent, stove, food, kerosene, and my sleeping bag—went into my pack, a thirty-kilogram load for my shoulders. The physical stress of my adventure was increasing in inverse proportion to the amount of money that I spent, but here no weak clients or partners were tying my hands. I understood the facts perfectly well, and it gave me a sense of freedom that I had never known before when climbing a high mountain. My ambition, readiness, and desire would determine all my actions.

With that psychological momentum, I shouldered my pack and began the trek to Base Camp in the early-morning twilight on September 18. The mountain looked amicable; all day the sun illuminated the summit in a cloudless sky. Nightfall found me climbing an upgrade of rocky scree. Though the route was unfamiliar, it felt as if

I were home. Seven hours of climbing brought me to the foot of the northwest crest of the eighth-highest mountain in the world.

Somewhere on the rubble at 5,700 meters among the tents belonging to different expeditions were the Russians. In the past, as members of the Combined Team of the USSR, we had climbed many mountains together. Among the group was a countryman from the Urals: Evgeny Vinogradski, a veteran of the traverse of Kanchenjunga. Locating them was easy. Only they were not sleeping at that hour; the men enjoyed playing cards late into the night. The whole team was in camp resting for their imminent summit bid. Our reunion was emotional. We had endured a long separation. Oblivious of time, we talked long into the night. I did not get to bed until the early hours of the morning.

My friends had prepared their high camps and acclimatized in spite of unstable weather. The eighteenth was only the second day since their arrival that it had not snowed. The nineteenth was a magnificent day. Feeling good, I loaded my pack and at 3 P.M. was on my way up a well-beaten trail. My intention was to continue up to the altitude where my body and mind gave the signs that I was not ready for a further increase in elevation. Four hours later I stopped for the night at 6,500 meters. I was sleepy after the eight-hundred-meter height gain, but I did not feel nauseated nor did I have a headache. Skipping supper, I drank hot tea from my thermos and fell asleep quickly. The next morning I took my waking pulse. It was a little faster than my normal forty-five beats per minute. Other than a loss of appetite, I had no symptoms of altitude sickness. Three hours later I arrived at Camp II at 7,000 meters. Apathy and muscle fatigue were new sensations, but I still felt no nausea or headache. My muscles were somewhat cottonlike because of the rapid ascent. I decided against pushing my luck, though there was enough light in the day for me to climb higher.

I stashed my equipment for the summit bid in a waterproof bag. In one hour I was back at Camp I, changing into my leather trekking boots. There I deposited my crampons and heavy plastic boots. Two hours later back in Base Camp, I continued to have no appetite, but that I took as a normal sensation during my body's adjustment. For supper I drank tea and ate a little dried fruit. I went to bed early, too fatigued to enjoy the interesting stories my friends were sharing about the events in their lives since we had last been together. Our reality had changed 180 degrees since 1989. It was especially difficult for professional mountaineers and other sportsmen to adjust to the abrupt process of commercialization that followed the collapse of the Soviet Union.

Despite the pressure of rapid ascent, the two days of hard labor had improved my *samochuvstvie*. That validated a personal theory I have that it is better to acclimatize by working hard and stressing the body. I had spent three and one-half months recovering from Lhotse, my last 8,000-meter success in the spring. Before that rest, in the period between May 17, 1995 and May 17, 1996, I had climbed Everest twice, Dhaulagiri, Manaslu, and Lhotse—five peaks higher than eight thousand meters. (I know of only one other climber, Carlos Carsolio, who has summited four 8,000-meter peaks in twelve months.) My body felt ready for the hard work, and I had no doubts it would tolerate the rapid acclimatization. Still, I had to pay attention because I did not want to fall prey to some infection that would compromise my respiratory system or, worse, my gastrointestinal track. Dramatic environmental change, dry mountain air, and physical stress leaves no one immune to these illnesses when climbing.

I slept that night without any problems, a good indicator for me that my body was functioning properly. The next day I enjoyed a rest, only allowing myself a walk around Base Camp. Stable weather continued; the sky was cloudless, the air calm. It was pleasant hiding from the strong mountain sun, lying with my muscles relaxed in the luxurious warmth of my tent. I could hear the Russians busy with preparations for the next day's summit bid. Should I begin the assault tomorrow as well, I wondered, or should I give my body another day of rest?

Part of the team left camp early on September 24; others waited to begin after the benefit of a good lunch. When questioned about my plans, I answered vaguely. I was enjoying my freedom and independence. I could follow my impulses. I was consciously trying to keep my actions in line with my body's feelings of readiness. Camp was empty when about three in the afternoon I decided to begin. Packing took an hour and I was on my way.

Russell Brice, the experienced English guide, took advantage of that day of good weather and led his climbers to the summit. At 7,800 meters a huge snow pack rolled off the slope, thundered down the mountain, and ran out only two hundred meters before Camp II. Russell's team was barely above the avalanche's point of origin. The famous Japanese alpinist Yuko Tabey was in that lucky group. (Some years ago, she became the first woman to summit Everest; she has not given up her hobby, continuing to climb 8,000-meter peaks in her old age using bottled oxygen.)

Traveling light, I arrived at Camp I in time to admire the incredible colors of the sunset reflected in the sky above the mountains. After supper I quickly fell asleep inside my small one-man tent. At 9 A.M. the next day, I began climbing along the easy crest to the next camp, on the way encountering some familiar faces. Henry Todd and his team were going down to rest after two nights of acclimatization at Camp II. The combination of brilliant sunlight and heat robbed me of enthusiasm and energy—the disadvantage of perfectly calm weather at high elevation. By the time I arrived at 7,000 meters the Russians were finishing tea and preparing to leave for Camp III. With the weather in the afternoon showing signs of impending change, they hoped to reach the summit the next day and descend before it started snowing again. Headed for their high camp at 7,300 meters, they crossed the fresh pattern of snow left by the huge avalanche.

The brother of the famous Polish climber Maciej Berbeka joined me. From our conversation, I learned that he, like me, had arrived on the eighteenth and was making his first trip to 7,000 meters. He had come directly from Pakistan after an unsuccessful attempt to climb Nanga Parbat. In response to his suggestion that we try for the summit together, I shrugged my shoulders, answering that I would see tomorrow. My actions had to depend on how I felt. The situation for him was less complex because of his good acclimatization on Nanga.

We agreed it would be a shame to ignore that the gods had favored us with good weather, but I would only go as high as my body told me was permissible. Berbeka went to bed early.

As a precaution against strong winds, I invested a lot of time digging a wide depression in the snow to shelter my tent. I fixed a late dinner and prepared for the morning by melting a good quantity of snow into water. Feeling good, I climbed into my sleeping bag about 9 P.M. and slept well during my first night at that altitude. About three in the morning, my Polish campmate could be heard putting on crampons, followed by the clanking of equipment and the crunch of snow as he left for the summit. For another hour, I dozed in the warmth of my sleeping bag, then began to make my own preparations. Instant oatmeal and a huge mug of instant coffee sufficed for breakfast. Dried fruit, a chocolate bar, a thermos of tea, and a thermos of water were stashed in the roomy pockets of my old down suit. About 5 A.M. with the beam from my headlamp illuminating the slope, I started up, digging my crampons in the snow, balancing with my ice ax and a ski pole.

The tents of Camp III were deserted when I arrived at 7 A.M. Away off ahead, I saw bobbing lights and dark silhouettes ascending a steep belt of rock at 7,500 meters. The stars were dying into the fantastic colors that illuminated the morning sky. At my pace, I would quickly overtake the group of backed-up climbers who were taking turns negotiating that dangerous section of steep snow and rock. It seemed like a stupid idea to push ahead only to wait in the cold behind them. A lack of sleep and the new elevation made me drowsy. The best way out of the situation seemed to be to wait in the Russian tent. Protected from the wind and warm in my down suit, immediately I was asleep. When I awoke at 9 A.M. restored, it validated a good conditioning program.

The twenty meters of steep rocks were put behind easily. With no one to be seen ahead, I continued at a deliberate pace, taking no more breaks for rest. About 11 A.M., two figures appeared in a halo of sun rays. My altimeter recorded 7,800 meters. Men from St. Petersburg were returning from the summit; we stopped to talk. In the past

I knew them as high-altitude mountaineers. Now they are examples of a new generation of entrepreneurs in Russia: men who tear themselves away from the tenacious grip of business for a month and pay their way to the Himalayas. They estimated that I had four hours of climbing ahead of me to the peak. The route became less steep, crossing a long plain. My pace was slow and steady and I encountered a few people descending, mainly Russians. Just before the top I caught up with Vinogradski. A team of Koreans going down breathing bottled oxygen passed us. Their Sherpas followed, loaded down with equipment, food, and water. Without much strain or effort, Zhenya and I arrived at our goal at 1 P.M.

Suddenly the weather changed; snow started to fall and thick clouds swirled in from all sides, reducing visibility. Denied the majestic views of Everest and Lhotse, our neighbors to the east, after a few summit photos we moved down into the fog. I caught up with a large group of climbers negotiating the section of steep slope above Camp III. Past that obstacle, I continued down to the security of my tent below.

I slept that night delighting in the fatigue that comes after such hard physical work. In the morning after a leisurely breakfast, I packed up and moved carefully down the crest, my balance secured by crampons and ski poles. At Camp I, I met the Kazakh climbers who had arrived at that elevation for their first night of acclimatization. Astonishment and disbelief registered in their eyes when I told them I had been on the summit the day before.

After that, we had several days before the yaks would arrive to transport our gear down to the waiting Jeeps. During that interval, I rested and poured out my open heart to my Russian friends. For a long time I had missed their presence in the high mountains. The Kazakh climbers were acting as guides for five Japanese men who had prepared for Cho Oyu by climbing in the Tien Shan. To my surprise these Japanese men were open and sociable; we celebrated the birthday of the strongest one in their group. He planned to summit without the use of bottled oxygen. After a festive dinner, we listened as a harmonious choir from the Land of the Rising Sun sang songs about their homeland.

On the twenty-seventh the weather deteriorated: the temperature dropped, heavy snow fell. The following day the clouds were dissipated by gusts of wind and the sun broke through. Happily, I handed over my barrels of equipment to the yak drivers. Toward dinnertime, I left advanced Base Camp burdened only with a small pack. Five hours later I was at the trailhead. The Jeeps that would take us across the Tibetan plateau arrived the next evening.

Shisha Pangma, Tibet

Lounging on mats at our encampment on the wide Tibetan plain on October 2, we watched as the yaks appeared out of nowhere. To the sounds of whistles, bells, and barking dogs, they were soon loaded with our equipment and supplies. Shisha Pangma is the only 8,000-meter peak located totally in Tibet. Snow and wind conditions on her slopes had forestalled the success of a number of expeditions that season. A French team quit the day we arrived. On our way into Base Camp we met them retreating. The summit of Shisha beckoned us with its beauty; it seemed harmless and accessible. The weather had been sunny and pleasant since we'd left Cho Oyu. With no difficulty we crossed a pass and arrived in camp seven hours later, right after our yaks.

Ukrainian climbers invited us to lunch. The two most experienced members of their team were at that moment on their way to Camp II at 7,000 meters. Victor Pastukh and Gennady Vasilenko had been members of the 1989 Kanchenjunga team; via radio they said hello to me and promised that we would celebrate our reunion over a bottle of beer. The last time I had seen the Ukrainians together had been in the fall of 1994 after their attempt on Dhaulagiri. Now the Soviet Union is divided into many states and sovereignties, and it is easier for us, her mountaineers, to meet on the neutral ground of Himalayan land. Over lunch, the men in camp gave us the details of climbing Shisha's technically easy route. The main difficulties were the large accumulations of snow and the force of the wind above

6,500 meters. An Italian team had established Camp III at 7,300 meters using skis, which made the work of breaking trail through deep snow easier.

After setting up my tent between the campsites of the Russians and the Ukrainians, I sorted my equipment. My plan was to dedicate a day to rest, making only a short equipment carry across the glacier, and to begin the assault in earnest on October 4. That evening, mountaineers from the former republics gathered in the big Ukrainian tent to celebrate our reunion with drinking and talking. A climber from South Korea had joined the Russian team after their Cho Oyu ascent, and that night I noticed he was shy and seemed to be uncomfortable among our boisterous group of animated Soviets.

Seventy-year-old Vladimir Monogarov, the famous coach of the Ukrainian team, invited me to visit the *banya* that had been improvised next to a glacial lake near camp. So I enjoyed the luxury of bathing in a well-heated tent with hot water and a rest before packing up my equipment for the assault. The true beginning of the route up the north side of Shisha starts at about 5,900 meters, after you cross a glacier that flows down from the side slopes. It took two hours to pick my way through the rocks and arrive at the place where an ice ax and crampons were necessary to climb higher. I deposited my equipment, pleased that the next day I could cross that section quickly and unencumbered on a familiar path.

The weather took a sudden turn for the worse. Wet snow fell throughout the night. In those conditions, I had no impulse to climb out of my tent early. The Russians set out from camp after breakfast with heavy packs. The snow fell continuously with increasing intensity. There was nothing for me to do but dress more warmly and get going. In six days the yaks would arrive to take our gear back to the waiting Jeeps. There was no time to sit comfortably in camp. Perhaps the weather conditions would improve, but I was somewhat reassured because I knew that the Ukrainians who were now at Camp II were scheduled to come down. They would break the trail. Their tracks would help me avoid the danger of wandering off the route.

Blowing snow reduced visibility to a few meters ahead when I left Base Camp; it had also erased the tracks made by the Russians only two hours before. I reached my stashed equipment, but it had become impossible for me to assess the overrising slopes for avalanche potential. All my effort took me to just 6,000 meters, only a little higher than the previous day. I decided to set up camp in the first place that seemed reasonably safe. Hoping I had selected a secure spot, at about 5 P.M. I climbed into my tent and settled in for the night. Despite the foul weather, in the warmth of my sleeping bag I was comfortable and fell deeply asleep until morning. It snowed all night. By breakfast, the wind had calmed slightly. I peered out of the tent into a milky vapor and could only see a few meters. I cooked breakfast, then waited. The snowfall let up around lunchtime. Visibility seemed to improve.

Sometime later I heard voices . . . the descending Ukrainians? Victor and Gennady should be with them, I thought. I greeted the men, but my friends weren't with them.

"Gennady and Victor wanted to make it up to Camp III before descending to rest," I was told.

Two hours before, during a radio contact, they had reported they were on the way down, at about the level of Camp II. They said that they would try to catch up with their teammates.

When asked about my immediate plans, I said that I was going to wait a couple more hours and let the weather suggest what I should do. I could not see the side slopes of the mountain, and by that time avalanche danger was severe. Obviously I did not want to ascend without being able to judge that hazard, but going all the way back to camp meant losing precious time. After our encounter, I began to pack. I felt ambivalent about going up, but neither did I desire to stay where I was, waiting. Without the weight of my pack and supplies to carry, Base Camp was two hours away. Something was nagging me; the day before I had chosen my campsite in a dense fog. I wasn't at all certain I was in a secure spot. Seventy to eighty centimeters of fresh snow now burdened the slopes above me. Even gentle slopes will avalanche in such conditions, and that had become a big risk. I waited an hour in the tent; the snowfall was light, but did not totally stop.

Stepping outside the tent, I tried to judge the conditions on the side slopes of the huge icy, snow-filled couloir above me. It was 4 P.M. I remember thinking that apparently Victor and Gennady were not in much of a hurry to catch up with the rest of their team. Through the breaks in the low clouds and fog, I searched the mountainside for the trail left by the descending climbers. The oncoming cold of evening improved visibility significantly. The contours of the side slopes rose above me. I made out the fresh tracks bisecting the couloir. No one was on the slope. Judging by the elapsed time, if Victor and Gennady were coming down, they should have been visible on the face, descending toward my tent.

Surveying the relief, searching for the approximate location of Camp I, I watched as a huge snow slab collapsed off the right wall. It gained speed and strength, crossed the ascent route, and was headed straight toward my tent. The dull boom of the snow layer tearing off the mountain hit me; the front line of the avalanche was a kilometer away in a direct line. Though I had taken the precaution of placing my tent behind a three-meter-high ice wall, I understood instantly that I was in danger. An avalanche this size would blanket the base of the couloir with a layer of snow many meters thick. This analysis took place as I ran away from the approaching cloud in giant leaps. My thoughts separated from my body, as though my consciousness were objectively observing the outcome of my situation from a distance. The blast of air preceding the avalanche hit my back. It propelled me forward. Immediately a squalling wind, dense with suspended snow dust, plastered my back, head to foot. I pulled myself together, covered my face and mouth with my light anorak, and prepared to receive the main blow of snow. It did not follow. One hundred and fifty meters separated me from my camp and equipment. One hundred meters beyond my tent was a completely new relief. I estimated the depth of the avalanche snow. It took away my appetite for risk that day. Leaving behind my tent, my equipment, and my backpack, I ran away from that place, hoping to reach Base Camp before sunset.

An hour outside of camp, I caught up with the Ukrainians. They had no news from Gennady and Victor. I shared an optimistic assessment; maybe their radio batteries had died, which often happens on long trips; or after appraising the snow conditions, they might have decided to stay at Camp I with Russian friends for the night. At that moment, the possibility that my predictions were wrong did not occur to me.

The next morning, the day was beautiful; not a cloud was in the sky. Normally when the weather is excellent, it puts everyone in a good mood, but not this day for members of the Ukrainian team or for me. As the day progressed, our worries about our friends increased. The slopes of the mountain were clearly visible, with no sign of anyone descending from Camps I or II. Our alarm intensified when about lunchtime we could see a group of eight people (definitely the Russian team) climbing along the snowy rise between the two campsites. The groups had not arranged a way to contact one another in the event of unforeseen circumstances.

There was no way to find out if they had seen Victor and Gennady's tracks. Had they perished in the avalanche I'd witnessed, or in another? Perhaps descending in the fog, they had ventured into a zone of ice faults and fallen into some crevasse overladen with unconsolidated snow. The day before I had come close to making the wrong decision myself. I could easily have gotten lost or ended up in the avalanche if I had tried to ascend that fateful day. What had made me hesitate to climb along that slope just one hour before the avalanche? Perhaps it was intuition, perhaps it was just too much effort to go up. It was easier to climb down to the warmth of Base Camp. Did that inviting prospect entice my friends as well? They had survived many situations far more dangerous than the conditions we had been in the day before. It was difficult to accept that men who had completed numerous dangerous routes, who had a huge bank of mountaineering experience behind them, had disappeared into an abyss.

On October 7, three strong Italian alpine guides left Base Camp ahead of me, beginning their summit bid. I advised the leader of the Ukrainian team that I planned to climb directly to Camp II that day if I could. He gave me a radio with new batteries to deliver to our friends. If they were safe and sound, we had a way to reestablish communication. In the equipment in the Russian camp, I located a shortwave radio tuned to the frequency that they were using. That I handed over to Vladimir Monogarov before I left camp.

By 9 A.M. I had crossed the glacier and was close to the spot where I had left my tent and gear; there was evidence of a second avalanche. Had it buried my gear? After a moment of real concern, I could see that it, too, had stopped behind the snow wall. Looking up the couloir, just below the plateau where Camp I was located, I could see the Italians ascending, two of them using cross-country skis.

I heated up water for tea and quickly prepared some breakfast. Not wasting time, I packed up my tent and gear and headed up. I climbed out of the couloir onto the vast plateau above, only to be greeted by a bitter wind. The tents of the camp were battered and snow-burdened, but their location was completely free of avalanche danger. Hoping to find my missing friends in the Ukrainian tent, I pulled open the flap and disturbed the Italians, who were making tea. They reported they'd seen no tracks on the slope when they'd come up. I established radio contact with the Ukrainian Base Camp. To my surprise and joy, I learned that my friends were with the Russian team on the way to Camp III at 7,300 meters. Everything was okay, the guys had been found.

After eating a little I put on my down suit and decided to continue up to Camp II to spend the night. If the weather the next day was good enough for a summit assault, the Russian team would leave early from Camp III. I would be able to catch up with them. I thought how much easier it would be to break trail through this deep snow in our old group, our effort fortified by the strength of Victor and Gennady.

There wasn't a cloud in the sky. The only flaw was the wind. Crossing the plateau, I pressed myself low against the slope and faced the full pressure of the gusting squall. Two Italians followed me on skis; the third man climbed as I did. Midway across the plateau, the skiers passed me. Each meter was conquered with effort, every step I went up to my knees in new snow. At the beginning of the rise that would take us to the next step, the third Italian, Simone Moro, caught up with me. My pace was slow, and we changed positions. He worked well and fast; we covered the trail to the lip of the rise before Camp II in about four hours. There the wind increased to hurricane force. The weight I carried reduced me to a creep. At last I arrived at the tents of Camp II in pitch darkness. Generously, the Italians offered me tea and shared their plans. If the weather was favorable, they intended to leave for the summit that night at 3 A.M. They hoped to be at the beginning of the steep, dangerous summit crest by dawn. I predicted that the Russian team would also be on the route, and our possibility of success would be much greater if we all worked together.

Saying good-night, I situated myself next to the Italians' tent and climbed into my sleeping bag wearing my down suit. I pulled my bivouac sack up over my head, leaving only a small space for breathing. At 4 A.M. I heard my neighbors preparing for the assault. I heated up water for tea on my kerosene stove, made breakfast, and departed from camp about an hour behind the Italians. The hard crust of snow supported my steps across the plateau. In an hour and a half I reached the beginning of a ridge. When the first rays of sun hit me, I was protected from the wind in the lee of the steep ice slope, and I could move without difficulty. In an hour I had clambered to the crest and again faced a blast of hurricane force. I had to crawl. The wind was strong enough to rip me off the slope and throw me down like a piece of weightless fluff. Driving my ax deep into the snow with all my power, I moved forward by dragging my body anchored by the pick.

At Camp III there were only two Russian tents. Everyone, including the Italians, had to be in them. Without doubt, I knew that my friends had postponed their summit bid. I shouted a loud greeting, asking in which tent I could find Victor and Gennady, saying that I had their radio. Total silence was the response to my greeting. Then team leader Vladimir Bashkirov said, "Anatoli, they are not here." The Russians had contacted Base Camp only hours before. I understood that yesterday someone in camp had given me false information. Perhaps it was too much for him to accept that the two great mountaineers were dead.

The Italians, who were experienced mountain guides, climbed out of the tent to say good-bye to me. When I asked about their plans, they waved their hands in disappointment. Their Jeeps were arriving in two days, so they had no time to try again. After their departure, I spoke with my Russian friends about Victor and Gennady. Everyone knew these men and each was suffering their deaths. They had not been seen for four days. Two big avalanches had come down below Camp I, covering more than half that route in a mass of snow. Another avalanche had obliterated the route between Camps I and II. Probably the bodies of our friends were buried in one of those.

I stayed talking with the Russians more than an hour, then decided to descend to Camp II where I had left my tent. If the wind subsided, I would to try for the summit the next day. Seven Russian mountaineers and one Korean climber would spend another night at Camp III, hoping for a break in the weather. Two hours later, down on the plateau, I discovered the Italians and their tent were gone. I cooked some food and had a meager high-altitude meal. I reviewed my situation. That day I'd noticed right after lunch that the gusts of wind on the plateau had calmed down and the snow flags blowing from the summit crest had decreased as well. Projecting that the wind would continue to decrease, I thought the best time to reach the summit would be between 3 and 4 P.M. the next day. I rested a little more. Toward sunset I decided to move my tent to the end of the plateau and to set up camp in the shelter of the steep ascent to the ridge crest. That move would save an hour of time and effort the next morning. I had little strength left in me after that day's work. When darkness fell, I was in the new spot cooking dinner.

After fixing breakfast and filling my big thermos with tea, the next morning I strapped on my crampons, picked up my ice ax, and began my journey to the summit. It took one hour to reach the altitude of Camp III, but to my disappointment the wind was gusting to the same hurricane force as the day before.

The Russians were in their tents. I climbed in with Vladimir

Bashkirov. He told me that they had started out early, but had been unable to move far and had returned to the tent to wait for the wind to decrease. They planned to wait another night, though food and fuel were becoming critically low. I noticed that among this tent full of Russians, the Korean climber was sitting quietly at the back with his face to the wall. He was obviously uncomfortable in this circle of people he did not know. His English and the English of the Russians left much to be desired, so communication was limited. My Russian comrades regarded him with displeasure. When I asked how our friend from Korea was doing, they told me a funny story.

In the evening some uneaten soup had been left to freeze in a pot near the stove so it could be heated up again in the morning. In the darkness that night, the Korean climber could not find his pee bottle. He did not want to disturb his tentmates by moving outside. Groping in the darkness, he found what he thought was an empty pot and relieved himself. In the morning semidarkness the climber assigned to cook put the soup on the gas stove to boil. The unbearable smell of hot urine soon filled the tent. That was the end of breakfast. The Russians questioned each other and quickly determined who had urinated in the soup. They did not scold him, but the unfortunate Korean now suffered in silence with his face to the wall.

No one on the Russian team was interested in going out with me to face the crazy gusts of wind. I went alone and began to climb along the crest of the ridge, moving over along its gentler side where the wind had deposited a considerable mass of snow. After an hour's climbing, the angle of ascent became more acute. The danger of snow avalanching from the overburdened slope increased. I chose my way precisely, going exactly along the crest, never stepping off to the left or right. In places, forced off the ridge by a boulder, I immediately became aware of the instability of the mass of snow below my feet. I ceased being aware of the wind and the time. The slope, though steep, posed no technical problem. The difficulty was the snow; occasionally it was up to my waist, and I could not sense that I had solid footing. Total awareness followed each step down into the snow. Tuning in to the exact amount of pressure that supported me, my progress was agonizingly slow. Absorbed by an excruciating level of stress, several hours passed with all my intuition, all my focus, riveted to the feeling of the powder beneath my boots.

Looking up, I saw a ski sticking up from the snow on the crest above, as though someone had unsuccessfully tried to ski down from the summit. Before the summit, a rocky gendarme forced me to traverse below it to the left on a steep incline. The snow on the surface was crusted by the wind, but just under the crust it had the consistency of free-flowing powder. On the slope below my steps was the fresh track of a snow slab that had peeled away. I moved like a tightrope walker, finally coming onto a small, rocky shelf—the beginning of the snow-covered summit crest. There, next to the skis buried in the snow, was a backpack. From writing in a diary inside the pack, I learned that the climber had been Slovakian. A picture of a beautiful little girl was folded in the pages of the book, perhaps the daughter of the mountaineer who left these things.

After a short rest, I continued to the highest point on the summit crest. Half-covered tracks led to a landmark that was protruding from the snow. I arrived on the top at three-fifteen. As I had predicted, the wind had let up a little, though the gusts still had enough force to push me off-balance. I straddled the summit crest, riding it like a horse, and took pictures. Despite the wind the visibility was excellent; before me was the top of the mountain, a long, steep ridge that dipped and rose again. From my friends I knew that the southern point was 8,013 meters, by some calculations only five meters higher than where I sat. I considered the traverse, looking at the huge snowdrifts that had built up over the technically easy relief. They were weighted and ready to carry a person down despite every precaution. Experience told me that I had about a 10 percent chance of reaching the south peak alive. How the snow had felt coming up the ridge was fresh in my mind. I knew the conditions were not right for more gambling with my life. Inside me, as it would be with any mountaineer, ambition was raging, but continuing would go against all logic. I had put my life on the line many times in 1996, but for important reasons. I don't know how other mountaineers will judge my actions, but I left the ridge with the feeling that I had climbed Shisha Pangma. Descending, I comforted myself that any other course of action would have been moronic recklessness. I stopped on the rocky ledge by the backpack and skis. What had happened to this man? He could not have descended in slippery plastic boots without his crampons or skis. Maybe he had tried to traverse the crest under conditions similar to this day's. I turned my attention to getting down, and once again all my awareness was in my boots.

I paused when I reached the Russian tents. Standing outside, I drank a cup of tea and talked with my friends. The next day they would follow my tracks to the summit or go down. The time and energy for climbing this mountain was coming to an end.

I was in my tent before dark. After drinking copious amounts of tea and eating a light supper, I climbed into my sleeping bag. For a long time I did not fall asleep. I wanted to understand how I felt about the choice I had made on the summit crest. To me the top of Shisha Pangma was the ridge, which had a few meters of variability from one end to the other—a few meters that could not compare to the enormous scale of the mountain. The choice I had made to come down worked for me and only me. How would others assess this ascent? We go to the mountains to satisfy our own ambitions, not because others evaluate what we are doing. Perhaps that other question, the heightened concern for how we will be judged, leads to death in the mountains. I had been in a similar situation when I'd climbed Makalu in 1994. On my first ascent I was fifty horizontal meters away from the principal tower, and I'd climbed to a point fifteen meters lower than the main summit. Later I climbed Makalu again to satisfy my ambition, meeting the world's standards. However, the second Makalu ascent posed no risk to my life, and I never entertained any doubt that it was possible. Was it interesting to ascend the second time? Yes, but looking back I saw no important difference in the two efforts. Climbing high for its own sake is interesting, though to climb for the simple pleasure of contiguity with a mountain is difficult. To climb only as a means of ego gratification is stupid, though for humans that is a compelling reason. The important conclusions I came to that night were that I should not let my ego or my concern about what others thought of me kill me, or kill the deep joy I experience in communion with the mountains.

The next morning, the day greeted us with good weather and no wind. My friends were lucky, and their days of waiting paid off. I was certain they would reach the summit following my trail. I wondered if they would decide to traverse to the south end of the ridge. When I arrived at Camp II on my way down, I was surprised to see my Italian friends and their tents. They shouted a greeting; watching me through a telescope as I struggled had inspired them to try again, and they planned to attempt the summit the next day. We took group pictures, shared tea, and they helped me load my pack full of equipment onto my shoulders.

In spite of that weight, I negotiated the footing down to the glacier. I spent the night on a moss-covered spot about two hours from Base Camp. The next evening, members of the successful Russian team joined me back at our camp. After a sober evaluation of the snow situation on the ridge, my experienced friends had decided not to try the traverse. The Italians also reached the peak of the north crest. They ventured a short distance along the ridge; the conditions of the snow mass under their feet discouraged recklessness, and they, too, turned back from the South Summit.

What can I say in our defense? Those who hunger for blood will maintain the summit is the summit and not a meter less. Those are the rules of mankind. Each of us was physically capable of making that traverse under sane circumstances. The Italians had previously competed in a sky marathon, winning prizes for their efforts, so endurance was not the issue. The South Summit is definitely a little higher than the point we reached. Despite that, each of us was satisfied he had honestly climbed Shisha Pangma.

October 12 found both our teams at the roadhead where the Jeeps were waiting to transport us back into the warm valleys of

Nepal. We carried with us memories of the bright colors of Tibet. Somewhere on the slopes of Shisha Pangma are the bodies of my Ukrainian friends. On the slopes of Everest are the bodies of other people who are close to me in spirit. I learned that Everest had claimed others that season, young Lopsang Jangbu Sherpa among them. Lopsang had survived the tragic night the previous spring, but fate took him in the fall. People will always go to the mountaintops, led on by their ambition and the desire to test themselves against the powerful forces of nature. Individuals chart this course into the mountains. These summits do not give in easily. One must be excellently prepared for the challenge.

On Cho Oyu, my Kazakh countrymen with their Japanese friends continued their assault, and that expedition had a tragic end. The most experienced of the Japanese climbers insisted on climbing without bottled oxygen. He moved much slower than his team. Though the Kazakh climbers urged him to use oxygen, he refused. As a precaution they carried an emergency supply for him. At 8,100 meters he stopped to rest. After drinking tea from a thermos, for no apparent reason he fell forward into the snow, losing consciousness. Immediately the oxygen mask was put on his face and the flow turned on, but that did not improve his condition. During the tortuous descent, when the unfortunate man roused to consciousness, he would sing songs to them, but he demonstrated no lucid understanding of what was happening. About one hundred meters from Camp III, he died. In a heroic effort, the three Kazakh climbers carried him all the way to Base Camp. The previous year he had successfully ascended to seven thousand meters in Kazakhstan, yet eight thousand meters in Tibet proved fatal.

Many things at high altitude are dependent on the human organism's readiness to endure in that atmosphere. Every professional alpinist who climbs 8,000-meter peaks searches for ways to prepare the body so that it will adjust to the variables. The environment at extreme altitudes is as alien as outer space; the dynamics play out in ways that we cannot fully understand. In those extremes each person has a personal boundary between life and death. The exact cause of demise can be wondered at or debated in this or that case, but realistically a mountaineer can only hope that a commitment to constant training will prop up his or her ambitions to explore the earth's highest reaches.

9

EIGHTY DAYS, FLYING
AT NIGHT, 1997*

In October 1996 when I returned to Kathmandu after climbing Shisha Pangma, Ang Tshering Sherpa, the owner of Asian Trekking, approached me. He wanted to know if I was interested in working as a consultant and climbing leader for the first Indonesian Everest expedition, scheduled for the spring of 1997. Though ascending Everest via the normal route is no longer interesting to me as a mountaineering problem and sports objective, the idea of leading an expedition was appealing. There are many ways to grow as a professional. Unfinished emotional business made me want to return to the site of the ordeal we had endured the previous spring. Somehow, I hoped to make respectful burials of the exposed bodies of Scott Fischer and Yasuko Namba. As I continue to examine my recollections and the opinions of friends and other professional climbers in the hard light of reality, I search for the lessons in that experience. What other option is there—when you have lived

---

*A differently edited version of this expedition account appeared in *The Climb*. Included in that version are expedition details that I have omitted here to avoid repetition, and answers to specific questions that were posed by coauthor Weston DeWalt, which elaborate on points Anatoli did not cover in his original account of those events.

through a situation where the best you could do was not enough to prevent a disaster?

When I entered into discussions with Ang Tshering, I needed to define some position in mountaineering's emerging market that would allow me to earn a living. I wanted to work in ways that were congruent with my beliefs regarding climbing as a sport. The job for the Indonesians would let me clarify my role as a coach and climbing team leader. Admittedly my ego is as fragile as the next person's. I felt maligned by the voices that had captured most of the attention in the American press. Acknowledged as some kind of mountaineering "superman" who was not a very smart guide, my years of experience, intelligence, and character had been discounted. If not for the support of European colleagues like Rolf Dujmovits and Reinhold Messner, I might have been depressed by the American perspective of what I had to offer my profession.

After negotiating with Indonesian team organizers in Kathmandu, in late November I flew to Jakarta, where I met with General Prabowa Subianto. Suharto's son-in-law was the official sponsor of the expedition. During conversations with the general, in stark, graphic terms I said his prospects for success on Everest with inexperienced climbers were marginal. Realistically, I projected we had about a 30 percent chance of summiting one individual, while the chance of someone dying was about fifty-fifty. Such odds were not acceptable to me personally. I asked the general to finance a year of training that would allow his men to gain experience climbing progressively higher peaks before taking on Everest. That request was rejected out of hand; I was given three months to train the team.

My tradition of climbing promotes mountaineering as a sport, a reasonable sport, not a game of chance. The death of a team member always supersedes any summit success. There is an exponentially decreasing margin of safety for an amateur, even a well-conditioned amateur, in the atmosphere above eight thousand meters. In life each person bears the responsibility for his or her ambition. Gaining the top of the world's highest mountain is an enormous human achievement under any set of circumstances. On Everest, every bit of preparation you can make still leaves you in short supply on summit day. The general could buy the benefit of my experience. He could pay for my advice, my services as lead climber, and my strength as a member of a rescue team, but if he wanted the summit of Everest, I wanted him to accept responsibility for the hubris of that ambition with inexperienced men. I could make no guarantee about their personal safety. The general assured me that his soldiers were motivated and well conditioned. They were patriotically committed to succeeding for their countrymen even if they were facing the prospect of death. In some ways, that was a shocking declaration, but it was realistic. I was not trying to sell an adventure tour to dilettantes. No guarantee of success was pledged, and I refused to accept the job unless the general gave me absolute authority to call off a summit attempt if I felt the condition of his men or those on the mountain prevented us from proceeding with reasonable safety. Expending psychological energy debating trivial issues with people who have a limited understanding of the difficulties ahead still seems like a waste of time to me. I was reassured that the Indonesian team would not need a social director. The role I outlined for myself gave the Indonesians every possible benefit of my experience while promoting their organizational independence. Those were the terms of our agreement.

I left Jakarta for the United States on December 6. Doctors in the United States were going to evaluate and treat eye damage I had sustained in a bus accident in late October. For the ensuing three months, the organizational aspects of my job occupied my time. Colonel Eadi was the military commander of the expedition, and Monty Sorongan was his civilian liaison officer; these gentlemen made every effort to satisfy my requests and address my concerns. They provided us with the best possible support.

Communication had been a huge problem during the Mountain Madness expedition, a problem that I had failed to appreciate completely until it was too late. Not only was the language barrier a source of frustration, but the system of radio contact between guides and camps had not been well thought out. In 1997, as well as radios for each member of our summit team, I asked that our duty officer at Base Camp have a direct line to our support personnel in Kathmandu. Also I requested daily weather reports from the meteorological service at the international airport in the capital. Technical advances in clothing and boots have made it much safer for an inexperienced climber to endure extreme temperatures. I saw the difference good equipment made in limiting injuries in 1996. Needing every margin of safety, based on my recommendations, no expense was spared outfitting our climbers with state-of-the-art equipment from American, Russian, and European suppliers.

English would be the common language used between the team members, support staff, and me. That was some disadvantage. Among the responsible parties on the mountain, I wanted no room for misunderstanding. I requested that General Subianto contract the services of two respected Russian mountaineers, Vladimir Bashkirov and Dr. Evgeny Vinogradski. They would act as trainers, members of the rescue team, and provide a balance to my rather difficult personality. The challenge of preparing an Everest team in ninety days was obvious, but both men agreed to join our experiment. Behind the shoulders of forty-five-year-old Vladimir Bashkirov were twenty-eight years of experience in expedition organization and technical expertise on the great walls in the Pamirs and Caucasus Mountains. He had summited six 8,000-meter peaks including Everest twice. As well as having a good command of English, Volodia is a soft-spoken diplomat compared to me. I would rely on his personable communication skills and good judgment throughout the expedition. To his credit, fifty-year-old Evgeny Vinogradski, seven-time champion climber in the Soviet Union, had thirty-three years of high-altitude experience as an instructor, sports climber, and physician. He had climbed eight 8,000-meter peaks, including Everest twice, once as a personal guide. We had climbed Kanchenjunga together in 1989. In the worst situations the "Old Eagle," with his gentle good humor and steely calm, had proved to be a friend whom I could count on. His long history as an instructor and sports physician made him an indispensable part of our team.

Ang Tshering chose and hired our Sherpas. The division of labor was spelled out from the beginning. They would provide the usual Base Camp support, fix rope on sections of the route above the ice-fall, set up and supply our mountain camps, and carry extra oxygen on summit day. As sirdar, we were fortunate to have the skill and service of thirty-seven-year-old Apa Tenzing of Thame, a seven-time summiter of Everest.

The politics of the Indonesian expedition were unusual all around. Ang Tshering put us all together and made a bold decision when he bypassed established expedition organizations that usually run the commercial show at Base Camp. The Indonesian organizers and climbers had no experience, but they were motivated by a great deal of national pride. Malaysia also planned to undertake an expedition that spring. Suddenly, the normal competition between these Pacific Rim powers was focused on the top of Everest. Russians, though respected as strong climbers, have been out of mountaineering's commercial loop altogether. Only since 1995, financed by an emerging class of merchants in our countries, have our teams found their way back to the Himalayas. If Bashkirov, Vinogradski, and I were successful acting as the tactical and strategic leaders for a foreign expedition, it would be a coup that might secure us a means of making a living beyond the borders of our chaotic economy. Outsiders manned each component of the expedition, and each of us had something to gain. I hoped that would make us all more conscious of our objective and in turn inspire an extra degree of cooperative effort.

Our training program was to the point; one cannot invent experience on 8,000-meter peaks. In one season of winter climbing prospective team members could be exposed to severe cold and wind, they could acclimatize to six thousand meters in the Himalayas, and we could test their endurance and mental discipline. Civilians who had some mountaineering background and Special Forces soldiers made up the group of thirty-four candidates for the final expedition. During training climbs we intended to teach and observe their proficiency in the technical skills necessary for mountaineering. Bashkirov and Vinogradski met the group in Kathmandu on December 15, and they climbed 5,900-meter-high Paldor Peak; seventeen members summited. In January all but one of those men reached the top of Island Peak. During that exercise individuals were pushed to ascend and descend a thousand meters in less than five hours for several consecutive days. Beset by howling winter winds, they camped near the 6,000-meter-high summit for seventy-two hours in frigid temperatures. That was the best we could do. Now I shake my head in disbelief—Paldor, Island Peak, Everest. I don't recommend this as a training program to anyone.

Back in Kathmandu on January 10, we met to discuss team selection. Bashkirov and Vinogradski ranked the men by the following criteria: speed, adjustment to altitude, general health, and attitude. Ten soldiers and six civilians were chosen for the final group. Though we advised the Indonesians to undertake only one expedition, in the end General Subianto hired Richard Pawlowski to head a simultaneous north-side attempt. Ten members were assigned to us and six men would go to Tibet to attempt the mountain with Richard.

On March 12, after a twenty-six day rest, an Asian Airlines, Russian-made helicopter lifted us out of Kathmandu's smog and headed toward Lukla. Returning to the Everest region always brings me a feeling of relief, for I love the mountains. Only those who have been there will understand this. After an early-morning flight you are dropped off on a precipitous aerie that sits in an embrace of bony mountains—jagged summits rise clearly outlined in the crystal air. Such majesty is humbling, and one is reminded of how small humans are in the scheme of things. A little more than an hour after our departure from Kathmandu, ten Indonesians and three Russian climbing advisers stepped down onto the small landing area. Armed with our ambition, we were headed for the top of the highest mountain on earth. Seven days later we would be in Base Camp, but on that morning I knew no matter what was ahead of me, I was at home, and that mountaineering is the only life for which I am fit.

Seventeen teams were camped on the glacier in 1997. The Malaysians and Indonesians would be the brunt of some jokes. Our expedition became the source of derisive comments by the American reporters; I had some training for that. Certainly it would have been a pleasure to have David Breashears's IMAX staff members taking my blood pressure at Base Camp, but I was not invited for that honor. The Indonesians were full of determination and I needed to work. We had enough to do, so I tried to keep our team out of the politics in camp.

After our arrival on March 19, the icefall was ahead of us. That is always an important step in psychological adjustment to the task of climbing Everest. Our climbers were shaky at first, but they did well. By the second trip up, they were moving with confidence and at a much faster pace. With that obstacle mastered, we settled into the routine of climb and rest that is acclimatization. On April 6, on our fourth trip up, we climbed to 7,300 meters for a second session of ac-climatization at that elevation. My original plan called for us to go on and spend one night on the South Col, then climb to 8,200 meters before we attempted the summit. Due to a mutiny in the Sherpa team I had to abandon that idea.

Because we were the first climbers on the route, we had no help for the work of fixing line above the icefall. To stay ahead of our team, the Sherpas had a huge burden of work. Though I lobbied the other expedition leaders for extra financial support or labor to assist them (since every expedition would later use our path on their way to the summit), my requests fell on deaf ears. I foresee a time when the entire trail to the summit of Everest will be fixed by a team of ex-perienced Sherpas, who will be paid by every expedition that uses the route. This change won't happen without the protests of those who until now have benefited exorbitantly by the hard work of un-derpaid men.

Having failed to get our men help or more money, as a compro-mise I worked with Apa fixing the route up to the Col. His cowork-ers had limited strength and skill, and my demands put too much pressure on them. In the end only eight of our sixteen Sherpas were able to work at high altitude. Apa Sherpa is an extraordinary man, a hard worker; always he gave more of himself than he expected of the others.

On April 8, eight of the team climbed to an elevation of 7,500 meters and returned to sleep at Camp III for one more night; on the ninth we descended to Base Camp. We saw a difference in individual performance and health after that ascent. Three men were obviously stronger than the others, and they moved easily at high altitude.

We descended to Deboche to rest at 3,770 meters in the forest zone. During our rest period, the Sherpas were supposed to climb ahead of us, fix the route above the South Col, and ferry supplies up to an emergency camp at 8,500 meters. The official director of the Sherpas' work was Captain Rochadi. He had no appreciation for how bad things can be when they go wrong at high altitude, so there was no consistent support for my requests. I am in a continual state of watchful apprehension climbing these mountains; everything looks easy until it is too late. Rochadi's lack of concern was an ongoing threat to the effectiveness of my backup safety measures. There was no one to blame; it takes years of repeated ascents and consistent monetary support to develop a team of Sherpas who can work together in equal strength to assist an expedition. Our manpower crisis worked itself out, but not optimally.

Several personal problems interrupted my concentration and took away my energy. A filling in one of my teeth cracked, an abscess formed, and that required a trip to Kathmandu. Were the ravages of time telling on me? Other questions haunted me. How would I function at high altitude after the bus accident? Minus a tooth, I rejoined our team back at Base Camp on April 21. My return trek from Lukla took one and a half days, which was a speed record on its own. In my absence the Sherpas never left Base Camp. Apa assured me that he would see that his men supplied the emergency camp while we made our summit assault.

We finalized a plan. Bashkirov, Vinogradski, and I would each carry a radio. One of us would be with team members at all times, and we had prescribed intervals to make radio contact with every camp below us. Two Sherpas would wait on the South Col. Members of Bashkirov's Lhotse team, all strong Russians who were acclimatizing at 7,400 meters, agreed to provide emergency support if we needed it. The second-strongest members of the Indonesian group would be stationed at Camp II.

Weather reports from Kathmandu were encouraging. We were at the end of a small weather disturbance, but the five days ahead of us looked stable. *Stable* is a relative term in the Himalayas. At the summit of Mount Everest you are at the apex of long river valleys; the gorges become steeper as the elevation increases. Below, the warm daytime temperatures cause water to evaporate; clouds form and naturally rise, flowing up the valleys each afternoon. There always seem to be some clouds around the summits late in the day, and even these benign weather changes can pose a challenge. We knew that we were going to be slow, and Camp V at 8,500 meters was our solution for that unsolvable problem.

Late afternoon of the twenty-first we gathered for a puja ceremony at the chorten above our tents. Buddhist prayer flags and smoke lifted in the thin, cold air. Every day during our time on the glacier, the Indonesians remembered their God, much like the Sherpas with their morning offerings of burning cedar; I appreciated their respectfulness. Serious concentration showed on every face that afternoon, and the evening was spent in private organization. That is always a tense time, loaded with expectation. A meditative calm comes over me and I feel excitement as I get ready for the challenge ahead.

At midnight on April 22, in the light of a full moon, three Russians and six Indonesians left the safety of Base Camp for a journey into the unknown. Without any difficulty, our sturdy climbers moved well, ascending to Camp II in six hours. On the twenty-third we rested. The next day, Bashkirov, Vinogradski, I, and the three strongest Indonesians—Misirin Sersan, Asmujiono Prajurit, and Iwan Lentnan—left for Camp III with Apa and seven other Sherpas. There wasn't much idle chatter and the men didn't need reassurance. Evidence of hard winds could be seen at the level of the South Col. After contacting Kathmandu, Rochadi assured us that forecasters did not indicate a change in the weather, and the prediction called for the wind to decrease during the next forty-eight hours. We held the team at Camp III for a day. On the twenty-fifth the Indonesians used oxygen to climb to the Col and arrived coherent, coordinated, and self-motivated.

During our summit attempt each of them would use bottled oxygen, as would the Sherpas, who were supposed to carry nine extra bottles for the three Indonesian climbers. Only Apa and Dawa were going all the way to the summit. Vinogradski, Bashkirov, and I each planned to carry a twelve-hour supply of oxygen, which we intended to use sparingly; we were in good enough condition to work without it if we had to. The weight of the equipment and the oxygen that had to be carried and the number of men we had to do the job did not add up. Knee-deep snow covered the route between 8,100 and 8,600 meters; we were in for some hard work. Apa continued to reassure me that the tent, stove, and supplies for Camp V were going up with us.

Midnight on April 26 we set out from the South Col. Utilizing oxygen, I broke trail. Loaded down as they were, it was unfair to ask the Sherpas to do that work. Bashkirov and Vinogradski climbed with the Indonesian members. After nine hours of wallowing through snow above my knees, with progress slow and difficult, I was fatigued when I arrived at the South Summit. Apa was below me at 8,600 meters fixing the last section of steep slope. It was 11 A.M. when the whole group arrived. Our speed was the same as it had been the year before. Discussing the next move, Apa asked me to break trail and fix the Hillary Step. I asked for rope. We had only forty meters left, he said. I was incredulous; where was the rope? Apa apologized; he had not calculated enough rope for the conditions we faced. Because of the snow, some sections that are normally safe without it had had to be secured with line. Fatigued as I was, I had no inclination to cross the ridge to the Step without a belay.

The margins for success are so close. The shadows of problems you perceive below are all-consuming on summit day; success or failure is in the balance, and you can complain or deal with them. All the reassurance I had been given in conversations evaporated. Time was of the essence. Apa offered to go down and recover the necessary meters of rope. The clock was ticking; we had to go forward or down. Realizing the gravity of our situation, and how this compromised our position, Apa did a brave thing. He took the last forty meters of rope, crossed the ridge before the Step, and pulled old pieces of exposed rope to the surface. In the interval it took for him to complete that work, I gratefully rested, and my overall sense of well-being returned. Dawa arrived at the South Summit and informed us that an emergency camp at 8,500 meters had a tent, oxygen bottles, and a stove.

At 12:30 P.M. Apa cleared the top of the Hillary Step. The weather was good and our emergency camp was supplied. Bashkirov, Vinogradski, and I decided to attempt the summit, though we projected we would arrive late in the day, about 3 P.M. I evaluated our team. Misirin was slow but functioning on his own. Asmujiono moved well but was focused like a zombie, consciousness somewhere deep inside. Iwan was alert but slow, and his coordination was suffering. Misirin was in the best shape, though all three demonstrated a kamikaze-like determination; when asked, each demanded the opportunity to go on. My vote was to take only Misirin, turning the others back, but I allowed myself to be convinced that we could postpone that measure until after we had surmounted the Hillary Step. Because I felt that Asmujiono's mental deterioration would be a critical factor, I assigned him to Dr. Vinogradski. Bashkirov and Misirin went out first, then Iwan and I, followed by Asmujiono and Evgeny. The ridge was much different than it had been in 1996; it was steeper. Iwan moved slowly, then fell; he stopped sliding by hanging tenuously from the old rope. I demonstrated how he should move to right himself, how to use his ax properly so he could regain the route. Realizing I was giving lessons on technique at 8,700 meters to someone who had been introduced to snow for the first time only four months earlier, I could only wonder what the experience meant to this man.

I am a sportsman, and for me a mountaintop is not worth the sacrifice of my life. I would not have ventured into a world so different, unfamiliar with the skills that would preserve me. Soldiers have a different mind-set, and these men felt that they represented the aspirations of a whole nation. In that role they were more committed to striving than they were to life. Iwan regained his footing on the ridge, and we resumed our careful journey in a deep track, coming to the bottom of the Hillary Step. There, tangled in the ropes, we came upon the body of a man, his crampons and feet protruding in our way. With features erased by the harsh conditions, all I could say for certain was that his down suit was blue. Though respect is always due fallen climbers, I could not afford to focus on him. That vision had a sobering effect on each of us. At that moment, the end of our ambition was in sight, but our situation was anything but stable. At the top of the Hillary Step, I looked down and watched Iwan and Asmujiono climbing slowly up; gingerly they circumnavigated the obstacle created by the body. Apa and Dawa had gone on ahead. Vinogradski tried to turn Iwan back, but none of the men were willing to admit defeat. My concern was that they were fast approaching the end of their physical resources. If they were going to get down, they had to move under their own power. Above the Step I advised Asmujiono and Iwan to go down. They refused. The whole team moved off toward the summit. I knew for certain that we would be spending the night at 8,500 meters. The weather was calm. Each step required one minute of rest for the Indonesians. On top I congratulated Apa on his eighth successful trip to the top of Everest. We watched as the Indonesians struggled with the last steps. Bashkirov and Misirin were thirty meters away, Asmujiono was behind them. We saw Misirin stumble and collapse in the snow. Asmujiono raised his head, and his eyes focused on the summit marker. Charging, doggedly running in slow motion, he came toward us, falling and embracing the tripod that is the official top of the mountain. He ripped back his down hood, replaced it with his army beret, and unfurled the flag of Indonesia. The determination of all Indonesians was affirmed by the last efforts this young man could wrench from his body. The others inched their way closer; Misirin was only twenty meters away from the tripod.

I felt fine; the exhaustion that swept over me at the South Summit had passed, and my reserves were intact. Bashkirov and Vinogradski were strong and thinking clearly. Our young men were running on bottled oxygen and autopilot, not capable of offering much in the way of self-reflection regarding reserve power. If they collapsed, we all knew we would be in dire straits. With all due respect to their focus and determination, I had seen enough; someone else could pass judgment on this Olympian effort. We were going down. I photographed Asmujiono at 3:30 P.M., and Bashkirov and I started down with him and Misirin. Vinogradski turned away from the summit and went back to aid Iwan, who was eighty meters from his goal. Apa was sent to set up the emergency camp. Every minute became critical, as descending in the light of day was mandatory.

The group moved slowly across the ridge below the Hillary Step. I followed. Misirin fell several times below the South Summit. Iwan was put on Vinogradski's last bottle of oxygen after he had carelessly disconnected himself at a juncture of fixed rope and fallen. Had Zhenya not grabbed him and reconnected him to the line, he would have slid about one hundred meters down the slope. With Bashkirov and Vinogradski following behind slowly because they had given up their oxygen, I went ahead with the three Indonesians along a route lit by my headlamp. At the tent, I removed the crampons from the boots of my charges and pushed them inside onto the insulated Karrimats. The sun was setting; it was easily thirty degrees below zero centigrade. Apa went down to the South Col with Dawa. Then began what Bashkirov in his diplomatic way describes as a very dramatic night. The full moon lit our tents; outside the night was still. Great silence was broken only by our voices. Showing his true colors, Zhenya brewed hot water continuously. We kept this up in shifts throughout the night. The reassuring flow of heat into our guts backed off the numbing cold. The oxygen mask was rotated across the faces of the three Indonesians, who cried or prayed if deprived of the bottle for too long. We made it though the night working together.

Dawn brought a splendid array of color and no wind. From that isolated aerie, the views of Makalu, Lhotse, and Kanchenjunga were spectacular. Morning sun bathed Everest in a blinding glory of light and us with warmth. The mountains below us were spread out like whitecaps on the ocean. We had survived. With a cautious descent the tenuous victory on the summit would become a true one when all our members walked into Base Camp.

We brewed one last round of water. Iwan, Misirin, and Asmujiono were more collected psychologically. They were out of oxygen, but good acclimatization and a night being weaned off the bottle had spared them from the worst effects of dependence. No one had frostbite. They moved slowly, but they moved! At the pleasure of the mountain we lived. We were going down without injury or the burden of tragedy.

By that time I felt secure enough in the stability of our situation to address my personal agenda. At 8,400 meters I began to search the slope for Scott Fischer's body and located it half-covered with snow about thirty meters from the trail we had made going up. Ascending, I had carried a flag inscribed with farewells from Scott's wife, children, and friends. I had wanted to wrap him in this cover before burying him. Ascending, given the physical shape of our team, I had not been sure that I would be able to find him or accomplish that mission, so I'd left the flag flying from the summit marker. I hope that Jeannie Fischer understands that was the best I could do. Evgeny helped me pack snow and rocks over the exposed parts of Scott's body. We marked the spot with the shaft of an ice ax that we found nearby.

Evgeny and I arrived at noon on the South Col. Our Indonesian members had been reassured they would survive by a resupply of oxygen at the level of the Balcony. Back in the tents drinking tea among the debris of former expeditions, they were convinced.

The morning of the twenty-eighth I crossed the Col over to the edge of the Kangshung Face, where I had left Yasuko Namba during the terrible night the year before. Her body was partially covered with snow and ice; her pack was missing and its contents were strewn among the rocks. Standing there again, I experienced the confusion that I have about her death. For a time I was lost in those complex, difficult emotions. They are unavoidable and their lessons are burned in my memory. Slowly moving stones, I built a cairn over her body, marking it with the shafts of ice axes. Those acts of respect are all that I have to offer her family and Scott's family to show my sadness over their losses.

I think of how ready Iwan, Asmujiono, and Misirin were to die, and I remember how the families I know who have left loved ones here bear their sorrow. Our success can only encourage other inexperienced climbers. With all my power I wish I had another way to make a living. I am a sportsman, with many objectives in the high mountains that I would like to try. Any man who has a capability wants to explore the limits of his potential. It is too late for me to find another profession, but I have great reservations about bringing inexperienced men and women into this world.

This may sound harsh, but I don't want to be called a guide. I don't want the responsibility of choosing between a person's ambition and his life. Each individual alone must bear the responsibility of that choice. The distinction between *guide* and *consultant* will be mocked by some, yet that is the only protest I can make about the guarantee of success in these mountains. I can be a coach and adviser; I will spend my strength as a rescue agent. But I will not guarantee success or safety for those who take up the challenge of complex natural phenomena and physical debility that waits at high altitude. I have accepted that I may die here. Our team descended to the sweet embrace of victory. Many people contributed to our success, but above all, we were lucky in playing our game of Russian roulette. The expedition had an ending that does not burn in my heart.

•　•　•

Seventeen four-star Indonesian generals flew to Kathmandu to debrief our expedition members and staff. As Major General Prabowa Subianto and I were discussing the details of our success, the conversation strayed to the status of the Malaysian expedition. They were stuck in Base Camp, their progress stymied by the rotten weather that characterized the climbing season. I needed to point out what we had gone through and what the general had gambled in this competition. I observed that his rivalry with the Malaysians reminded me of my own country's competition with America during the late fifties and the sixties, when the two superpowers were in the "space race."

"When we launched *Sputnik*, it caused a general degree of panic in America," I said. "Russians had the same feeling when U.S. astronauts walked on the surface of the moon. One of our generals gathered the cosmonauts.

"'To outshine this American accomplishment we will have to undertake a mission that is truly spectacular, something definitive,' he told his captive audience. 'Gentlemen, our next mission is the sun. After this, no one can doubt our superiority.'

"The hushed silence was broken when one of the cosmonauts spoke up: 'But, General, we will burn.'

"'Don't worry, comrade,' he replied, 'you will fly in the night.'"
General Prabowa was not amused.

Lhotse–Everest Traverse

In the spring of 1997, Anatoli and his climbing partner, the Italian Simone Moro, had their names included on three permits that allowed them to consider traversing the summits of Lhotse and Everest. After the Indonesian celebrations in Kathmandu, Bashkirov was also returning to the Khumbu as the leader of a team of Russians who were climbing Lhotse.

My original plan had been to follow the Everest climb with the Indonesians with a sports ascent, a south-to-north traverse of the peaks of Lhotse and Everest. That turned out to be too ambitious. The Indonesian expedition proved to be a tremendous challenge for us. After fighting for the lives of our charges on the slopes below the summit of Everest, Vinogradski, Bashkirov, and I went back to Kathmandu and spent two and a half weeks in that dirty city waiting for a group of Indonesian generals to arrive so we could get paid. During that time, the toll our work had taken in psychological and emotional energy registered on me. Though I had spared my physical resources for the traverse by using supplemental oxygen during the Indonesian summit bid, back in Kathmandu I had no juice. I felt like a squeezed lemon. A series of expensive permits had been paid for, and my Italian friend Simone Moro was gaining acclimatization and would soon be waiting for me to return to Base Camp. The traverse was my main sports objective for 1997, and success would have set a milestone in high-altitude endurance. Just having my name on the necessary permits, which made the climb legal, made attempting the route irresistible. Other psychological pressures urged me on. Before leaving America, I had responded to questions posed by an interviewer from *Men's Journal* magazine. He was curious about how my bus accident and the subsequent operations on my eye had affected my abilities as a mountaineer. That interview supercharged the issue of performance for me. When no one pays much attention, you climb according to the dictates of your own judgment. But when your life and behavior become the focus of interest and comment for thousands of people, you start to feel that you must constantly prove yourself, that you must present a good face even if you don't feel like it. For me that was a new and difficult situation.

While I was waiting in Kathmandu, my body sank into the lethargy that characterizes my physical rehabilitation after hard climbing. The capital city, with its polluted atmosphere, is not the best destination for a rest. If you go to Nepal to climb, you are better off getting out of town as soon as possible. Though there was a lot of celebrating after we arrived, I avoided drinking alcohol. That drew some sarcastic remarks from my Russian friends. Again the scars on my lungs from the 1991 Everest expedition let me know of their presence—bronchitis developed and my throat became sore.

Time ticked away. In the back of my mind I knew that Simone was waiting. Finally on the fifteenth of May, Bashkirov and I flew back to Lukla. His Lhotse expedition members had been left on the glacier to acclimate. The group of Russians had an interesting objective—they planned to traverse the three peaks on the Lhotse Massif. When I decided that I needed an extra day of rest in Namche Bazaar, Volodia mocked me a bit, saying I was sick because I had refused to drink vodka with the group in Kathmandu. In a hurry to rejoin his group, he went directly to Base Camp. On the seventeenth, surveying the summit of Everest from the village of Pangboche, I could see an arc of snow suspended in the wind across the top that would prevent anyone from making much progress above eight thousand meters. So I rested there for another two days, sending word of my planned date of return to Simone with passing Sherpas. I suspected that he was nervously waiting for me. His sponsor had paid for his opportunity to climb; it represented a lot of money for him and I felt responsible for the agreement we had made. My respiratory condition improved and I pushed on up to Base Camp. When I arrived, Simone had some minor health problems, but he was well acclimatized.

Though I sensed I was not in perfect form, my sickness seemed to be over. I would allow my intuition to lead and started to climb. Leaving Camp II at 6,800 meters at about midnight, we arrived at the Russian assault camp about 5 A.M. The tents were empty, for earlier that morning Bashkirov and other members of the team had begun their summit bid. Simone and I brewed tea and rested for about two hours. I began to cough—the bronchitis again. Until that time Simone and I had climbed at the same pace, but when we left camp, Simone went out ahead of me. Soon we caught up with the Russians, and as we climbed with them for a while, I spoke with Bashkirov.

"How are you, Volodia?" I asked.

"I didn't sleep well. I had a low fever during the night, and now I feel a little tired," he responded.

Nothing in his demeanor made me worry. He spoke normally. I confessed that my own condition left me wanting for better.

Simone arrived at the summit first, then I came up. My illness was progressing rapidly. I advised him that I would not be able to attempt the traverse. We began to descend. Encountering Bashkirov about thirty meters below the top, protected from the wind in the couloir, I asked how he was feeling.

"Not too well," he replied, "but as leader of the expedition I need to wait for the slower ones, Bagomolov and Pershin, who are coming. Waiting will give me time to do some filming for my sponsors."

When he asked how I was doing, I told him that I found myself falling asleep on the top, drifting away from reality. I was not in any sort of normal condition and felt that I had to get down quickly. Now I think that I was lucky to get down alive.

Bashkirov waited another two hours for his climbers. He did not make it back to camp. When I spoke to the other Russians about his descent, they said he simply became ill, then lost consciousness. His condition deteriorated even though he was supplied with bottled oxygen. Well or not well, Volodia was able to ascend to the summit of Lhotse in three or four hours less time than the men he was leading. Weaker people lived and he did not—why was that?

As a coach I know that when you have achieved peak athletic form, the body's defense mechanism becomes weaker. You are more susceptible to illness. Any exposure to a bacteria or a virus makes you sick. There is a balance in the human body. You work and work, but strength is not limitless. If you train for speed, then endurance suffers; if your strength improves, your endurance decreases. At high altitude a similar reversal occurs: as your acclimatization improves, you feel better with the elevation but your strength decreases. Too much time at altitude weakens your defenses and you are more susceptible to illness, yet your body has no energy available to fight disease. That day I had a simple sore throat, a cough, but I knew that I could not make the traverse. I did not feel sick necessarily; I simply felt that if I fell asleep, I would never wake up. Bashkirov's situation deteriorated fast; waiting those few hours caused his death. When I spoke with him after the summit, neither of us had any sense that events would take such a tragic turn. He did not feel well, I did not feel well, that is all; it did not seem too bad.

If you are a professional high-altitude climber, your body adopts a rhythm for dealing with prolonged stress and recovery. We worked hard with the Indonesians, and in the two weeks we had waited in Kathmandu our bodies had begun to retune. During the period of recovery, which I feel usually corresponds to the same length of time the body has been above six thousand meters, we again attempted a challenging climb. Interrupting your body's period of recovery and remobilizing physical resources before rehabilitation is complete is a bad idea. That is what Bashkirov and I did by returning to Lhotse after working with the Indonesians.

High-altitude mountaineering is the most dangerous kind of sport; it has the highest rate of fatal consequence. Most of these tragedies happen because human response is so unpredictable at high altitude. Though I have enormous potential at altitude, I am not protected. I know that if I get sick, I, too, can perish. You can't accurately calculate all the odds; maybe God is unhappy with you one day. You get yourself into the situation with your *samochuvstvie,* your overall readiness, then fate plays its hand. To say that one person is stronger than another and that is the reason one survived and another did not is the same as saying nothing. Comparing Bashkirov's strength to that of the men on his team who survived, is like comparing the sky with the earth. Logically the strongest would have survived, and that was not the case.

The same situation occurred with Scott Fischer. A professional level of training allows you to overwork your body. Competitive conditioning increases your ability to perform because it teaches you to wring out the last reserves of your energy. For an untrained athlete it is almost impossible to push so far and hard that all physical reserves are exhausted. On some unconscious level the body protects itself. Those are the very margins the superathlete overrides.

Broad Peak and Gasherbrum II

I rested for ten days after the summiting of Lhotse and then flew to Pakistan, arriving on June 14. I did not have a lot of ambition, but I had paid for my part of the expedition cost earlier in the year. Using Thor Kieser's Base Camp at Broad Peak for rest, I intended to support myself and ascend alone.

On June 27 I climbed to 6,900 meters carrying my shovel, down suit, sleeping bag, and tent. I cleared a campsite, secured my tent, and descended to Base Camp at about 9 P.M.

On June 28 a cataclysm of weather prohibited further progress. I had never seen anything like it; the sky was clear, then in a few hours it began to snow heavily. Delayed until July 6, at 3 A.M. I left camp and crossed the glacier to begin climbing the mountain proper about four-thirty. The slopes were burdened with snow. No one had climbed above the level of Camp II. I met Ed Viesturs descending with his partner and I continued up, breaking trail to the level of my tent. After shoveling it out, I climbed inside to rest. One of Thor Kieser's clients, a young man named Mark, poked his head through the door. He announced that he wanted to accompany me to the summit as the next day was July 7, and he believed the numbers 7-7-97 would be auspicious. Mark had never climbed an 8,000-meter peak, and this was his first ascent to the level of 6,900 meters. Gently I advised him that his idea was crazy, that he should simply descend to Base Camp the next day. This provoked an emotional response. Weary and incredulous, I packed my bivy sack and thermos and quietly slipped out of the tent. Climbing until I reached 7,200 meters, I bivouacked on the slopes about 9 P.M. and slept.

Waking to start in the darkness of a still morning, I climbed an unknown route burdened with snow and arrived at the bottom of a steep couloir. Standing on the pass below the summit about 8:30 A.M., I took off my down suit. Sun-warmed on that windless day, I positioned my black overboots so as to melt snow to water and rested. About 1:30 P.M., dressed in light clothing, I began ascending the summit ridge. The route was not technically difficult, but the new snow made it dangerous. Near the top a cornice broke off under my feet. Jumping off the falling island, miraculously I landed on solid rock. At four-thirty, from the peak I surveyed the relief around me. The other end of the dangerously snow-burdened ridge looked to be about the same elevation as where I stood, give or take a meter. For me, I was on the summit. Empty, I descended. One hour later back on the pass, I caught my breath and redressed in my down suit. Darkness came on the mountain. Following the vague trail of my own footsteps, I descended in the light of my headlamp, stopping to doze as I felt like it. The cold would wake me and I would resume climbing down completely unaware of and unburdened by the pressure of time. About midnight I arrived at my tent. Mark was distraught, thinking he had killed me.

The morning of the eighth, I made coffee and hot chocolate and life returned. Lower down, I met Thor Kieser, his partner Katerina, and Ed Viesturs. Thor joked with me, asking if I was sure that I had been on top of the mountain. For me it was the top.

I rested, enjoying Thor's hospitality until the twelfth. That day, after some discussion with my liaison officer, Major Baig, we decided to move up to the location of the supply camps for Gasherbrum I and II. On the thirteenth I crossed the glacier to Gary Neptune's Base Camp located at 5,800 meters at the beginning of the route up GII. Beginning my assault the morning of July 14, I arrived at the 8,068-meter-high summit of GII in nine and one-half hours. The round trip from Base Camp and back took thirteen hours.

No one keeps track of records on these mountains. Each climb is different because the conditions are different. You might say the competition is held and each person achieves a personal result. Mountaineering is a struggle with yourself, a struggle to face a natural situation and take what comes.

Borrowing a satellite telephone, Anatoli called from Gasherbrum Base Camp to let me know that he was alive, not to worry, and that he expected to see me at the airport in Almaty in two weeks. He had summitted four 8,000-meter peaks in eighty days—never before had anyone achieved those results in such a short time.

10

LETTERS FROM
ANNAPURNA

In July and August of 1997, leading an expedition from New Mexico, Anatoli traversed Myramornya Stena and climbed Khan-Tengri. That trip inaugurated our new business, Hi-Altitude. The opportunity that he provided was his way of repaying a debt of gratitude to several friends, Jack Robbins and Martin Adams among them. Though visibly tired, Anatoli was relaxed and obviously pleased to be sharing his beloved Tien Shan Mountains. Serendipitously, Reinhold Messner arrived at Khan-Tengri Base Camp while we were camped there, and Anatoli passed most of a day talking with him. During September, Tolya rested, taking time to travel home to Korkino to visit his sister. On September 25 he returned to Santa Fe.

While he enjoyed a respite harvesting the apple trees in my yard and jogging a bit, storms racked up record snowfalls in the Himalayas. We did not know that. The Climb was recently published, and Anatoli was scheduled for a two-week publicity tour to begin on November 1. A speaking engagement took him to the Banff Festival of Mountain Culture. Attending that event was a great pleasure for us. The book tour was a trial. He came home tired but feeling liberated from the Mountain Madness expedition. The final sad explanation had been made at an emotional appearance in Seattle. Jim Wickwire, representing the American Alpine Club, had met him there and advised

Anatoli that he had been awarded the AAC's prestigious David Sowles Award, an honor bestowed in recognition of the courage he had demonstrated while selflessly attempting to rescue Scott Fischer in 1996. Anatoli returned to Santa Fe the next morning. Sandy Hill, her partner Steve, and Martin Adams, another Mountain Madness client, joined us for dinner.

Events were compressed and accelerated. Tolya railed at having so little time to say good-bye. But there seemed to be no way to slow things down.

Planning for the Annapurna Expedition began in September 1996. As an objective, Anatoli found the majesty of the peaks that create the great bowl of the Annapurna Sanctuary compelling. Before his death Vladimir Bashkirov had described an unclimbed route on the South Face that was intriguing. After Volodia's death on Lhotse in May 1997, attempting this route became more important. Based on his 1995 Manaslu experience, Anatoli expected that the steep avalanche-prone slopes on the South Face of Annapurna would be more stable in early winter. Normally the season's falling temperatures reduce the avalanche potential. Earnings from the Indonesian Expedition had provided Tolya with the first real financial cushion in his life. The constraints and danger that he associated with guiding 8,000-meter peaks were very frustrating for him. He hoped to liberate himself from the need to earn his living that way by finding commercial sponsorship for more interesting alpine objectives.

Over the course of their association, Simone Moro had become a friend as well as a trusted climbing partner. The thirty-year-old Italian climber was personable and strong, and both he and Anatoli worked long and hard to find financing for the Annapurna expedition. The original proposal included a list of seven international climbers; however, circumstances forced the other members to cancel one by one. In September when old friend Kevin Cooney told us that he and his wife, Annie, were expecting their first child, Anatoli took him off the expedition roster. "Kevin is no longer invited," he said. Kevin's growing family responsibility was more important than the opportunity to climb an 8,000-meter peak. By December 1, 1997, a Polartec Grant and contributions from Italian and Kazakh sponsors amounted to about one third of the expedition cost. Anatoli was very pleased that his efforts to find funding for an original idea had been at least partially successful and he wanted to live up to the commitment that accepting the sponsorship implied. Interviews, tele-

phone calls, and letters written during that time tell his part of the Annapurna story.

Excerpt from Anatoli's letter to Jim Wickwire dated November 15:

I very much appreciate your coming to see me in Seattle. I am sorry I was so disturbed; I was so tired after the publicity tour that I may have seemed crazy to you. I could never have imagined how difficult it would be; reviewing that sad story was more difficult than climbing Everest.

It is very important for me to tell you how much I am honored by the idea of this award from the American Alpine Club. I have many friends in America who are climbers and their friendship and respect means a great deal to me—Scott Fischer was one of them. With respect I recall what spirit let Scott try to work with and understand a climber from another culture. I understand this award is extended in that same spirit. I feel very fortunate to be recognized this way.

I will be in Nepal preparing for an attempt on the South Face of Annapurna when you have your meeting. Again I apologize that I could not be more attentive to you at the end of the book tour. Now, I am a little rested and must express my gratitude to you and to all the members who thought of me.

Interview with Alex Severnuk, November 18, Almaty, Kazakhstan:

Applying *to conquer* as a verb for a mountain was an invention of the propagandists of the Soviet Union—who thought of conquering a country, conquering people, conquering a summit. To me *conquer* means something like rape—to take by force. I don't think anyone should aim at conquering anything, and it is the wrong word to apply to our climbing achievements. At best a person is able to rise to the same level as a mountain for a short time.

I have climbed eleven different 8,000-meter-high peaks in nineteen or twenty-one successful attempts, depending on how you count the summits of Kanchenjunga. Of the fourteen highest peaks in the world, only Nanga Parbat, Gasherbrum I, and Annapurna remain unclimbed by me. Messner was the first person to summit them all, and four other men—Jerzy Kukuczka, Christof Wielicki, Erhard Loretan, and Carlos Carsolio—have repeated his work. For me this goal is interesting, and though it has been done before, it will complete a certain stage of my life.

Speaking honestly, I do not feel fear climbing high; rather, my shoulders straighten, square like a bird stretching its wings. I enjoy the freedom and the height. Down below, when I become immersed in the problems of ordinary life, there is fear sometimes, or the pettiness of human behavior can weigh heavily on my shoulders.

After spending time with Anatoli in Kathmandu, mountaineer Charlie Fowler, on his return to America, delivered this letter to me:

NOVEMBER 26, 1997

It's difficult for me to make contact with you; we did not give much money to the trekking agency for their help and they don't pay much attention to us. I just received your fax, thank you. I will be working on Annapurna until January 15. Don't worry if there is no telephone call before then. We need to think about the summer; hopefully I will be on a Kazakh permit to climb Gasherbrum I. Try to find a place for me on a permit for Nanga Parbat. I will be available to climb Gasherbrum II with clients in June, but remember we cannot find high-altitude porters in Pakistan. For $10,000 per person we can organize just a nonguided expedition; that is, permit, base camp support with food, and fixed line up a secure broken trail to the summit. If no one likes that, then maybe we will have enough money and we can go alone.

The title of the slide show at Gary Neptune's is "Challenge 8,000 in 1997." Make plans with Monty Sorongan for us to climb Karstenz and go to Bali from March 25 until April 25.

During the evening of November 30 my phone rang. It was morning in Pokhara. That charming lakeside town blessed by Annapurna's watershed

*was one of Tolya's favorite places. He was in good spirits. Kazakh moun-
taineer Dima Soubelev and Almaty artist Andre Starkov were going to join
Anatoli and Simone during the early stages of the expedition. Later that
morning, all of them were flying to Base Camp in an Asian Airlines helicopter piloted by Anatoli's old friend Serge Danilov. Snow was deep on the mountains, he said, and few expeditions had been successful that fall.*

*After talking about schedules and business, my children and animals, we
said good-bye, but both of us held the line. There was a long silence and he
asked again, "Linda, how are you?"*

*"Think about Annapurna, Anatoli, I am afraid of this mountain. Have
you had dreams?"*

*"No, no dreams," he said, then wistfully adding, "I have been so much
in the mountains this year, Inshallah, we will rest in the spring."*

*On December 18, Andre Starkov bid Anatoli, Simone Moro, and Dima
Soubelev good-bye at the hot springs lodge below the Gurung village of
Chomrong. Andre returned to Almaty with exposed rolls of film and letters
to mail.*

Today is the eighteenth of December; we came down to 1,760
meters to the settlement of Tatopani to rest near the hot springs.
Tried to call but the phone doesn't work in Gandruk. For the last two
weeks the weather here has been unusual for Nepal. We have three
and one-half meters of new snow and have had to break trail from
the last teahouses at 4,100 meters up to our Base Camp at 5,000 meters. We lost two tents to the snowfall. Tomorrow we are going back
up. My expectation is to finish the expedition about January 16, be
back in Almaty by the twentieth, and in America before February 20.

First I must survive this. If possible we will summit, but it is more
important to come back with my sticks.* This expedition has cost a
lot of money so I will be fighting until the last drop of strength is spent.

*When the phone rang at midnight on December 26, Simone was on the line
and the news was bad. While he and Anatoli were fixing a route up the low-*

---

*Leki ski poles, which climbers use for stability on snow.

est section of slope along the ridge between Annapurna South and the summit of Annapurna I, a cornice had collapsed. Simone was waiting on the fixed line in the lead position. Anatoli was bringing up the fifty meters of rope needed to secure the last section of the route. Car-sized blocks of ice fell, missing Simone, but they pulled out the fixed line below and jerked him off the route and down the slope in a wake of debris. Before being swept down, he shouted an alert to Anatoli and Dima. Simone recalled his last view of Tolya, face up, his eyes judging the trajectory of snow and stone as he began moving to the side below the path of the rushing avalanche.

EPILOGUE:
SMALL PIECES OF PIE
WITH BITTER GRAVY

*W*ritten in the summer of 1996, this piece recalled the morning on the Mountain Madness expedition when Anatoli and Neal Beidleman had set out to fix rope on the route between Camp II and Camp III.

Three hundred meters from the beginning of the fixed ropes on the Lhotse Face, I deviated a little to the left of the usual path through that place, selecting a lower-angled slope and cutting a zigzag trail up. After climbing about thirty meters, I noticed something unusual in the snow. The early-morning rays of the sun illuminated a dark form. It did not resemble a stone. At first I thought that I was looking at an empty equipment case that had fallen from the upper camps. But approaching, I could make out boots with crampons attached. Moving closer, I discovered the form was half of a human body.

Where was the upper part of the body?

Probably the person had broken loose from the upper reaches of the mountain, falling a considerable distance along the rock faces and ice; as a result, I was looking at a maimed body.

What caused this tragedy and who was this person?

The magnitude of the mountains' enduring power penetrated deep inside me. These mountains do not forgive mistakes, and human ambition means nothing on this part of the earth's territory. I dropped my pack not far from the body, trying to compose myself while I waited for the members of our group who were spaced out climbing up the slopes below me. Reflecting on the short duration of human life and what remains after life on earth, I recalled an ancient custom. I don't remember exactly if it was a Greek or a Roman habit, but at the height of the victory banquet after a battle, the music stopped and into the hall were carried the troops who had perished. In the mountains I often encounter bodies. It makes me think about the significance and the desire to ascend into the zone of danger—to an altitude that is unnatural for a human body, where the price of mistake, failure, or even triumph can be measured in a human life.

The incommensurable value of mountaineering experience, it would seem, exists alongside the danger. Why? For me, though I have devoted myself to climbing mountains as objects of passion for twenty years, this has always been a straightforward question. What is it that pushes a person to climb? Clients on our expeditions pay great sums of money to endure the hardships of camp life, a life that in no way resembles the ordinary civilized life to which we have grown accustomed. Of course, inside each one of us is the ambition to reach the summit, to realize that you are stronger than obstacles, that it is within your power to do something uncommon and indeed impossible for most people. But one must be prepared to face those obstacles.

It would be far better if ambition compelled people to train, to commit to preparation that went from simple to complex, hardening the spirit. The individual should derive pleasure from the process of physical and mental development. The payment for ambition should be made in preparation, in training and improving oneself, not in the loss of a life. The greatest significance of our efforts—and it is after all only of importance to the individual—is to have a way to evaluate our actions in life. Climbing gives you a way to define the significance of events and your surroundings. I wondered if the people coming behind me were really evaluating the upcoming ascent and their preparation for it. Paying a large sum of money is much easier than gaining altitude.

During the Makalu expedition two years before, at about 7,500 meters, team climbers had a similar encounter with the remains of a deceased person. Weather conditions were worse and our team was climbing without the help of Sherpas. A strong wind blew, and Makalu's steep slopes wore out our people. For many of them the encounter with the mountaineer's remains was a significant warning. It created a psychological barrier that compelled the majority of them to turn around and head back down. Subconsciously they were pushed to avoid a critical situation. At the time, it seemed to me that this incident had played a positive role. That day on the slopes of Everest, I hoped that the vision of the broken person would provoke each person behind me to ask, "Am I prepared for this ascent, can I realize my ambitions without becoming a victim of them?"

This excerpt is from the unedited text for an article titled "Oxygen Illusion" that Anatoli completed in February 1997. The article was selected by American Alpine Journal *editor Christian Beckwith for publication in the 1997 edition.*

Nowadays the popularity of ascents up Everest is increasing despite the fact that permit prices have gone up dramatically. People go there to test themselves with hardship and altitude. Utilizing the best technical advances in equipment and extensive outside support, they climb a mountain that is much more approachable than the one Hillary and Tenzing summited in 1953. Success today cannot be compared with the milestone those men set or the achievement represented by Messner's solo ascent. Easier and more approachable does not mean that the mountain is lower.

Everest is no less dangerous, especially for those who have insufficiently trained their bodies and spirits. Many of today's ascenders have nothing to test because they have devoted so little to preparing for the challenge. It's worth thinking about—both for the individual who climbs with a guide, for the guides themselves, and for anyone who makes money from what we do. Commerce has stepped up to the big heights; now vertical meters are calculated in dollars. The use of oxygen canisters has become one part of a profitable business. Supplemental oxygen makes the industry profitable for the canisters' manufacturers, guiding companies, and publications that reap the benefit of advertising. But is it profitable for the individual who pays big money and knows nothing about high-altitude reality? Money and oxygen make it possible to ascend into a zone where it is easy to die, to a place where no one can rescue you if suddenly your own strength is insufficient. The myth of safety is a delusion for dilettantes. It is better to shatter that myth than perpetuate it with the notion that supplemental oxygen or a top guide can save you.

It is impossible to stop the growth of business around Everest. Now commercial expeditions have a firm hold. But can any of these ascents claim to be "guided" as Americans want to define this term? Anyone going to Everest should understand that no guide can give a 100 percent guarantee that the client's life is safe. If such a guarantee is made, then it is a deception. The last word will always belong to the mountain.

This is the poem Anatoli left with me before leaving for Annapurna. It was written after his successful summit of Everest in 1995.

SUMMIT

Daybreak stars interface time with space.
On the summit's altar
Light falls like rain from black sky,
Pouring down purifying my body,
Washing my soul with serenity.
Will and every act of kindness emanates
Traveling for centuries
Carried on cosmic winds.

Life is a trifle
And you have risked all earnestly.

Earthly compassion,
Conscious comprehending
Strength overcoming
Mindfulness discerning good and evil.
Live fully heart at one with the Earth.

Returning home, I breathe easier.
My life appraised from the vantage of Himalayan slopes
Healed are the doubled agonies of my bloodless wounds.
No summit is gained without pain.
Walking a knife-blade ridge to the summit
Cold steel light illuminated your image.
Next to me, climbing with me were a troop of men
Their past lives marching.
Lives cut short by love that was true.
Songs left unfinished
They could not tell you why love
Sacrificed life for the blue mountains.
I came down to you
Bearing thoughts and dreams
To live their unfinished melodies
So you would hear and understand them.

—Anatoli Boukreev

CHRONOLOGY OF

ANATOLI BOUKREEV'S LIFE

1958   January 16, born in Korkino, Chelyabinsk Oblast, Russia

1970   Began mountaineering and rock-climbing education in the Ural Mountains

1974   Began high-altitude training, Talgar, Tien Shan Mountains, Kazakhstan. First ascents of 5,000-meter peaks. Earned Mountaineer of the First Category rating, USSR

1975   Graduated Korkino High School, Russia

1979   Graduated Chelyabinsk University for Pedagogy, bachelor of science, physics, and bachelor of science, physical culture, specialty cross-country skiing

1979–81   Lieutenant, Army of the Soviet Socialist Republic, Central Asia Military District, Almaty, Kazakhstan, Mountaineering Division

1980   Communism Peak, 7,459 meters; Lenin Peak, 7,134 meters. First summits of 7,000-meter peaks. Earned Master of Sport, Mountaineering, USSR

1981   Suffered a debilitating three-month bout of meningitis

1981–91   Head coach and program director, Cross-Country Ski Program, collective farm in Mountain Gardener, Kazakhstan

1981–97   Reserve officer, instructor, and coach of high-altitude mountaineering, Seventh Asia Military District Army Sports Club, Almaty, Kazakhstan

1981–93   Successfully completed over thirty ascents of 7,000-meter peaks and two hundred other peaks above four thousand meters in the Tien Shan, Pamir, and Caucasus ranges with the national climbing team of the USSR or Kazakhstan. Four-time Snow Leopard

1986   Climbing leader, first Romanian expedition to Lenin Peak

1987   First round-trip speed ascent of Lenin Peak; eight hours to summit, fourteen hours round-trip

First place, national competition, speed ascent of Communism Peak

First place, national competition, speed ascent of Mount Elbrus, 5,642 meters, Caucasus Mountains

1988   First traverse of the Pobeda Massif, twenty-two kilometers above seven thousand meters, West Summit to Peak Topografov

1989   April–May, traverse of the four 8,000-meter-plus summits of Kanchenjunga, Ylung Kang to South Kanchenjunga, supplemental oxygen used. Summited Kanchenjunga, 8,586 meters. New route to Central Kanchenjunga, 8,489 meters, Central Couloir, South Face

June, Awarded Honored Master of Sports, International Class, USSR (this class was reserved for Olympic gold medalists or for athletic achievements of equivalent endeavor) and the Order of Personal Courage, USSR, by Mikhail Gorbachev in Moscow

July, auto accident on returning from climbing in the Pamirs

First place, speed-ascent competition on Mount Elbrus

1990   February, first winter ascent of Pobeda Peak, 7,439 meters. Summit attempt abandoned at 7,100 meters to rescue disabled climbers

April–June, first trip to America

April, Mount McKinley, 6,194 meters, summited via Cassin Ridge route

May, Mount McKinley, solo speed ascent, ten and a half hours

August, Khan-Tengri Peak, 7,199 meters, summited

August, Pobeda Peak, first solo ascent, thirty hours

October, first place, International Elbrus Race, Caucasus Mountains

October–November, second trip to America

1991   Dhaulagiri, 8,172 meters, summited May 10, new route via West Wall, first Kazakh expedition to the Himalayas

July, Lenin Peak, Communism Peak, summited with Balyberdin's St. Petersburg team

Mount Everest, 8,848 meters, summited October 7, South Col route, member Russian-American Everest expedition

Collapse of the Union of Soviet Socialist Republics, privatization of sports

1993   May 14, personal guide to seventy-year-old Jack Robbins, summited Mount McKinley

July 30, K2, 8,611 meters, Abruzzi route

Fall–winter 1993–94 spent in Telluride, Colorado

1994   Makalu, 8,481 meters, climbing leader, Condor Adventures commercial expedition, summited first tower, April 29

Alpine ascent of Makalu with Neal Beidleman, summited main summit in forty-six hours, May 15

September, guide and climbing leader, Condor Adventures, Cho Oyu expedition. Commercial expedition aborted due to refugee problem on Nepal-Tibet border

October, guide, Himalayan Guides (Edinburgh, Scotland) commercial expedition to Island Peak

1995 Mount Everest, summited via North Ridge route, Tibet, May 17, climbing leader and guide, Himalayan Guides commercial expedition

Myramornya Stena traverse, 6,500 meters, and Khan-Tengri, guide with Simon Yates and Peta Waite for Himalayan Guides expedition

Dhaulagiri, summited October 8, solo speed ascent, seventeen hours and fifteen minutes; round-trip, twenty-four hours and thirty minutes

Manaslu, 8,156 meters, summited December 8, Kazakh National Expedition, third successful winter ascent of Manaslu

1996 Mount Everest, summited via South Col route, May 10, guide, Mountain Madness expedition, Scott Fischer, leader

Lhotse, 8,511 meters, summited May 17, solo speed ascent, twenty-one hours and sixteen minutes

Cho Oyu, 8,153 meters, summited September 25, self-supported solo ascent

Shisha Pangma, summited North Summit, 8,008 meters, October 9, solo ascent

"The Roads We Choose" published in *American Alpine Journal*

Letter of Commendation, U.S. Congress, for rescue on Mount Everest

Bus accident between Tashkent and Almaty, October 25

May 17, 1995–May 17, 1996, successfully summited five 8,000-meter peaks

1997 January 13, contract with St. Martin's Press for *The Climb*

Mount Everest, expedition climbing leader and coach, first Indonesian Everest expedition, summited via South Col route, April 26, supplemental oxygen used

Lhotse, summited with Simone Moro, May 26

Broad Peak, 8,047 meters, July 7, solo ascent, thirty-six hours. First ascent of the season

Gasherbrum II, 8,068 meters, July 14, solo speed ascent, from Base Camp at 5,800 meters to summit, nine hours and thirty-seven minutes

"Oxygen Illusion" published in *American Alpine Journal*

July 25–August 25, summit and traverse of Myramornya Stena and Khan-Tengri, leader of New Mexico expedition

Publication of *The Climb,* St. Martin's Press

December, awarded American Alpine Club's David Sowles Award for 1996 rescue of clients and attempted rescue of Scott Fischer

Annapurna attempt with Simone Moro and Dima Soubelev, via West Ridge and Annapurna Fang

Disappeared in an avalanche with Kazakh sportsman Dima Soubelev on December 25

Posthumously awarded the Order of Personal Courage, Republic of Kazakhstan, by President Nazarbayev

ACKNOWLEDGMENTS

Anatoli won my affection and loyalty because he was a good man, not because he was a great mountaineer. Finishing the project that we had started has been both a pleasure and an honor. I have our agent, Kathleen Anderson, and our editor at St. Martin's Press, George Witte, to thank for this opportunity. There are not enough words to express how gently I was supported while writing and rendering this book. Marie Estrada, George Witte's assistant, was my patient ally throughout the production of the final manuscript.

I was not a writer, and if this effort has made me one, Tony Colwell, my mentor, deserves much of the credit for my evolution. Tony passed away on Thanksgiving Day, 2000, after climbing his own Everest. He did that demonstrating as much style and courage as Anatoli. My neighbor, artist Julie Kandyba, created the maps and the graphic used on the dedication page. The graphic is her imaginative rendering of Nicholas Roerich's logo for Pax Cultura. Julie read my manuscript repeatedly, each time as though new, and I owe her a trip to Central Asia for her interest and support. Writings in Russian provided most of the rich palette that I had to paint from, and they were translated word for word by the conscientious efforts of our friends Natalia Lagovskaya and Barbara Poston. The thoughtful readings and votes of confidence that Galen Rowell and Jed Williamson have given this effort would have been counted by Anatoli as the highest praise.

By a fortunate alchemy of birth Anatoli was liberated to explore the extremes of human potential, and thus he experienced a greater measure of what is possible for a human being on earth. I cannot communicate fully what it was like to be a woman with a man in our circumstances. Most often we were encompassed by geography that was humbling in its magnificence. The reflection of that beauty lit us and our time together. I will say that I am grateful that it was so difficult and that so much was required. Neither Anatoli nor I was given to canonizing cults of personality, and this book is not about that. Degrees of his wit, sturdiness, and humanism that I have encountered in so many of his countrymen (his sister Irina, Vladimir Frolov, Natasha Bashkirova, and Valeri Khrichtchatyi's sons to name but a few) have made me believe that these are characteristics of Russian culture. I hope that I have lived up to Anatoli's standards for honesty and attention to detail, and that my work translates something beneficial about a man, his culture, and the contributions of his generation of Soviet mountaineers.

The Anatoli Boukreev Memorial Fund was established in 1998 and is dedicated to the promotion of mutual understanding and friendship across cultures through shared love of mountains and mountaineering. A portion of the revenues generated by this book goes to support fund projects. For more information contact:

Anatoli Boukreev Memorial Fund
P.O. Box 737, Boulder, Colorado 80306
Or visit the fund Web site at *www.boukreev.org*